THE
MILLION
DOLLAR
DUCHESSES

THE

MILLION DOLLAR DUCHESSES

How America's Heiresses
Seduced the Aristocracy

JULIE FERRY

For James, Evie and Arlo

Brimming with creative inspiration, how-to projects and useful
information to enrich your everyday life, Quarto Knows is a favourite
destination for those pursuing their interests and passions. Visit
our site and dig deeper with our books into your area of interest:
Quarto Creates, Quarto Cooks, Quarto Homes, Quarto Lives,
Quarto Drives, Quarto Explores, Quarto Gifts, or Quarto Kids.

First published in Great Britain in 2017 by Aurum Press
an imprint of The Quarto Group
6 Blundell Street
London N7 9BH
United Kingdom

www.QuartoKnows.com

This paperback edition first published in 2018
Text © Julie Ferry 2017

ISBN 978 178131 787 7
eBook ISBN 978 1 78131 820 1

2022 2021 2020 2019 2018

10 9 8 7 6 5 4 3 2 1

Typeset in Adobe Garamond Pro
Printed and bound by CPI Group

MIX
Paper from
responsible sources
FSC® C020471
www.fsc.org

Contents

Characters (in order of appearance)

Minnie Paget (Also known as: Minnie Stevens, Mrs Arthur Paget, Lady Paget) Favourite of Bertie, the Prince of Wales, Paget is an American living in London. An accomplished society hostess, she assists transatlantic marriages between the British aristocracy and American heiresses. Married to the untitled but well-connected Captain Arthur Paget from the aristocratic Paget family. Mother to four children, Albert Edward (godson of Bertie, the Prince of Wales), twins Arthur and Reginald and daughter Louise.

Sunny, Duke of Marlborough Emotionally repressed English aristocrat with a title for sale to save his beloved Blenheim Palace.

Consuelo Vanderbilt American debutante and one of the most eligible heiresses in society. In love with a dashing older man but totally dominated by her controlling mother, Alva.

Alva Vanderbilt (Also known as: Alva Smith) Wife of the wealthy Willie K Vanderbilt and ambitious mother of Consuelo Vanderbilt.

Alva is determined that her imminent divorce won't affect her hard-won place in society.

Arthur Paget Minnie's husband, who makes his money through horse racing and his role as Bertie's bookmaker. Arthur is not in possession of a hereditary title but with his wife, Minnie, they make a formidable team in society. As one of Bertie's favourites, he's almost guaranteed a title when Bertie becomes king.

Lily, Dowager Duchess of Marlborough (Also known as: Lilian Price, Lily Hamersley, Lily, Duchess of Marlborough) Twice widowed heiress who hopes to find love in England. Kind and rich, Lily is a favourite aunt of Winston Churchill.

Marietta Stevens (Also known as: Mrs Paran Stevens, Marietta Reed) Mother of Minnie Paget, widow of wealthy hotel magnate, Paran Stevens, sister of the always entertaining Fanny Reed, and New York society matron.

Mrs Astor New York society leader with the power to accept or shun social climbers into the fashionable set.

Bertie (Also known as: the Prince of Wales, King Edward VII) Leader of the Marlborough House Set. Fond of Americans.

Ward McAllister Self-styled social arbiter of New York and inventor of the Four Hundred.

Consuelo Manchester (Also known as: Consuelo Yznaga, Lady Mandeville, Dowager Duchess of Manchester) One of the original buccaneers, cigar-smoking Consuelo Manchester hails from the American South. Her family, the Yznagas, is of Cuban heritage and finds it difficult to be accepted into New York society. After her marriage to libertine Kim, the future Duke of Manchester, Consuelo

Manchester has three children; Little Kim, heir to the Dukedom, and twin daughters, Lady Mary and Lady Alice. Perpetually broke owing to her husband's gambling debts, Consuelo Manchester acts as a social sponsor for the daughters of American plutocrats desperate to acquire a title.

Kim, Duke of Manchester Impoverished English Duke who becomes one of the first English aristocrats to marry into American money when he marries Consuelo Manchester. A spendthrift and a rake, he is forever avoiding the shadow of bankruptcy.

Jennie Chamberlain Wife of Sir Herbert Naylor-Leyland and former mistress of Bertie. One of Minnie's first proteges.

Josephine Chamberlain Jennie's sister who is keen to follow in her footsteps and marry into the British aristocracy, becoming one of several pairs of sisters to do so during the transatlantic phenomenon.

Winthrop Rutherfurd Dashing sportsman and one of New York's most eligible bachelors.

Mary Leiter Popular Washington heiress who counts President Cleveland's wife as one of her best friends.

George Curzon The pompous heir to English country estate Kedleston with a passion for studying the East.

Maud Burke Vivacious San Francisco belle with a questionable background but a wealthy guardian who is prepared to furnish Maud with a tempting dowry.

Sir Bache Cunard English aristocrat with American connections. After a run of bad business decisions, Cunard finds himself in need of a cash injection to sustain his country estate.

Lord William Beresford Confirmed bachelor and accomplished soldier.

Pauline Whitney Young American heiress from the politically powerful Whitney family.

Almeric Paget Aristocrat from a historic English family and brother of Arthur Paget.

Wealth and Money in 1895

While it is very difficult to give an accurate comparison between monetary values in 1895 and the present day owing to fluctuations in currency values and the gap between relative values and purchasing power, we can estimate the figures based on the Retail Price Index to highlight the huge amounts of money that accompanied American heiresses to their new life in Great Britain. This also gives an insight into the money that was spent by Gilded Age hostesses on events like costume balls. In 1895 a British pound was equivalent to around $125 US dollars. One pound in 1895 could buy the equivalent of goods that in 2015 cost around £100. One dollar could buy the equivalent of goods that in 2015 cost around $30. To find out more about such comparisons, visit the website www.measuringworth.com.

We Britons born beneath a duller star,

Knew that her wit could blaze exceedingly bright,

But scarcely fancied it would reach so far

As literally make the house alight.

We hear of those who vainly do their best

By craft to set on fire our native Thames,

But here's a charming lady from the West,

Whose intellect turns Warter into flames.[1]

POEM ABOUT MINNIE PAGET WRITTEN BY LORD CREWE
DURING A STAY AT WARTER PRIORY IN 1896

Prologue

June 1894, London

*'The American girl comes along, prettier than her
English sister, full of dash, and snap, and go, sprightly,
dazzling, and audacious'* – CHAUNCEY M DEPEW

To those who didn't know Minnie well, the faintest hint of a smile that
passed over her face would not have been cause for note. But those
in her inner sanctum who attended such private affairs would have
been quietly waiting for such a sign. For it demonstrated the hostess's
obvious pleasure at the course of the evening's events and hinted
that tonight was an occasion not to be missed. Before the guests had
arrived she must have taken one last look at the seating arrangements
and silently congratulated herself on a job almost well done. She had
placed Sunny, the Duke of Marlborough, next to herself, with the
Vanderbilt girl situated immediately on his right. Admittedly it wasn't
a subtle placement, but Minnie didn't have time for subtlety. This was
her chance to introduce the two parties in an intimate setting, and

who knew whether such an opportunity would arise again before the end of the London Season.

One of the capital's most prestigious addresses, 35 Belgrave Square was the perfect place to entertain two single people at the pinnacle of their social worth. Minnie was riding high on the continued attendance of the Prince of Wales at her infamous soirées and card parties, and every heiress who wanted to cement her place in society was clamouring for an invite to the Mayfair boudoir. It was rumoured that Minnie had spent close to six million dollars entertaining the Prince, but it was worth it, she would have reasoned; besides, it was a well-known fact that spending to accumulate was essential for a successful business and this was a simple extension of that philosophy.

The Vanderbilt girl was not just another heiress seeking Minnie's introduction to society and ultimately a titled husband. At seventeen, she was refined and cultured, her journey to this meeting having begun many years ago, masterminded by her enterprising mother Alva, an old friend of Minnie's from her days in Paris and New York – a distant memory from the grand London house. Now, there were no doors in British or American society that would not open on Minnie's command. She had conquered both sides of the Atlantic and it was this unique position that lay at the heart of her social power. It was also what interested Alva Vanderbilt, who was undoubtedly wealthier than Minnie, but had only managed to secure a place as a *grande dame* of the New York elite. She had fallen short of total acceptance into the increasingly international upper classes who spent their time endlessly moving from fashionable resorts to chic cities. Domination of American society wasn't quite enough for Alva or her beautiful daughter, Consuelo. So they looked to Minnie, who had married into one of England's most prestigious aristocratic families when she had wed Captain Arthur Paget in 1878, to introduce them into society. Using the tried and tested manoeuvres they had applied as outsiders in New York, Alva and Minnie would get their way.

Back in her luxurious Fifth Avenue mansion, Alva had selected the Duke of Marlborough as a potential husband from a list that included marquesses, lords and obscure European princes, because she believed he 'could give my daughter that which her equipment invited'[1]. So, after briefly stopping in Paris to hone Consuelo's social skills, Alva made her way to England, where her daughter was told she must not fail in securing an aristocratic husband, and that the Duke was the ultimate prize. However, gaining access to such men was difficult, especially for a vulgar American debutante portrayed by leading social commentators as a slave to the latest Paris fashions and lacking in taste. 'She is fond of "frocks and frills" – and wears an enormous quantity of jewels, "stones" as she calls them. She "pushes" herself in every possible social direction, and wherever she sees she is not wanted, there, more particularly than elsewhere, she continues to force an entry,'[2] wrote the popular British writer Marie Corelli in her book *Free Opinions, Freely Expressed*.

The beautiful Jennie Churchill, who would become the mother of Winston Churchill, had been one of the first transatlantic brides, marrying Lord Randolph Churchill in 1874. Her father, Leonard Jerome, had made his fortune speculating on the stock market and she was well versed in attending opulent and elegant social occasions. However, when she first arrived in England, she was immediately faced with hostility, prejudice and ridicule from the upper classes.

'In England, as on the Continent, the American woman was looked upon as a strange and abnormal creature, with habits and manners something between a Red Indian and a Gaiety Girl. Anything of an outlandish nature might be expected of her...' Jennie wrote. 'As a rule, people looked upon her as a disagreeable and even dangerous person, to be viewed with suspicion, if not avoided altogether. Her dollars were her only recommendation, and each was credited with the possession of them, otherwise what was her *raison d'être*?'[3]

Although money was often the principal motive for impoverished aristocratic bachelors to admit swathes of American debutantes to their elite social circle, when they actually spent time with the vivacious young ladies who were determined to make their mark on English society, many dukes and earls were simply captivated by their charm.

Chauncey M Depew, a US senator who was a famous raconteur of the day, wrote in *Titled Americans*, a guide to eligible English nobles published in 1890, of the differences between American and English debutantes.

'I should say that the American girl has the advantage of her English sister in that she possesses all that the other lacks... the American girl comes along, prettier than her English sister, full of dash, and snap, and go, sprightly, dazzling, and audacious, and she is a revelation to the Englishman. She gives him more pleasure in one hour, at a dinner or ball, than he thought the universe could produce in a whole life-time. Speedily he comes to the conclusion that he must marry her or die.'[4]

Despite such appreciative American views, it was the perception that Jennie Churchill remembers of the heiresses as unrefined and crass that pervaded the upper echelons of British society and so posed a conundrum for girls like Consuelo and their determined mothers. Alva fully expected Consuelo's ascent into the British aristocracy to be a tumultuous one. She had been warned by Minnie to expect a great deal of opposition from English *grandes dames* to another American heiress in their midst. In a 1905 article, *Harper's Bazaar* described the atmosphere that heiresses could expect to encounter, surmising that a newcomer 'had to be trebly armed in indifference to the inspired scandal and abuse that will instantly centre on her'[5], warning that she 'must be prepared, even under the happiest circumstances, for a good many Seasons of relentless opposition'[6].

In Edith Wharton's last novel, *The Buccaneers,* the aristocratic Lady Brightlingsea encapsulates the views of the British upper class towards the American invaders when she comments: 'Their ways are so odd, you know... so very odd. And they speak so fast – I can't understand them. But I suppose one would get used to that. What I cannot see is their beauty – the young girls, I mean. They toss about so – they're never still. And they don't know how to carry themselves.'[7] Faced with such mounting obstacles, it was to one of the original buccaneers that Alva turned.

Consuelo had been presented to her mother's friend a few days before the dinner where she would meet Sunny for the first time. In her autobiography, *The Glitter and the Gold*, she recalls the meeting.

'Once greetings had been exchanged I realised with a sense of acute discomfort that I was being critically appraised by a pair of hard green eyes. The simple dress I was wearing, my shyness and diffidence, which in France were regarded as natural in a debutante, appeared to awaken her ridicule. My lack of beauty, for I was still in the ugly duckling stage, made me painfully sensitive to criticism. I felt like a gawky graceless child under her scrutiny.

'"If I am to bring her out", she told my mother, "she must be able to compete at least as far as clothes are concerned with far better-looking girls."

'It was useless to demur that I was only seventeen. Tulle must give way to satin, the baby *décolletage* to a more generous display of neck and arms, *naiveté* to sophistication.'[8]

Such scrutiny must have felt unbearable for Consuelo, but Minnie would have been all too aware of the importance of the meeting and what it would mean for all of their futures. She knew that she would quickly have to teach Consuelo the pillars of behaviour upon which women who entered the English aristocracy had to stand. A reporter from *Harper's Magazine* wrote about what was expected of an American invader, reminding every heiress to 'keep her emotions in unwonted check… to stop asking questions, and to wear the famous English society mask'[9]. The ultimate goal for American debutantes seeking success in England was to become 'more English than the English themselves'[10].

Minnie knew these social skills would be pivotal to Consuelo's success. It was simply imperative that she perform to her best abilities. A perfectly executed dinner party could signal the beginnings of a pairing that could eventually elicit an engagement and, for Consuelo, a title. For Sunny it meant securing his family seat by using his bride's millions. And for Minnie it marked another successful introduction, another transatlantic marriage, affirmation of her social standing and a little financial reward from the grateful parties.

For the Duke, affectionately known as Sunny, the stakes could not have been higher. In the 1870s the great agricultural depression had decimated the incomes of many of England's most distinguished families and the Marlboroughs were no different. Sunny's father, the 8th Duke, had attempted to alleviate the family's financial problems by offloading eighteen canvases by Rubens, a collection of Van Dycks, Titians, Rembrandts and paintings by Claude Lorrain, Poussin and Watteau, but the sale barely made a dent in the family's debts. He then decided to marry wealthy New York widow Lily Hamersley in 1888 and, although the union provided temporary respite, the cost of maintaining Blenheim Palace, which now only yielded £37,000 in income a year, coupled with declining rents from his tenants, forced Sunny to look again to America to solve the crisis when he inherited the dukedom after his father's death.

Indeed, all over England the landowning classes were feeling the pinch, squeezed by industrialisation and the growing and upwardly mobile middle classes. In 1895, no fewer than nine aristocratic British bachelors married American heiresses, the most matches of any year during the transatlantic marriage phenomenon. The dollars flowed over the pond and shored up English coffers. The Vanderbilts alone were estimated to have contributed $15 million to the Marlboroughs over the course of Consuelo and Sunny's marriage. Many in society benefited from the matches, not just the immediate families involved, and Minnie and other social godmothers were perfectly placed to take their share. In 1882, Parliament passed the *Married Women's Property Act*, which outlined a married woman's right to retain and control her own property, rather than automatically surrendering it to her husband, as had previously been the law. For women like Minnie, it provided an opportunity to earn and keep their own money and develop some independence from their husbands.

In Wharton's *The Buccaneers*, Miss Jacky March is described as 'the oracle of transatlantic pilgrims in quest of a social opening'[11]. Jacky

March was of course based on Minnie, a contemporary of Wharton's and someone she knew personally. Indeed, Wharton had been engaged to Minnie's brother before Minnie's mother, Marietta Stevens, had delayed the marriage and ultimately thwarted the union. Wharton writes of March: 'These pilgrims had learned that Jacky March's narrow front door led straight into the London world, and a number had already slipped through it... and if her services were sometimes rewarded by a cheque, or a new drawing-room carpet, or a chinchilla tippet and muff, she saw no harm in this way of keeping herself and her house in good shape.'[12]

Although she didn't have first-hand experience of the machinations of her buccaneers and their families, the social manipulation employed by Minnie and her friends was common knowledge throughout high society on both sides of the pond. Indeed, days before his wedding, Sunny would rather unromantically tell *The New York Times* that his engagement had been 'arranged by his friends and those of Miss Vanderbilt'[13].

In her autobiography, Consuelo describes Minnie as 'Becky Sharp incarnate'[14]. That Consuleo would compare Minnie, someone who practically invested her as a duchess, to one of Thackeray's most conniving but arguably greatest characters, indicates the complexity of the marriage market in the late Victorian era. Unfortunately for those involved, such transactions, while achieving their initial goal, would prove unpredictable – unlike simple property exchanges. With the hearts and minds of passionate and often impetuous young people on the line, the reverberations from the matches would be felt for generations to come.

However, on this night, the stage had been set for a great union to be arranged. As Minnie glanced around the table, she would have discovered Sunny and Consuelo locked deep in conversation – an achievement that would have merited a little raise of her newly bought crystal wine glass. A schemer she might be, but always on her own terms.

1

Society Gathers

January 1895, New York

'A girl of eighteen, she married old, stupid Stephens [sic]. They say she was a Lowell factory girl...' – MARIA LYDIG DALY

Mrs Marietta Stevens, swathed in a sealskin rug and seated on a plush velvet cushion, gave the signal to her footman that she was ready to go. Central Park was enveloped in a beautiful blanket of crisp white snow, which sparkled under the dazzling light of the winter sun. The air was cold and fresh, the everyday sounds of the park muffled, so that there was an eerie sense of stillness all around. Marietta was, as usual, one of the first to arrive. It had long been her way to lead New York's elite when on parade and today was no different. She had always found it preferable to survey the scene in advance, to take a moment to catch one's breath before Society descended on an occasion.

Today, the Stevens sleigh had been prepared to display its full magnificence; after all, it was the beginning of a new year. Its runners had been highly polished, the brightly coloured red paintwork was freshly applied, and the footmen and coachmen looked resplendent in their livery, their black collars trimmed with piping that matched their red-topped boots. Marietta, in all probability, would have reflected that it had been the right decision to discard the yellow livery of old, and the new style had been much remarked upon – even the *Chicago Tribune* had called it 'unique'[15]. With the elegant aigrettes unfolding magnificently from her horse's heads, there really was nowhere like New York in the winter to display one's finery.

A sleigh ride in Central Park was, of course, an informal occasion. Coinciding with the usual round of afternoon calls, it served as a departure from the normal routine of carriage rides and provided a chance for society to flaunt another opulent addition to its stable of transport. As the first sleighs began to gather in the distance, Marietta could instantly tell which families would be gathering on that fine January day. In as much as the red-and-black display she had created marked her out as Mrs Marietta Stevens, equally distinctive was the maroon livery of the Vanderbilts or the dark blue of Mrs Astor. For all those who were 'in society', appraising oneself of every detail of New York's most prestigious families was a skill that was honed over many years, along with memorising the names of old families and new, those who were on the rise and those who had retreated to the fringes, those who entertained lavishly and those who clamoured for invitations. Retaining and using this information was part of the game; if it was played successfully, those in the fold kept their highly coveted place among the elite. Ladies and gentlemen who made mistakes could expect to slowly descend the social order, their names reduced to drawing-room whispers, until they faded away altogether, reduced to living in some unfashionable part of town, never to return.

Marietta may have shivered at the memory of her own beginnings on the edge of New York society. Even after years at the top, she must have remembered her past with the clarity of one who had so often been shunned: how she had meticulously planned her rise and the sacrifices she had made to be considered one of society's foremost matrons. And there was Minnie. Without Minnie she might never have cemented her position. Minnie now lived far away but her influence was felt and respected by ambitious mothers and impressionable daughters throughout polite society. So if Marietta could help her now-powerful daughter's business – matchmaking eager and rich heiresses with titled but poor English nobles – from her position in New York, by suggesting a mutually beneficial transaction to the parties involved, she was more than willing. After all, she had had plenty of experience of the marriage market.

Marietta Reed was only nineteen years old when she met Paran Stevens while visiting a friend in Boston. She was the daughter of Ransom Reed, a wealthy merchant of Lowell, Massachusetts, and Paran was a much older widower, twenty years her senior and the father of a daughter the same age as his future wife. It was 1850 and Paran was captivated by the tall, handsome brunette who quickly established herself amongst Boston's younger set. They were soon married, with two children, Harry and Minnie, added to the family shortly afterwards. Paran had made his fortune as the proprietor of several smaller hotels, including the Revere Hotel in Boston, The Continental Hotel in Philadelphia and The Battle House in Mobile, Alabama. He was known 'widely and favourably for his business activity and enterprise'[1] and he used his instincts to pursue his dream of building a modern establishment in the then unfashionable uptown district of Fifth Avenue, New York. Believing the area would soon be populated by the *nouveaux riches* who had made their money off the back of the Civil War, Paran staked his fortune on the success of the opulent Fifth Avenue Hotel.

For old New York, the uniformity and distinctive colour of the brownstone houses around Washington Square on the lower edges of Fifth Avenue provided safety and security. They were a nod to tradition, having been where the first Dutch settlers, known as Knickerbockers (an Americanisation of a common Dutch surname), had chosen to make their homes, and became a proud rebuke to the ostentatious mansions of the so-called Swells that were blighting the uptown landscape. Swells were millionaires from all corners of the United States, recently flushed with indescribable wealth gained from fortuitous investments and speculations on the success of the industrial age. They were the parvenus converging on New York, irrepressible social climbers desperate to buy their way into the respectability that the proud Knickerbocker families represented, but boasting instead gaudy homages to Italian palazzos, French chateaus and English palaces.

The Knickerbockers stood firm, hiding behind a curtain of conventionality and tradition. Society would not be moved into welcoming the Swells and their new money with open arms, nor would it relocate uptown and live next to profiteers attempting to show their refinement by building increasingly vulgar mansions in the European style. But what Paran and his ambitious new wife understood, that the New York elite failed to grasp, was the pace of change gripping the city. Life before and after the Civil War was markedly different, and the trickle of new money that quickly became a flood would gamble on cheap real estate to carve out its own fashionable quarter where the rest of society would follow. That quarter was Fifth Avenue.

In June 1856, construction began on the Fifth Avenue Hotel. Amos Richard Eno, a dry-goods merchant who had moved into the real-estate business and owned the site, wanted to build a hotel that resembled a white marble palace. It covered the whole of the Fifth Avenue block between 23rd and 24th Streets and took three years to build. Labelled 'Eno's Folly' during construction, the project was widely believed to be doomed to failure, but Eno doggedly continued and found that, on completion, Paran Stevens shared his vision, leasing the hotel with the intention of turning it into the most luxurious of its kind in New York. *The New York Times* praised the vast white marble frontages in the Italian style that illuminated Madison Square and 23rd Street, declaring it the most opulent hotel offering within New York City. No expense had been spared by Paran on the lavish interior, with every eventuality accounted for. The hotel included a reading room, telegraph office, barber shop, ladies' tea room and restaurant, as well as boasting a 'perpendicular railway', one of the very first elevators in the country. The Fifth Avenue Hotel was a triumph, whose reputation was cemented whe, in 1860, the young Prince of Wales, Bertie, chose to stay there on his first visit to New York. This provided a magnificent opportunity that Marietta was able to capitalise on. She ensured that Paran redecorated the Prince's suite of rooms, even borrowing a Rubens and a Rembrandt from respected city art dealers to adorn the walls. Neither Marietta nor her husband could have possibly predicted how the success of this single visit would transform their lives but it was the Stevens family's initiation into pleasing the Prince of Wales, something that would become an almost full-time occupation for their only daughter, Minnie, in the years that followed.

However, for now, Marietta set about establishing herself as a society hostess, quietly observing that Sunday nights among the pious families of the Knickerbockers were deliberately left free of social occasions, so that they could respectfully spend the Sabbath at home. She had by now realised that the patronage of a royal prince at the Fifth Avenue Hotel was not enough to gain a foothold into the inner circle that counted Rhinelanders, Joneses and Belmonts as New York's elite. She would need something more to force the issue of her acceptance. Suspecting that it was the female members of the ruling class who most objected to her humbler origins, Marietta set about enticing their husbands away from their prayer books by holding *musicales* at her home at 244 Fifth Avenue.

The chief draw was Marietta's talented sister, Fanny Reed, who, it was later said, 'sang her sister into society'[2]. This view gives little credit to Marietta. If it was Fanny who had the voice, it was Marietta who had the 'magnetic personality'[3] and social savvy that quickly saw her parties become the talk of the city. Of course, society matrons were outraged and shunned her parties. As far as they were concerned, her flagrant challenge to the traditional order was shameful and branded her a parvenu of the worst kind. Mrs Mary Mason Jones, a formidable matriarch from one of New York's oldest and most respectable families, declared, 'There is one house that Mrs Stevens will never enter. I am old enough to please myself, and I do not care to extend my sufficiently large circle of acquaintances.'[4]

Mrs Jones couldn't have known that after her death Marietta would have the last laugh by taking over the lease of her adversary's palatial mansion, permanently taking her place in a residence to which she was so often denied admittance. At the time, one of Mrs Jones's heirs commented, 'I assure you I was actually afraid to give my consent to the lease. I felt that I might be visited by grandmamma's reproachful spirit.'[5]

Opponents like Mrs Mary Mason Jones only made Marietta redouble her efforts and eventually, lured by the intoxicating combination of champagne, enchanting music and an end to long tedious evenings at home, husbands from the city's patrician families began to frequent her salon. At first, they came almost grudgingly, as Frederick Townsend Martin, a society leader and author, wrote when remembering a conversation between Marietta and a gentleman at one of her *musicales*:

'Well, Mr Travers, I was beginning to think you had quite forgotten me….' 'My dear lady, it is impossible for me to resist the magnetism of your charming society, although I know it only draws me back to cold tea, hot Apollinaris and bad music.'

'Never mind these trifling drawbacks. I think you find ample compensation for them when you know that at my *musicales* you meet all the most charming and civil people of the day.'[6]

Despite such reservations about the quality of her hospitality, which seem at odds with the Stevenses' experience as luxury hoteliers, Marietta's star was on the rise. Martin would also describe Marietta as 'dressed in exquisite taste, and whose position as a hostess was unassailable'. [7]

It would take some time before the rest of New York society came around to Marietta's particular brand of entertainment. Maria Lydig Daly, the wife of the Chief Justice of the New York Court of Common Pleas, who herself came from Old New York stock, attended a party with Marietta on 6 December 1864 and wrote about the encounter in her diary: 'Mrs "Fifth-Avenue-Hotel" was there, of course, with her sister. I would rather dispense with the music than have to take Mrs Stevens with it.'[8]

Two years later, Marietta had still failed to be admitted into Maria's good graces, but the rhetoric appeared to have cooled: 'Mrs Paran Stephens [sic], the wife of the keeper of the Fifth Avenue Hotel and formerly of the Tremont in Boston…is decidedly a leader of fashion, although Mrs Belmont doesn't visit her… A girl of eighteen, she married old, stupid Stephens [sic]. They say she was a Lowell factory girl, educated herself after marriage, being clever found that music was the open sesame to society. Could not hope to be visited in Boston. Cultivated her sister's voice. Went to Europe…returned and set up in a society establishment in New York.'[9]

All her life, Marietta had to contend with such rumours about her beginnings. The accusations that she was a grocer's-shop girl or a chambermaid in one of her husband's hotels before becoming Mrs Marietta Stevens never quite went away, despite her years firmly in the centre of high society. Gossip magazines repeated them, society matrons made thinly veiled references to the stories when talking to young debutantes, and servants sought to emulate the girl from Lowell who had conquered New York. Marietta chose to ignore them, secure in the knowledge that she was in a much stronger position now. Since Minnie had become a favourite of the Prince of Wales, Marietta had extended her reach beyond all expectations in New York society. Together, mother and daughter had established a transatlantic pipeline, funnelling wealthy friends and acquaintances, who were too 'new' to be accepted into the exclusive circles of New York, from America to England, where Minnie would begin the careful process of introducing them to the British aristocracy, slowly improving their social kudos both at home and abroad. Whereas once Marietta had fretted about how she would infiltrate the aristocracy to win Minnie a place among the elite, she now used this experience to do the same for others, for a fee. Historian Leonore Davidoff wrote that an education in the English aristocracy 'could be bought by the *nouveaux riches*, especially the American variety. It was alleged that some impecunious insiders were even introducing *nouveaux riches* in return for gifts of carriages, horses or gifts to charity in their name.'[10]

The simplicity of it all must have rather amused Marietta. As the sleigh swiftly glided through the snow, its soft tinkling bells mingling with the thunder of horses' hooves, its occupant was surely very conscious of the change in her position. The display of wealth congregating *en masse* in front of her were *her* people now. As society maven Ward McAllister had commented in his book *Society As I have Found It,* 'If you want to be fashionable, be always in the company of fashionable people.'[11] Marietta Stevens had instinctively realised the same thing many years before, and through her appreciation of what was missing in New York society she had become one of its leading lights. Understanding that the new class of Swells had a desperate need for acceptance, and that Marietta and Minnie could provide a solution to their problems, had only enhanced her status. Refinement could be bought for the right price and the English aristocracy knew just how to put their titles up for sale. *The New York Times* had commented at the beginning of the Season, 'The majority of society people are in the best of spirits. There is the brightest kind of a Season before them. There is not a cloud even the size of a man's hand on the social horizon.'[12] As Marietta took her place at the front of the parade, it was evident that 1895 was going to be a good year.

The Art of Discretion

January 1895, New York

'His cult of snobbishness was so ardent, so sincere, that it acquired dignity; it became almost a religion.' – ELIZABETH DREXEL LEHR

The first Patriarchs' Ball of the new year was held on 14 January 1895 at Delmonico's. The fashionable restaurant on Fifth Avenue and 26th Street had long been established as the preferred location for Ward McAllister's exclusive entertainments. McAllister, self-appointed arbiter of New York society, had, as usual, carefully selected the guest list, agonised over the invitations and ensured the menu and wine list reflected the expensive tastes of the elite. Everything had been arranged with the precision and care that was symbolic of the Patriarchs – but something was amiss.

McAllister, a pompous Southerner who had married an heiress and then fortuitously secured the friendship of Mrs Astor, the doyenne of New York society had sensed for a few Seasons that his influence was on the wane. He longed for the days when all of New York society looked to him to set the tone and provide guidance on the *right* way to behave. In the frenetic social jostling between Old New York's Knickerbockers and the new millionaire Swells in the years that followed the Civil War, McAllister and Mrs Astor had stood tall and led the way. They set the rules and declared through their guest lists who was in and who was out. They navigated the minefield that lay between the acceptance of vast new wealth and the preservation of the old order, and ensured that the social battles that dominated Fifth Avenue ballrooms were conducted in a proper and decent manner.

In the early 1870s, McAllister and Mrs Astor had realised that New York society was in a state of flux. The rise of the Swells was becoming impossible to ignore and the sheer wealth they commanded gave them a presence that constantly challenged the high society of Old New York. As always, it was down to them to manage an acceptable transition, allowing in just enough of the upstarts to maintain stability. In an attempt to bridge the gap between the two groups, McAllister had founded the Society of Patriarchs, a collection of gentlemen that represented both old Knickerbocker families, otherwise known as Nobs, and successful speculators who had sufficiently proved themselves socially to be of the right stock for McAllister's vision of a new American aristocracy. The Patriarchs included McAllister, John Jacob Astor, William Astor, Lewis M Rutherfurd, Lewis Colford Jones, Alex Van Rensseler and William C Schermerhorn. In total there were twenty-five Patriarchs, whose position enabled them to use their superior judgment to invite four ladies and five gentlemen each to events. McAllister later explained in his book, *Society as I Have Found It*: 'Patriarchs were chosen solely for their fitness; on each of them promising to invite to each ball only such people as would do credit to the ball.'[1]

In addition, McAllister, with the approval of Mrs Astor, could extend fifty additional invitations to those he deemed socially acceptable, enabling him to bring certain Swells into the fold. They had become a social force that was impossible to ignore, so with his typical pragmatism, McAllister decided that if he could not push the Swells to the sidelines, it would be prudent to hand-pick them instead. In the creation of the Patriarchs, he had provided a benchmark that indicated to high society, the press and the wider world, who had really made it. It gave those in the inner sanctum the power to make or break reputations, and those whose star and bank balance was on the rise something to aspire to. McAllister wrote, '… the whole secret of the success of these Patriarch Balls lay in making them select; in making them the most brilliant balls of each winter. In making it extremely difficult to obtain an invitation to them and to make such invitations of great value; to make them the stepping-stone to the best New York society.…'[2]

Of course, McAllister positioned himself at the centre of this social manoeuvring, taking responsibility for selecting unrivalled food, drink, musical accompaniments and even who would take part in the increasingly elaborate cotillions that were favoured at such social occasions. Elizabeth Drexel Lehr – wife of another wannabe social arbiter, Harry Lehr, who came to prominence in the 1890s – commented on McAllister's reverence for society in her memoir, *King Lehr:* 'His cult of snobbishness was so ardent, so sincere, that it acquired dignity; it became almost a religion. No devout parish priest ever visited his flock with more loyal devotion to duty than did Ward McAllister.'[3]

McAllister, whose family had traded Savannah, Georgia, for California to make their fortune practising law in the heady days of the Gold Rush, had married an heiress and then spent several years touring Europe, where he studied the culture and trappings of the aristocratic Old World with a judicious zeal. These early years refined his tastes and perfected his conduct, ensuring he was equipped to bring his own brand of pretentious etiquette to an American elite floundering in the face of an invasion of *arrivistes*. However, Mrs McAllister, the former Sarah Taunter Gibbons, did not seem to share his love of entertaining and suffered from poor health, so McAllister formed an enduring alliance with a distant relative through marriage,

Caroline Schermerhorn Astor, otherwise known as *the* Mrs Astor, a nod to her total domination of the New York elite.

Mrs Astor had Old New York running through her veins. As a member of the Schermerhorn family, who could trace their lineage back to the original Dutch settlers of New Amsterdam (later to become New York), she had made a desirable match in 1853 by marrying William Backhouse Astor Jr, whose father had made his fortune in the fur trade before moving on to New York real estate. The Astors had five children before Mrs Astor, concerned by the pace of social change incurred by the expansion of New York City after the Civil War, began to define the parameters of social acceptance. Through complex rules and etiquette, she sought to preserve the establishment against the threat of the new industrialists and speculators who were eroding all that the Knickerbockers held true, such as family lineage and tradition, while having an innate understanding that the time for change was coming. Accepting that her husband was more interested in business and spending time at his gentlemen's club than policing society, she enlisted the help of McAllister, and together they began to create a new social order that didn't ignore the changes but instead contained them. They became a power couple whose iron grip on society throughout the 1870s and 1880s kept the undesirables out and those who were accepted permanently on their toes. 'For years, whole families sat on the stool of probation, awaiting trial and acceptance and many were then rejected, but once received you were put on an intimate footing with all,'[4] said McAllister when describing the long and arduous road society hopefuls were required to tread to gain admission.

McAllister quite clearly adored Mrs Astor, calling her his 'mystic rose', referring to Dante's *Paradise,* and using any opportunity to pay deference to her. When planning a Patriarchs' Ball he would constantly seek her approval, noting, 'Whenever we required advice and assistance on or about them, we went to her, and always found ourselves rewarded in so doing.... Quick to criticise any defect of lighting or ornamentation, or arrangement, she was not backward in chiding the management for it.'[5]

No stranger to entertaining, Mrs Astor had established her lavish annual ball, given on the first or second Monday of January, as one of the New York Season's most coveted events. Guests were greeted by the hostess in her drawing room, where she stood resplendent under a huge portrait of herself. She glittered in a profusion of diamonds, which clustered around her neck, snaking up to a dazzling tiara embellished by diamond stars atop her black pompadour. She performed her duties with consummate skill, watching her guests from one end of the ballroom perched on a red velvet banquette that could accommodate six carefully chosen ladies. Those chosen to sit on the 'throne' could receive no greater honour; their position was assured. A decadent sit-down midnight supper would follow and then the hostess would simply retire for the night. Mrs Astor did not dance. Mrs Astor did not deign to mingle with her guests for hours while Lander's orchestra played from the balcony. In fact Mrs Astor did not dine out in public, give interviews to society reporters about her many entertainments or let herself be photographed. She knew that her success depended on creating a majestic superiority that ensured she was just far enough removed from her subjects to maintain her mystique. 'Always dignified, always reserved, a little aloof. She gave friendship but never intimacy. She never confided. No one ever knew what thoughts passed behind the calm repose of her face.'[6] McAllister was in awe of her, declaring, 'She had the power that all women should strive to obtain… calling forth a loyalty of devotion such as one imagines one yields to a sovereign, whose subjects are only too happy to be subjects.'[7]

Securing an invitation to Mrs Astor's ball became a Gilded Age obsession, preoccupying old and new money alike, with many families putting in months and years of groundwork to ensure their name was on the list. If they were denied, 'life could hold no more bitter mortification'[8]. Families went to great lengths to hide the humiliation of not being invited to the ball from friends and acquaintances, knowing that such a slight would inevitably encourage gossip. Instead, they would enlist the help of sympathetic doctors who would recommend immediate trips for their patients to the nearby Adirondacks as a cure for ailments that did not exist. Alternatively, 'maiden aunts and grandmothers living in remote towns were ruthlessly killed off to provide alibis for their relations.'[9] For society, there was no greater disappointment. It was far preferable to be out of town, however spurious the reason, than be forced to admit that an invitation had not been forthcoming from Mrs Astor.

Mrs Astor's carefully crafted image was threatened when the man she had placed her faith in succumbed to the overtures of the press. The increasingly popular newspapers laid siege to an upper class far removed from the tenement slums so many New Yorkers called home and began to tread a fine line between denouncing the elite for their frivolity and celebrating them for their splendour. McAllister opined that there were 'only about four hundred people in fashionable New York society'[10] and later admitted that four hundred was indeed the capacity of Mrs Astor's fabled ballroom. This rather indiscreet comment marked the beginning of the press's fascination with a group which they termed The Four Hundred, and saw a growing obsession among everyone from the elite to the New York masses with who was in and who was out.

For Mrs Astor, who prided herself on discretion, McAllister's hand in creating the myth of The Four Hundred was a grave mistake. She had credited him with impeccable taste and breeding, and now he had overstepped the mark. He became known not only as the arbiter of New York society, earning the mantle 'despot of the Patriarchs'[11], but also as an eager informant for newspapermen, with whom he was 'constantly in touch'[12].

McAllister's self-assured proclamations on the great and the good and his absolute belief in his own social position were further confirmed when he published Society As I Have Found It in 1890, much to the horror of the elite, who valued their privacy and did not appreciate the realities of their social struggles and triumphs being laid bare for the world to ridicule. The reviews for this social handbook poked fun at The Four Hundred's self-styled leader and his pompous and convoluted set of rules. McAllister appeared in a cartoon entitled 'Snobbish Society's Schoolmaster' in *Judge* magazine in November 1890, depicted as an ass lecturing Uncle Sam on how to be a gentlemen. For Mrs Astor the embarrassment that McAllister had caused was too great. Their friendship cooled and the partnership that had once ruled society was no more. *The New York Times* later wrote that McAllister had 'acquired the habit of writing what he thought, and his social set had punished him somewhat severely for it'[13]. Society highly valued discretion, so much so that when socialite Eleanor Belmont confided to a friend that she hoped to write a book entitled *The Outlaws and In-Laws of Society,* she was wisely advised to forget such a scheme. She reported her friend's cautionary words in her memoirs: "'If you don't tell the truth, there would be no point in it – if you told the truth, the points would make you and everyone else uncomfortable," and she quoted a saying attributed to Mark Twain, "A little truth is a dangerous thing; a great deal is fatal."'[14]

If it was not shocking enough for McAllister's revelations to lift the veil on the complex social manoeuvres that were the very lifeblood of the upper classes, he had also incurred the wrath of those who were in society but did not appear to be part of The Four Hundred. For those society ladies who had almost fifteen hundred names on their 'at home' calling list, McAllister's proclamation took away their air of exclusivity. For those firmly ensconced in The Four Hundred, the undercurrent of ill feeling created by McAllister's actions indicated that his tenure was coming to an end.

An alternative to the Patriarchs' Ball, the Assembly Ball, was introduced by some leading matrons who, concerned at McAllister's influence over society, sought to take away some of the Patriarchs' cachet. By creating the Assembly Balls, purported to be even more exclusive than the Patriarchs', female society leaders showed they were closing ranks and making the notion of The Four Hundred obsolete. If you really belonged to the inner sanctum, you were graced with an invitation to the Assembly Balls; if you were simply a member of the elite, then you were more likely to receive the call to the Patriarchs'.

Rumours also abounded that McAllister had received compensation for including names on his guest list. These were confirmed when the newspapers ran a story about McAllister and the railway tycoon Collis P Huntington. Huntington had agreed to pay McAllister $9,000 for an invitation to the Patriarchs' Ball and an introduction to Mrs Astor, but had reneged on the deal and only offered $1,000 after the event. McAllister was furious and poured the whole story out to a journalist friend, only to be mortified when the scandal appeared in print.

By November 1894, *The New York Times* was openly telling its readers about the type of service that McAllister provided. 'For introducing rich persons into "society", there are "society leaders" in the United States of whom like things are darkly said. But these things are mostly done in corners.'[15] Although these kinds of services weren't only provided by McAllister – in fact they were an open secret in society – it was increasingly felt that, for him, the game was up. He had pushed the boundaries of what was acceptable too far, and had failed to act with the discretion that was required to live and operate among the elite.

There was little doubt that McAllister's American aristocracy was casting him aside, and even Mrs Astor, who had for so long been his most formidable ally, now supported the matrons. By the early 1890s he faced a challenge to make the Patriarchs great again. Society still came – after all, there were twenty-five influential families represented at every occasion and they still had the power to give and withhold invitations. Society families wisely reasoned that to sustain their position they simply must be invited to and attend all of the key functions during the Season, as well as be seen at the opera on Monday and Friday nights, host lively dinner parties and continue the round of monotonous afternoon calls. However, the prestige of the Patriarchs had undoubtedly diminished. After almost two decades at the pinnacle of society, McAllister was under intense pressure, although one newspaper noted, 'Mr McAllister has been a great deal maligned by some of those who criticise him. There is no more genial host, entertaining guest, or "jolly good fellow", as he has often been voted by his many friends.'[16]

And so it was amidst this atmosphere that the best of New York assembled again on that Monday night in January 1895. Despite his experiences, McAllister had clearly not learnt the art of discretion and had gleefully informed reporters of the details of the Patriarchs' Ball. They had congregated at his house at 16 West 36th Street, sitting expectantly around the dining table, pen and paper in hand. McAllister had been in his element, at ease in a revolving office chair, comfortable carpet slippers and a desk-worn sack coat, plying the press with titbits of gossip and details about the menu, the decorations and the guests they could expect to see. At the beginning of the Season he had predicted another influx of *nouveaux riches*: '… there are a host of new people cropping up among us, don't you see?… I think a good many have been living in seclusion right in this city. They have suddenly or gradually made money, and are now entertaining every one and being received everywhere. Look at some of those in the opera boxes, for instance. The other night I cast my eyes from box to box, and bless me, if there weren't at least a dozen "new" people receiving a vast amount of attention and admiration.'[17]

However, he had responded by closing ranks. This ball was to be more exclusive than previous Patriarchs', limited to 275 guests. McAllister had thought it prudent to ensure only the very best of society graced the ballroom at Delmonico's. The first guests would arrive after the opera and he had directed the renowned Hungarian Band to play as soon as they appeared in the red anteroom. They would then make their way through the smaller red ballroom, which he had instructed would be adorned with spectacular flower garlands of yellow roses, daffodils and acacias, draping over every mantel and mirror. The corridor leading to the main ballroom would be massed in green with great palms standing in the corners and the walls covered with Southern clematis interspersed with the soft mauve of the Cattleya orchid. Finally, the main ballroom would be festooned with fourteen cone-shaped baskets overflowing with great white lilies, pink roses and vines tumbling over the edges. He could almost hear the audible gasps of wonder from the debutantes as they took in the display. It was not the grandest decor he had ever put together, but it was stunning and tasteful and just might remind society how he alone would continue to set the tone for all to follow, despite their doubts.

McAllister must have been gratified to see that Mrs Alva Vanderbilt and her debutante daughter, Consuelo, would be in attendance, along with Mrs Marietta Stevens. Both women were subscribers to the Assembly Balls, but were savvy enough to be seen at all the fashionable entertainments. Of course there had been rumours swirling around them for months. Alva Vanderbilt was contending with gossip about the state of her marriage to Willie K while simultaneously launching her only daughter onto the social scene, and Marietta Stevens was said to be having money trouble again. However, neither woman had ever been the type to shy away from scandal. In fact, like McAllister, their ability to play the game had seen them rise from Swells to *grandes dames* with terrifying speed. Now, as they all faced threats to their positions, it occurred to McAllister that maybe they could use their tenacity and each other to stay on top. Of course McAllister and Marietta already had much in common and had helped each other before in their endeavours. Both had come to the aid of the *nouveaux riches* languishing on society's sidelines many times, for a little fee of course. Yes, they understood each other well, and Alva Vanderbilt, with her ascent from nobody to somebody, knew what it took to get on in their world.

So tonight was the perfect opportunity for McAllister to bask in the triumph of another magnificent social occasion while a few complimentary words from Alva and Marietta to their extensive network of friends would ensure that his name was once more associated with the highest levels of decorum and taste, and the tawdry newspaper business would be forgotten. In return, McAllister would use his press connections to dispel the unseemly fabrications about the women that were gracing the pages of every newspaper in town because, as he had learnt to his detriment, in New York only the right kind of publicity would do.

Fortune Favours the Brave

January 1895, New York

> *'I gave blow for blow.*
> *I accepted any challenge.*
> *I stopped at nothing attempted.'*
> – ALVA VANDERBILT

It was two days after the Patriarchs' Ball when the story broke in the *New York World*. The front page confirmed that Mrs Alva Vanderbilt and Mr William K Vanderbilt would be divorcing and that Willie K had fled America for the safety of Europe.

'Mr William K Vanderbilt will sail for England this morning on the White Star steamer *Teutonic*… Mr Vanderbilt came from Europe just one month ago. His stay has been almost entirely devoted to arranging his family affairs. There has been no reconciliation of him and Mrs Vanderbilt. It is understood though, by friends of both parties, that he leaves behind him papers signed and sealed… It was Mrs Vanderbilt's reception day yesterday but none of the Vanderbilts called.'[1]

The news that one of the heirs to the Vanderbilt fortune had finally decided to dissolve his marriage caused a sensation, although nobody among New York's elite could pretend they were surprised. For the nearly one million readers who devoured every morsel of gossip they could about Gilded Age society, the story was irresistible. It had scandal in the form of two protagonists who were rumoured to have had affairs, and one of New York's most powerful families whose loyalties were now divided between a scheming society matron and a submissive husband who had sought refuge from daily domestic battles in the salubrious underworld of Paris. All of New York was braced for a fight of epic proportions over the Vanderbilts' millions, but who would come out on top?

Alva Vanderbilt would have been confident it would be her. As a little girl, growing up on her father's cotton plantation in Mobile, Alabama, she had revelled in terrorising the slave children, while proving more than an equal to the boys from neighbouring farms that dared to cross her. She later remembered, 'I gave blow for blow. I accepted any challenge. I stopped at nothing attempted.'[2] Alva was a survivor and she was no doubt determined that her divorce from Willie K and the furore surrounding it would not distract her from her main focus, the launch of her daughter Consuelo into society. Indeed, she had been masterminding that journey since the day her daughter was born, and now she would not let Willie K and his indiscretions derail her plans.

Alva was long used to engineering her own success. She had ridden the ups and downs of fortune since her days as one of the four Smith girls from the South, suddenly uprooted from their privileged life by the chaos of the Civil War. Murray Smith, her father, had been a very successful cotton merchant and had shown foresight in moving his family to New York before the Civil War. He could see the city's central role in the industrial age fuelling its expansion, with outsiders both rich and poor trying to take advantage of its increasingly important role in America's economy. At first the Smiths seemed to have no problem in assimilating into New York society. Although they were outsiders, they had the right genteel background, were well travelled and obviously had the funds to match their lifestyle. Murray was a member of the New York Cotton Exchange and was elected to the first of New York's gentlemen's clubs, the Union Club, in the early 1860s. However, as the realities of the Civil War began to hit home, the Smiths increasingly bore the brunt of the North–South divide and found themselves at both a business and a social disadvantage. As the war drew to an end and the family were trying to operate within a toxic atmosphere of recriminations, they fled to Paris.

The Paris of the Second French Empire (as the reign of Napoleon III, 1852–70, was known) was an alluring prospect for Americans. The lavish court of Napoleon III and Empress Eugénie provided a glittering opportunity to mix with European aristocracy and respite from the strain of constantly striving for social acceptance that had become a daily burden in New York. It became clear to the Smiths and many others in their position that, in Paris, whether you had new money or old didn't matter as long as it was spent with aplomb. Whereas keeping up appearances on a reduced income proved a real challenge in New York, where new money was consistently upping the ante, in Paris it was possible to rent a fine house on the Champs Elysées and enjoy all the opulent trappings of high society that the Empire demanded. Paris also enabled Alva to mature into a young woman ripe for the marriage market. In many ways she was still the independent and strong-willed child who had afforded those daily beatings in Alabama and was often a headache for her parents, but her experiences in Europe opened up another world for Alva, one of luxury, frivolity and an aristocracy who made the rules.

By the end of the 1860s, Murray Smith found his businesses under real threat and decided that the family must return to New York. His self-imposed exile from America had seen a reduction in tensions but, as a Southerner, he was still at a disadvantage in the new era. He also found it difficult to adapt to an economy that favoured speculators and profiteers like Cornelius Vanderbilt, Willie K's grandfather and the head of the family, who took advantage of the industrial age by investing heavily in the railways that were opening up the country.

By 1871, when Alva's mother Phoebe died from an acute attack of rheumatoid arthritis at the age of forty-eight, the Smiths had been forced to rent houses further and further away from the fashionable Fifth Avenue abode they had once owned. When the stock-market panic of 1873 hit what remained of Murray's fortune, Alva realised the family were in serious trouble.

'Through change of circumstances he began not only to make no money but to lose it, so he notified us that we must move from 33rd Street to 44th Street,' recalled Alva in her memoirs. 'I could not understand the great worry and grief to my father because it did not seem to affect me. I remember hearing his saying when he was worried "we shall have to keep a boarding house" – at this my sisters would look dismayed but I would shout, "If we do keep a b.h. [boarding house], I will do the scrubbing."'[3]

This typical reaction by Alva to her circumstances was full of defiance and chutzpah and may have brought Murray Smith some comfort, but it belied his daughter's true feelings on their slide down the social scale. This experience would, in fact, colour Alva's attitude to money for many years to come. Faced with a life of relying on wealthier relatives to afford them kindness while scratching out a precarious existence of genteel poverty, Alva took action.

She scoured her circle of friends and acquaintances for any opportunities that would transform her fortunes. It was not long before she remembered two old school friends from her days at Madame Coulon's finishing school in Paris: Minnie Stevens and Consuelo Yznaga. Like Alva, both Minnie and Consuelo lived on the fringes of New York society. The very reason they had all congregated in Paris was because their families had chosen to seek refuge from the high-stakes social manoeuvring that characterised New York. In Paris they could partake in the very best society and give their daughters a valuable training ground to hone their skills. After experiencing first-hand the humiliation of being barred from the ballrooms of the establishment at home, they resolved to create something better for their daughters. They had the money to funnel into European pockets, which afforded them the taste of an aristocratic lifestyle Ward McAllister and Mrs Astor could only seek to emulate.

Minnie, Consuelo and Alva, together with Jennie Jerome soaked up the heady atmosphere of the French court. Although they were not yet old enough to make their debuts, their families were welcomed into the Empress's inner circle and the sights they were exposed to had a profound effect on them all. They had much in common. They were young, beautiful, well educated and fun, and while Minnie and Jennie provided a considered foil to Alva and Consuelo's lively personalities, their early days in Paris would lay the foundations for long and enduring friendships.

Alva, who now found herself motherless and without the funds to launch even a minor assault on New York society, knew she would have to use these alliances to her advantage. She had known Consuelo's family, the free-spirited Yznagas, since childhood – when she would tumble over sand dunes at Newport, Rhode Island, with Consuelo's brother Fernando. The Yznagas had a Cuban background, but both families came from the South and so understood the now herculean challenge that lay before them in trying to gain access to the social elite. They were outsiders bonded together through their experiences in Paris, their fluctuating fortunes and their need for acceptance. Mrs Yznaga, with three daughters of her own, and Mrs Marietta Stevens, who had already had some success parading Minnie around Europe's drawing rooms, were well aware of the perils of the marriage market. They took pity on the feisty eighteen-year-old who had nobody to guide her through her most important years and, despite her circumstances, included her in their circle.

Waiting patiently in the wings, Alva made herself indispensable to her friends. She ensured that, along with the Stevenses and the Yznagas, she secured invitations to the so-called bouncers' balls, filled with Swells on the sidelines, a younger, faster set who were not yet accepted by The Four Hundred but were making their case to Mrs Astor for inclusion. Alva was not the most beautiful, a title that Consuelo Yznaga, with her soft blonde ringlets, would surely challenge for. Later, Alva would be described as 'a little too short, a little too plump, her face a little too severe, her mouth a little too set, her long brown hair, which reached the ground, tinged with gray even in her twenties. Some remarked that she looked like a cute Pekingese. But intelligent? Yes, without question.'[4] She would have to rely on her irrepressible energy, her undeniable charm and fierce intelligence to place herself at the heart of the *arrivistes*, and then she would make her move.

Alva didn't have to wait long before Consuelo Yznaga introduced her to Willie K Vanderbilt. The Vanderbilts' rise to the top had been swift and alarming for New York society. Cornelius Vanderbilt, also known as Commodore Vanderbilt, Willie K's grandfather, was the eldest of nine children, born in humble circumstances on Staten Island. His father diligently worked his small farm but the family often lived on the poverty line and the young Cornelius had very little formal education, eschewing literacy while searching for the practical means to change his circumstances. He demonstrated his entrepreneurial talent early by establishing a passenger-ferry service from Staten Island to Manhattan. When this proved successful, he expanded the operation and took advantage of new technology in the form of steamships, creating a network of routes along the Hudson River and the New England coastline. It's perhaps a testament to the Commodore's natural entrepreneurial ability that after making his first million dollars, a considerable amount at that time, he again looked around for how he could exploit the fruits of industrialisation. His answer was the railroad, in which he invested heavily, capitalising on its convergence in New York. From that moment, the Vanderbilt fortune was secure, although the Commodore would tell his son and successor, William Henry, 'Any fool can make a fortune. It takes a man of brains to hold on to it after it is made.'[5]

The Commodore cared little about ingratiating himself with New York society, preferring to occupy himself with business matters and intimidating his family with his imperious personality. His lack of interest in the establishment was a source of relief to the Knickerbockers, who saw the Vanderbilts as uncouth upstarts who had been fortunate enough to predict the rise of the railroad. William Henry, who proved a diligent and talented successor, and his wife, Maria Kissam, did not seek the approval of New York society either, although their rapidly multiplying fortune was proving a challenge for The Four Hundred to ignore. However, Willie K, a third-generation Vanderbilt who had been educated in Europe and so exposed to society at an early age, sought acceptance. He wanted the Vanderbilt name to match its millions and to do this he would have to marry well.

There's little doubt that, given the time and the inclination, the charming Willie K could have made a more strategic match than Alva Smith. However, despite her family's fall from grace, Alva had managed to position herself at the epicentre of the younger set who were determined to climb all the way to The Four Hundred. She knew that to secure her family's future and achieve what she really wanted, an unassailable social position, she would first need money, and Willie K, as one of the heirs to the Vanderbilt fortune, certainly had that. For his part, he saw Alva's Southern heritage, her style and grace perfected in Paris and her indomitable wit as an irresistible combination. Years later, she was described as 'pert, sassy, a tease, she was a bundle of energy'.[6] When the two found themselves at the popular Virginian resort, White Sulphur Springs – whether by accident or by Alva's design – in the summer of 1874, it wasn't long before an engagement was announced.

The wedding itself took place on 20 April 1875, under the shadow of Alva's father's declining health. Although unable to attend the wedding, Murray Smith gave his daughter his blessing and congratulated her on a marriage that would ensure a future free from financial worry. The wedding was a smart affair, although Alva still had to make do with a wedding dress made out of flounces from one of her mother's old dresses. She would maintain that her intended dress had not arrived from Paris, although this explanation seems unlikely, given her family's financial situation. Of course one of her bridesmaids was Consuelo Yznaga, Alva's friend from Newport and Paris, who had first introduced the couple and whose mother had taken Alva under her wing. Minnie Stevens's mother, Marietta, had also offered Alva social protection and her friendship with Minnie had led to an invitation to be a bridesmaid; on the day, however, Minnie was too ill to attend and had to be replaced by Consuelo Yznaga's sister, Natica.

The church was filled with society people, although very few of The Four Hundred were present, however the wedding was clearly the beginning of a new chapter for Alva. One when she would lead and others would follow. In spite of all the challenges she had faced, she had managed to secure one of the wealthiest men in the country, while her school friends with money and connections had yet to attract a suitor. 'I always do everything first,'[7] Alva would remark, but twenty years later, as she faced down the scandal of her divorce, blazing a new trail may not have seemed such a smart thing to do.

The Young Pretender

January 1895, New York

*'We have no right to exclude those whom the growth
of this great country has brought forward, provided
they are not vulgar in speech or appearance. The time
has come for the Vanderbilts.'* – MRS ASTOR

Mrs Astor had taken pity on young Consuelo Vanderbilt and decided to invite her to dinner. Tonight she would be entertaining in honour of her great niece, Helen Kingsland, before her guests would move on to the first Tuesday dance of the year at Sherry's. Of course she had heard the news about the Vanderbilts' separation. Although she didn't like to listen to gossip, it had been unavoidable. Alva Vanderbilt had decided to divorce her husband and the newspapers were gleefully speculating about possible causes. There were rumours of Willie K's affair with a certain Nellie Neustretter, a *demi-mondaine*, whom he had been seen flaunting around Paris and the South of France. The notorious scandal sheet *Town Topics* had reported the story in July the previous year, describing Nellie somewhat surprisingly, given the situation, as 'one of the prettiest and nicest of the high-class *horizontales*'.[1] Willie K appeared to do nothing to conceal his affair, parading the courtesan around the Tuileries Garden and ensuring the couple dined out in the most fashionable places of the day. The rumours surrounding Alva's own affair with Willie K's friend Oliver Belmont, a dashing and accomplished sportsman from the Belmont banking family, had also been gathering pace during the summer of 1894. It was clear that both of the Vanderbilts wished to abandon the marriage, and their inability to be discreet about their emotions had resulted in press coverage that now made it impossible to continue the façade.

Mrs Astor felt sorry for young Consuelo. After all, it was her first Season out in society but, instead of taking her rightful place among the establishment as one of the most elegant, cultured and wealthiest debutantes of the age, she would be forced to show immense fortitude in the face of a flurry of media reports and drawing-room whispers. It wasn't at all certain that Consuelo Vanderbilt had the tenacity to see off the gossips. There was no doubt she had an ethereal quality about her; she was almost regal in the way that she carried herself and appeared removed from the minutiae of life. Indeed, the young girl likely had often reminded Mrs Astor of herself, rising above life's challenges, never concerning herself with the details of society. Thankfully, Consuelo was nothing like her mother and her band of presumptuous Swells, who had infiltrated New York's elite and turned what were once dignified and restrained entertainments into pretentious affairs that increasingly resembled a circus. Initially, Mrs Astor had attempted to discourage their rise, decreeing that they never appear on guest lists associated with the Astor name and, together with Ward McAllister, ensuring they were ostracised from the impenetrable citadel of The Four Hundred. But McAllister had quickly realised that this new generation of Vanderbilts would not be kept out of society for long. They were ambitious, socially astute and knew how to use the press to their own advantage, a new and crucial element of the game that Mrs Astor had declined to master. Slowly, she had been compelled to acquiesce and the Vanderbilts had been granted an invitation to a Patriarchs' Ball, but even that did not satisfy the ambitious Alva. She was not content with simply appearing at one event after another as the winter Season marched on. No, she had wanted all of New York to grace *her* ballroom.

And so it was that Mrs Astor came to attend her first Vanderbilt ball. The evening must have been forever etched on her memory, for Alva's notorious costume ball on 26 March 1883 changed everything. It was on a scale of opulence New York had never before witnessed and would become an aspirational touchstone for hostesses as they sought to plan rival entertainments to yield the same impact on their world. Looking back on it, Mrs Astor would have had to admire Alva: she had played her hand to perfection and had used the ball to claim her place as a leader of the elite. She had invited all of polite society to a costume ball at her newly built and exceptionally lavish residence in honour of her good friend Consuelo Manchester (née Yznaga), generally known now as Lady Mandeville, on her first visit to America since her marriage. In so doing, she had offered New York's nobility the opportunity not only to meet a member of the British aristocracy but to finally discover what lay inside the Beaux-Arts mansion that dominated Fifth Avenue.

Alva and Willie K had commissioned the renowned architect Richard Morris Hunt to build 660 Fifth Avenue, which was situated on the northwest corner of 52nd Street and Fifth Avenue. He had been slowly gaining a reputation among New York's elite for his designs and had recently completed the architecturally accomplished New York Tribune Building, which was noted for being one of the first high-rise-elevator buildings. In 1878, he embarked on an ambitious project for the W K Vanderbilts to create a French Renaissance-style chateau that would be an embodiment of the couple's ambitions. Drawing on the time she had spent in Paris as a young woman, Alva was an exacting client who took a keen interest in Hunt's designs, vigorously challenging the architect at every turn to ensure the mansion lived up to her inflated expectations.

The Fifth Avenue house was the second time Hunt and Alva had collaborated on a project, after completing Idle Hour, the Vanderbilt's Long Island country estate. This project was to be on a much grander scale and naturally would require more of the Vanderbilt millions to ensure its completion. Alva was confident it would be a good investment and, after the Commodore's death in 1877, it was Willie K's father, William Henry, to whom she turned to bankroll the project. When she presented her plans for an ambitious three-and-a-half-storey mansion to him, he is reported to have said, 'Well, well, where do you expect to get the money for all this?'[2] Alva's reaction was to slap her father-in-law on the back and reply, 'From you!'[3] Whether William Henry was now wise to his daughter-in-law's dogged persistence or whether her grit and self-confidence reminded him of the Commodore, who was always fond of Alva, he agreed to the plan and the money was soon made available.

Hunt immediately got to work building a mansion that would not only be a symbol of the W K Vanderbilts' immense wealth, but would also be architecturally revered. The house was situated next to the residence of William Henry, who had purchased an entire block of land from 51st to 52nd Street on Fifth Avenue to build his 'Twin Palace'. Unusually, he engaged Herter Brothers, who were renowned for working on interiors, to design and build two identical Italianate-style mansions, one to be occupied by himself and his wife Louisa, and the other to be divided in half for two of his married daughters to live in. At the same time, William Henry's eldest son, Cornelius, Willie K's brother and principal heir to the fortune, was embarking on his own project on West 57th Street, a French Renaissance-inspired palace conceived by the architect George Post. It meant that the Vanderbilts were now occupying a huge block of land on Fifth Avenue, soon dubbed 'Vanderbilt Alley', an immense demonstration of strength and unity by the family and a clear signal to society that they now had the real-estate portfolio to match their fortune. However, while the mansions built by William Henry and Cornelius were large and imposing, they had not been well received. Fitting the usual model of mansions funded by new money, they were considered ostentatious and unrefined; critics and old Knickerbocker families took pleasure in deriding them from their simple and tasteful brownstones. One critic wrote of Cornelius's house that it 'suggests rather a pretentious family hotel than a luxurious and elegant home'.[4]

The property rush uptown, driven by the Swells who were also driving Manhattan's economy, did not go unnoticed by visitors to the country. The French writer Paul Bourget did not appreciate the American pastiche of European architecture, musing: 'Here and there are vast contraptions which reproduce the palaces and chateaux of Europe... The absence of unity in this architecture is a sufficient reminder that this is the country of the individual will, as the absence of gardens and trees around these sumptuous residences proves the newness of all this wealth and of her city. This avenue has been willed and created by sheer force of millions, in a fever of land speculation, which has not left an inch of ground unoccupied.'[5]

Alva and Willie K's mansion was the final Vanderbilt palace to be completed. Where William Henry and Cornelius had failed, Alva would not. She was determined that her house would be a very different prospect and would gain the approval of both society and any distinguished visitors to New York. It was inspired by the gothic and perennially chic Château de Blois in the Loire Valley in France and its position ensured it was in a prime position to be admired by New Yorkers both rich and poor. Inside, its polished marble floors and grand Caen stone staircase fifty feet high formed a dramatic and commanding entrance for every entertainment that Alva would host. In fact, entertaining was this French palace's *raison d'être*, and every detail had been planned to astound and amaze guests. It had to be unlike anything New York society had ever seen before, Alva instructed Hunt, whatever the cost.

In the end the project would cost the Vanderbilts around three million dollars[6] to complete. The interior would indeed be the most sumptuous that society had been exposed to. It boasted oak-panelled ceilings and walls that were adorned with wainscoting of richly carved stone and antique seventeenth-century Italian tapestries. Hunt also constructed a fifty-foot banqueting hall with a first-floor gallery specifically built for the musicians that would entertain at balls. At one end of the banqueting hall there was an imposing bay window filled with an ornate twenty-five-foot-wide stained-glass window by the renowned French artisan Eugéne Oudinot. It was divided into three sections and depicted Henry VIII's meeting with François I at the Field of the Cloth of Gold – a dramatic backdrop for the smart set to admire. Everything about 660 Fifth Avenue was luxurious and impressive. Its beautiful façade stood proudly on the most fashionable street in the city, fascinating society as it made its daily calls. Like a fairytale palace, it beguiled and intrigued the elite to such an extent that it became impossible to resist an opportunity to peek behind its doors. Amid this atmosphere of intense curiosity, Alva took her chance and duly dispatched the invitations to her ball.

It had been Consuelo Manchester who had first suggested a costume ball. Now firmly ensconced in the British aristocracy after her marriage to Kim, the heir to the Dukedom of Manchester, she had on her return for the Season, been immediately accepted into the upper echelons of New York society and was revelling in her new status. Her ascent from outsider to darling of The Four Hundred had been achieved by an English title; now her Cuban background and questionable breeding didn't seem to matter to the establishment, not when they had a member of the aristocracy in their midst. This newfound sense of power delighted Consuelo Manchester and, knowing how her friend longed to replicate her success and finally be accepted by Mrs Astor, it occurred to her that her presence might help to accelerate the process. Journalist William Croffut suggested that Consuelo Manchester's 'society experience, cleverness' made the ball 'the grandest ever given on this continent, and one which fully established the Vanderbilt family as social leaders'.[7]

While this view may give a little more credit to Consuelo Manchester than is perhaps warranted, there is no doubt that the friends planned the ball together and quickly realised that one of their greatest assets was to highlight the guaranteed appearance of a member of the British aristocracy. For Alva, it was a coup, and the realisation that they had tranformed from Southern misfits to actual power players within the tangled webs of English and American high society, was almost unreal. The night of the ball would be the night they would force the *grande dames* of New York to smile and pay deference to their hosts, while all of New York watched. If only Mrs Astor wasn't such a problem.

There was little doubt that Mrs Astor had started to welcome the Vanderbilt family into society. They had duly been invited to a couple of Patriarchs' Balls, she sat on various charitable committees with Alva and they often moved in the same circles. However, this dance of decorum was very much on Mrs Astor's terms. She knew she couldn't stop the rise of the Vanderbilts, but she would accept them gradually. They would wait their turn and be accepted only when they had proved themselves to be acceptable. Memories of Commodore Vanderbilt and the stories of him spitting out tobacco juice on the drawing-room floors of Old New York families that had offered him the hand of friendship were relatively recent, a reminder of how dreadfully 'new' the Vanderbilts still were. Granted, the old man was not around anymore to make such a social faux pas but the clan still demanded caution. Willie K was certainly charming and had at least been drilled in the arts of society through his European education, and Alva hailed from old Southern stock so was in theory reliably genteel, but Mrs Astor had noticed a steely ambition in the young woman more akin to the impertinent profiteers who certainly wouldn't be joining their ranks. Clearly, the Vanderbilts' transition from outsiders to fully-fledged members of the inner sanctum must be managed very carefully.

What Mrs Astor's astute perception of Alva Vanderbilt hadn't extended to was her sheer impatience for change and the force of personality she would put into play to achieve it. The ball was announced for 26 March 1883, falling at the end of Lent and straight after Easter, the perfect time… for society to unburden itself of pious duties and have fun. After weeks of denying themselves in the name of the Lord and their reputations, people would certainly be ready for the kind of decadence that such an occasion demanded. Alva and Consuelo Manchester pored over the guest list – more than sixteen hundred invitations would go out, but who would dance the quadrilles, a set of themed and intricate square dances by a chosen few that would give a focal point to the evening? They had to be elegant, original and perfectly executed. There were many accomplished gentlemen and ladies to choose from, but the hosts had to think strategically: who would garner the most attention and influence? The answer was Carrie Astor.

As Mrs Astor's youngest daughter, Carrie was the perfect choice to lead the Star Quadrille, a dance that would be populated with the youth and beauty of the city. She was young, impressionable and would surely be swept up in the excitement of being on display at *the* event of the Season. The invitation was extended and immediately Carrie began to practise her steps and be measured for her sumptuous costume.

Meanwhile, the buzz surrounding the event intensified, leading some to surmise that the press were being briefed by Alva Vanderbilt herself or by one of her most intimate circle. *The New York Times* wrote: 'Since the announcement that it would take place... scarcely anything else has been talked about. It has been on every tongue and a fixed idea in every head. It has disturbed the sleep and occupied the waking hours of social butterflies, both male and female, for over six weeks.'[8] And it wasn't just the guests that became consumed by the ball. Like a growing obsession, looming as large as the Vanderbilt mansion, dressmakers, artisans, florists, caterers and musicians were all spending every waking moment preparing for the occasion.

Carrie Astor, who had by now been busily practising the Star Quadrille with her friends for weeks, was just one of the guests eagerly anticipating her starring role in Alva's unstoppable performance. However, just days before the ball, Alva played her trump card. She let it be known that Miss Carrie Astor couldn't possibly be invited to the ball, as her mother had never even called on the W K Vanderbilts, as was the accepted etiquette. Distraught at the prospect of being left to watch on the sidelines, Carrie appealed to her mother to relent and accept Alva and Willie K into the fold. An Astor carriage was duly dispatched with a calling card, the essential first step to establishing cordial relations, and an invitation to the ball was received in return.

Mrs Astor had been outwitted by the young pretender and, while the Vanderbilts were surely on their way to acceptance before this incident, the costume ball certainly accelerated the process. She declared in 1883, 'We have no right to exclude those whom the growth of this great country has brought forward, provided they are not vulgar in speech or appearance. The time has come for the Vanderbilts.'[9]

The society florist Klunder had been commissioned to produce a display for the ball that would highlight every inch of the palatial residence. In practice this meant thousands of long-stemmed roses in shades of pink from the darkest crimson to the palest blush, which were purchased at two dollars apiece and adorned the ground and first floors in gilded baskets and vases. However, it was the supper room that had been reserved for the greatest display. As guests stepped inside, they were greeted with a lush tropical garden complete with enormous palm trees and acres of orchids, with two beautiful fountains situated in opposite corners of the room to complete the effect. 'The walls were nowhere to be seen, but in their places an impenetrable thicket of fern above fern and palm above palm, while from the branches of the palms hung a profusion of lovely orchids, displaying a rich variety of color and an almost endless variation of fantastic forms... The doors of the apartment, thrown back against the walls, were completely covered with roses and lilies of the valley.'[10]

Guests were treated to a decadent supper, while the quadrilles were indeed the most magnificent New York had ever witnessed, with nearly one hundred guests partaking in the dancing. The press speculated that 'the drilling in these quadrilles has been going on assiduously in Mrs William Astor's and other private residences for more than a week,'[11] and the themes ranged from a picturesque Mother Goose offering, which included characters such as Little Bo Peep and Red Riding Hood, to the much-commented-on Hobby Horse quadrille, featuring life-size hobby horses that had taken artisans two months to construct. These were made out of genuine hides and sported large, bright eyes and flowing manes and tails. The gentlemen donned red hunting coats and yellow satin knee-breeches while the ladies wore red hunting coats and white satin skirts from the period of Louis XIV.

The guests – who had agonised long over their costumes, scouring books and paintings for inspiration – did not disappoint either, with costumes ranging from historical figures like Don Juan and Henry IV to a dazzling representation of the electric light and a bejewelled peacock. Of course the redoubtable Mrs Marietta Stevens, as one of the hostess's earliest champions and the mother of Alva and Consuelo Manchester's close friend Minnie, had been at the top of the guest list and instinctively grasped the importance of the occasion. Her choice of Queen Elizabeth I as the character she wished to portray was a nod to the scale of her own aspirations, which were gradually being realised. Ward McAllister attended as the Huguenot Count de la Môle, in a sumptuous costume of royal purple velvet slashed with scarlet accents.

There was no limit to the lengths some guests would go to ensure their costume was noticed, as *The New York Times* remarked: 'One of the most striking costumes worn was by a well-known young lady who represented a Cat. The overskirt was made entirely of white cats' tails sewed on a dark background. The bodice was formed of rows of white cats' heads and the head-dress was a stiffened white cat's skin, the head over the forehead of the wearer and the tail pendant behind. A blue ribbon with "Puss" inscribed upon it, from which hung a bell, worn around the neck completed the dress.'[12]

The evening's hostesses had no need to go to such extremes. Alva chose to appear as a Venetian princess, a luminous glow radiating from her as she savoured her triumph. The colour of her dress ranged from deepest orange to the lightest canary and her outfit was topped by a Venetian cap covered with magnificent jewels, the most noticeable of these being a superb peacock in exquisite gems. Consuelo Manchester stood regally beside Alva and Willie K as they received their guests in a costume copied from a picture by Van Dyck of Princess de Croy. She wore a petticoat of black satin heavily embroidered in jet with a body and train of black velvet, large puffed sleeves and an immense stand-up collar of Venetian lace, providing a stunning contrast to her fair colouring.

As the guests streamed in and stared in wonder at the Vanderbilts' chateau, it was obvious to all that a new era had begun. New York had turned out *en masse* and even Mrs Astor was part of the glittering menagerie of wealth on display in every corner of the mansion. The opulence on show was like no other ball before it and would mark the beginning of a Gilded Age form of competitive entertaining that would dominate the following years. Elizabeth Drexel encapsulated the profusion of wealth when she wrote: 'Those were the days of magnificence, when money was poured out like water... The new kings of trade might work at their offices twelve, fourteen hours a day but their wives would have something to show for it. Festoons of priceless jewels draped ample bosoms... the greatest dress designers of Europe vied with one another to create costumes that would grace some splendid ball for one night and then be thrown away.'[13]

Mrs Astor was faced with a problem. Much as she disapproved of the sheer scale of entertainment that Alva Vanderbilt had created that evening, she knew that to maintain her own social position as arbiter of New York society, she would now have to wholeheartedly accept the Vanderbilts or risk being eclipsed by them. Along with McAllister, she would open up the door to society just a little further to ambitious families who could demonstrate their social abilities, talents and all-important resources. And of course, she would have to examine whether her own entertainments were befitting for the new order.

Looking back on the decade since Alva and Willie K's acclaimed costume ball, Mrs Astor would inevitably have been aware how much had changed. Society had been transformed and, despite her best efforts, was becoming something she almost didn't recognise. Her proclamations on the right way to behave and her approval on *arrivistes* fighting to be recognised were still sought and given, but she was now just one of several society matrons who wielded influence. It was clear that the establishment had really changed now that one of those leaders was seeking a divorce and, despite some very public difficulties, was managing to ride out the storm and retain her place. Those who occupied the inner sanctum of society knew that Mrs Astor deplored scandal and yet on this occasion it didn't seem to matter. Was *the* Mrs Astor simply a spent force in the face of other more resourceful opponents? Whereas once she and McAllister had held all the power in the palms of their hands, even he was proving a conundrum, exposing the details of their world to an increasingly intrusive press. It all just seemed so dreadfully vulgar.

Yet she herself had changed too. After losing her husband William in 1892, followed by her daughter Helen and one of her sisters in 1893, she had retreated further from the dinners and parties that used to be her most comfortable domain. The vacuum left by her period of mourning had further opened up society to invaders. Now that her nephew William Waldorf's wife, Mamie, had also passed away just before Christmas, there was a pervading sense of loss, for her family and the life she once knew. Like Willie K, William Astor had been a slave to his indiscretions, a continued source of rumours, but together they had sustained their partnership and risen above the gossip. Divorce would have been truly unthinkable in *their* New York. However, the new generation, the fast set, was different.

In one of the only interviews Mrs Astor gave to the press she said: 'I am not vain enough to believe that New York will not be able to get along without me. Many women will rise up to fill my place. But I hope that my influence will be felt in one thing and that is, in discountenancing the undignified methods employed by certain New York women to attract a following. They have given entertainments that belonged under a circus tent rather than in a gentlemen's house.'[14]

In her later years, Mrs Astor would continue to attempt to bring New York back from the brink of excess but she was not so naive as to reject the new guard of society in doing so. She preferred to exert her influence from within. After so long keeping others on the sidelines, she knew how inconsequential that position could be. She would support Alva and Consuelo Vanderbilt for the time being, while continuing to entertain Willie K's side of the Vanderbilt clan. She still believed that squabbles and divisions among the upper classes did not set a good example to those less educated in the nuances of respectability. And setting an impeccable example was something Mrs Astor would always do. She had set rigorous standards that New York had followed for a generation and that kind of influence was something she would never relinquish.

Bertie's Whims

February 1895, London

*'She has the inventive genius of a social
Edison.'* – HARPER'S MAGAZINE

Minnie Paget sat at her writing table as usual, dealing with her correspondence. Today was a relatively quiet day: of the pile of letters, notes and calling cards, only around two dozen required an answer. It was just a temporary lull in proceedings, for when it came to the London Season, she would be inundated with invitations and urgent business that would need her full attention. The Season of 1894 had been particularly busy, with hundreds of missives appearing every week. Watching over her were portraits of the Princess of Wales and the Duke and Duchess of Connaught, permanent fixtures on her desk. She liked to keep them always in her sights, a constant reminder of how she had become one of the most renowned society hostesses in London and a steadfast member of the Prince of Wales's Marlborough House Set. A cursory glance at a member of the royal family could always steel her resolve when she was growing weary under the sheer volume of social formalities that required her deliberation; she would pick up her pen with renewed vigour and re-apply herself to the planning, proposing and solving that was necessary to stay on top.

The one thing that her mother had taught her above all else was that to maintain such a position as Minnie Paget had been fortunate enough to find herself, it was imperative to keep on evolving to be assured of entertaining an audience. For Minnie, her captive audience was Albert Edward, the Prince of Wales, generally known as Bertie. And everyone knew that, to stay in Bertie's good graces, producing imaginative and diverting entertainment at all times was essential. All of London society was a convoluted and never-ending performance. The unremitting rounds of formal functions were littered with the great and the good of the aristocracy, whom Minnie saw simply as props to be manoeuvred into the best position to produce a breathtaking show. It wasn't easy; the hedonistic middle-aged prince had seen it all, but Minnie was up to the task. 'She has the inventive genius of a social Edison,' *Harper's Magazine* wrote of Minnie. 'Is there a fancy-dress ball to be planned, tableaux to be arranged, a bazaar in aid of some charity to be organised? London turns to Mrs Paget for ideas and the ideas are always there and have always a commercial value.'[1]

The Prince of Wales demanded much of his closest friends. His appetite for decadence and diversion was insatiable, so for any member of the Marlborough House Set, so called after Bertie's principal residence in London, creating unique entertainments that would satisfy the Prince was a constant preoccupation. Bertie had a notoriously low threshold for boredom, and only the most innovative of hostesses could keep it at bay for any length of time. Minnie had been excelling at doing exactly that for over a decade: she had been anticipating Bertie's whims, keeping abreast of the latest novelties, and devising grand entertainments that would satisfy the royal appetite, just as her mother had done when the young Prince of Wales had visited the Fifth Avenue Hotel in New York for the first time years before.

She had found it surprisingly easy to navigate her way to the heart of the smartest set in London all those years ago. She had been preparing herself for the great challenge of winning over Bertie, but in the event he had capitulated rather easily and welcomed her into Marlborough House with open arms. Bertie loved Americans and particularly American women, much to the chagrin of the British nobility, who still considered them rather uncouth. He enjoyed the Americans' sprightly temperament and lively conversation and how they quickly accustomed themselves to the mannerisms of the aristocracy, as Lady Dorothy Nevill explained to *Town Topics* in 1895: 'The American has an irresistible "go" and dash about her which makes her fascinating, and it is wonderful how easily she adapts herself to her surroundings. She becomes in the case of marriage with one of our sons, more English than the English.'[2]

Bertie was also pragmatic and could no doubt see the usefulness of American money to sponsor his growing appetites. A reporter for *Vanity Fair* described the allure of the American hostess when they told their readers that these women 'entertain with an originality, an entrain, and above all, a splendid disregard for money, which our sadly handicapped aristocracy cannot afford to imitate'.[3] It was a simple decision for Bertie: Americans provided everything he desired and he would therefore champion and favour them relentlessly.

For Minnie, who was not one of the wealthiest heiresses, but gave a very good appearance of one, money remained a challenge. Entertaining Bertie was ludicrously expensive and neither Minnie's allowance from her mother in New York nor her husband's income stretched very far when it came to the Prince of Wales. An increasingly exhausted and overstretched aristocracy had almost gone bankrupt ensuring their crumbling stately homes were suitable to host the Prince and his wife, Princess Alexandra. A collection of alterations would have to be undertaken by an aristocratic host before they could embrace their royal guests, including the redecoration of Bertie's suite of rooms, the installation of a Post Office to meet his communication needs and the rearranging of staff quarters to accommodate his large entourage of servants. They began begrudgingly to accept the American invaders in the hope that they would be able to share some of the burden.

Fortuitously, this was one problem that the Pagets had managed to eschew. Captain Arthur Paget's father, General Lord Alfred Paget, was the fourth son of the Marquis of Anglesey, meaning that the hereditary title and large estates had not passed to him on his father's death. Thus Arthur and Minnie were not burdened with the intolerable pressure of maintaining a dilapidated pile, a fact that Minnie was increasingly thankful for. She had seen far too many aristocrats buckling under the strain of land that offered dwindling yields yet mounting expenses to make her yearn for her own piece of little England yet. Belgrave Square would do, for the moment, while she continued to capitalise on her little sideline in introductions. A modest house in the country where they could entertain at their leisure would come later.

The house at 35 Belgrave Square was perfectly situated. A short drive from Buckingham Palace and Marlborough House, it had a suite of reception rooms for entertaining the myriad of guests that walked through its doors. The L-shaped drawing room was filled with Louis XV and XVI period furniture upholstered in costly brocade and exquisite cabinets filled with rare china bibelots and antique silver. Marietta Stevens had generously given her daughter several rare French masterpieces to adorn the walls. It was vital that the Paget home emanated good taste and, while the New York society matron had never quite mastered the art of interior decoration, preferring to cram her home on Fifth Avenue with an extravagant collection of *objets d'art* that lacked sophistication, her daughter's tastes had been refined by years touring the palaces of Europe, and consequently she had achieved a sense of stately calm in her house. Her one nod to extravagance and frivolity was her husband's den. Filled with military paraphernalia, such as rifles, swords and other firearms, this space was designated as Arthur's domain, a place where he and gentlemen guests could retire, smoke and discuss the day's politics or Captain Paget's obsession – horse racing.

Minnie's opulent bedroom was her own private retreat when the strain of polite society threatened to overwhelm her. The beautifully carved white enamelled furniture was upholstered in pale pink satin, which complemented the sumptuous white satin bedspread embroidered in bouquets and festoons of perfect flowers. Then there was the desk that she sat at, undisturbed by the frenetic activity that occupied the rest of the house. Soon enough she would have to direct the day's proceedings, issuing careful instructions to the servants and beginning the elaborate process of dressing for royalty, but for just a few more moments she would continue with her work, diligently and effectively, as was her way. Perched atop the table was a motto that she read aloud to herself every day when she was in London. It was another habit, another indication of her true purpose. 'I expect to pass thro' this world but once. If, therefore, there be any kindness I can show, or any good I can do, any fellow being, let me do it now – let me not defer or neglect it, for I shall not pass this way again.'[4]

Her interpretation of this sentiment was somewhat unique. Thus far her life had been a mass of contradictions, her often good intentions consistently thwarted by practical considerations. With a mother like Marietta, who had been forced to rely on her innate resourcefulness to establish Minnie in society, it had long been clear that when you lived in the precarious world they had chosen to make theirs, sometimes social niceties had to be sidelined in favour of survival. And yet she had also grown up in an aristocratic Europe that valued *noblesse oblige*, with duty, honour and dignity all bound tightly together and espoused so vehemently by her schoolmistress, the delightful Madame Coulon; it ran through her like a constant moral compass. This dichotomy within meant that Minnie could never quite decide whether the services she provided were a string of selfless acts, born out of an interest in good relations between the country of her birth and Great Britain, or an ingenious way to bolster the Pagets' coffers while ensuring the greatest families on both sides of the Atlantic would always remain in her debt. More often than not, her motivation may well have been the latter. How could she possibly afford to dedicate her life to such demanding work if the only reward she could look forward to was a hollow gratitude that would soon fade to nothing?

An anonymous foreign resident living in London at the time could have been talking about Minnie and her progress from transatlantic bride to unofficial marriage broker when they gave their observations on the trend for Anglo-American marriages: 'The fair Yankee has no sooner made a conquest and led an English aristocrat to the altar than she commences immediately to consider what she can do for her compatriots with the leverage in her hands... Altogether she is an acquisition to society, though... her incessant efforts to advance by matrimonial alliances or otherwise the interest of her countrywomen, may sometimes prove fertile in mischief.'[5]

Introducing American families and, particularly, wealthy young heiresses, had provided Minnie with a substantial income. It was a trade shrouded in secrecy, involving clandestine meetings and conversations that only implied all that she offered a young lady hungry for prestige and power. She was never explicit about her methods or what she expected in return, but after the first invitations began to arrive at the rented Mayfair mansion of a family of Swells, it was never long before Minnie received a terribly expensive piece of jewellery or notification from her milliner that her account had been mysteriously settled.

'In England great wealth can, by using the appropriate methods, practically buy rank from those who bestow it,'[6] commented the British Ambassador to the United States, Lord Bryce, writing about the business of introductions. The wife of an American diplomat similarly described the practice, acknowledging that influential ladies 'will sell their entree to any American who wants to buy. They acknowledge that they cannot do without their accustomed rounds of pleasure, of dinners, balls and hunting. So they get it all and make a good living besides by bringing out their dear kinsman from the United States.'[7] It was a practice well known among the elite but one that very few would acknowledge. To publicly name such powerful society figures would put any aristocrat's social position in jeopardy.

Queen Victoria's first Court Drawing Room of the year fell on 20 February 1895 and, despite the freezing and inhospitable weather outside, Minnie knew she had to attend. Insiders who had experience of such events knew that while the Winter Drawing Room meant running the risk of catching a chill, it was an occasion less likely to draw the crowds of the summer events and more likely to be graced with an appearance by the Queen herself. Now that Queen Victoria was advancing in age, she often discharged her Drawing Room duties to the Princess of Wales as the year progressed. While Princess Alexandra performed her duties with charm and grace, a Drawing Room without personally being presented to the Queen herself was, to Minnie and many ladies like her, an abject failure. Court Drawing Rooms began at three o'clock in the afternoon but the magnificent finery required for such an occasion took time to assemble. Minnie applied all of her previous knowledge of Court, including the probable hours spent shivering inside her carriage, snarled up in a long queue that snaked from Buckingham Palace down The Mall, and called for her maid to help her get ready in good time. She had chosen an exquisite white satin gown for the occasion, embroidered in steel and bordered with sable. It perfectly flattered her lithe figure, complementing her smooth, alabaster skin and dark brown hair, which she wore swept away from her neck in a soft Newport knot, one of the most fashionable styles of the day. A rich black satin train fell from a deep collar of sable that Minnie hoped would keep the cold at bay.

'She had an almost imperceptible American accent, looked English and dressed like a Frenchwoman,'[8] observed J P C Sewell, a close confidante of Bertie's. Minnie glanced again in the mirror and finally adorned herself with her exquisite collection of diamonds, a pleasing symbol of her achievements to date. She was ready once more to meet the Queen.

Invitations to the Drawing Rooms were limited to two hundred and, weeks before the occasion, letters from past attendees nominating suitable ladies to be presented would bombard the Lord Chamberlain's office, in the hope of securing an invitation. For debutantes and those relatively new to British society, it was an essential stepping stone on the road to success and for Minnie, whose position depended on her ability to place young ladies at socially advantageous events, the Drawing Room provided a key opportunity to commence their journey. During the past two decades the number of well-connected ladies clamouring to be presented at Court had doubled, so that more Drawing Rooms had to be added to the already congested social calendar.

It was already becoming a busy year and Minnie knew she must leave nothing to chance: she needed to be visible at every important social event, as well as engineering some of her own to ensure that her compatriots were introduced to London society successfully. Of course she had been working with certain distinguished families for some time, but these things could not be rushed. However, she instinctively felt that other eligible heiresses could be placed quickly, without the need for several Seasons spent learning the complex etiquette of the English aristocracy. An heiress well educated, and fully aware of what it took to conquer European society, could and would progress quickly. 'The American girl who hopes to shine in Continental society must be versatile,' Minnie once said. 'She must be able to converse in all countries with all sorts and conditions of men with equal facility. She must be able to talk with the politician on politics, the artist on art… to accomplish this she must be a linguist.'[9]

In her experience, successful American heiresses immediately acclimatised to the English way of doing things. They were keen students of the aristocratic way of life and, crucially, used their American attributes sparingly but effectively, so that they provided an intriguing point of difference to any duke or marquess who crossed their paths. Like Lily Bart, the principal character of Edith Wharton's *The House of Mirth*, Minnie knew that beauty played an important but not vital part in the business of attracting a husband. That's why she encouraged any heiress she encountered to put her expensive education to good use when attempting to capture an English gentleman.

'Lily understood that beauty is only the raw material of conquest, and that to convert it into success other arts are required. She knew that to betray any sense of superiority was a subtler form of the stupidity her mother denounced, and it did not take her long to learn that a beauty needs more tact than the possessor of an average set of features.'[10]

Other heiresses, who either refused to take Minnie's advice or did not have the attributes to put it into practice, took much longer to be accepted by London society and therefore required a good deal more attention to secure them a prestigious match. By now, she could usually ascertain straightaway which category the debutantes fitted into and always gave an inward sigh when a challenging family of blatant Swells walked through her door. Unfortunately, the English aristocracy were also becoming wise to the American infiltrators. After a number of successful transatlantic marriages, including Minnie's, elements of society had begun to accept heiresses more readily into their ranks. However, as the historian David Cannadine observed, 'Others believed that these women were unscrupulous adventuresses, who were pushed forward by the calculating American hostess, Lady Paget, who spoke with unrefined accents, who were probably tainted by Red Indian blood, and who helped to make [society] shallower, more extravagant, and more vulgar than it ever was before.'[11]

They were long-held prejudices that were not unfamiliar to Minnie, and she reasoned that any heiress serious about buying her way into the aristocracy would have to overcome them – and of course she would be there to help. She relished a challenge and her contacts in New York would never recommend a completely unsuitable project. Besides, the greater the instruction that she was required to offer a young lady, the more compensation she could look forward to.

Marie Corelli wrote in *Free Opinions, Freely Expressed* of 'at least a dozen well-known society women' who accepted 'huge payments in exchange for recommendation or introduction to royal personages, and who add considerably to their incomes by such means'.[12] Minnie acknowledged that there were others offering similar services to her own but was quietly confident that her methods, along with her friend and ally Consuelo Manchester, were by far the most successful. When it came to aiding her compatriots, there really was no one better placed, and everybody knew it.

So far, the most glittering event of the social calendar had been the Countess of Warwick's Bal Poudré on 1 February. Warwick Castle had looked magical as it stood proudly lit against the freezing night sky, ensconced in several feet of snow. Five hundred guests had received invitations instructing them to wear costumes representing the French Court of Louis XV and XVI, causing whispers of expectation and excitement to reverberate around upper-class households across the country. Powder or white wigs were permitted and guests were directed to Auguste on Welling Street or Nathan on Coventry Street in London for drawings of costumes or advice to be sure of their historical accuracy, if required. An invasion of hairdressers and dressmakers had descended on Warwick, as the town prepared for its moment of triumph. The snow continued to fall steadily as the guests braved the freezing weather, approaching the castle in their carriages through the entrance gate, along the sweeping avenue and under the Great Gateway. There, in the courtyard with the castle's turrets and ramparts looming large above them, they appeared to take an enchanted step into another place and time. The dazzling court of the Second Empire awaited them.

Daisy, the Countess of Warwick, was dressed as Marie Antoinette, the Warwick diamonds wound around her neck in a breathtaking collar of sparkling jewels. Her blue velvet cloak, embroidered with gold fleur de lys, complemented the turquoise velvet cap clasped with jewels and pink and white ostrich plumes that perched on top of her elaborate white wig. Minnie had plumped for the Duchesse D'Orléans as her inspiration and Arthur dressed as a musketeer. Together they made a ravishing couple and, as close friends of the Countess, ensured their place at the hostess's table along with the Austro-Hungarian ambassador, Prince Francis of Teck, the Portuguese minister and the unmarried Duke of Marlborough.

Over two thousand wax candles had been used to create a subtle diffused lighting that illuminated the path of each guest as, utterly captivated, they made their way through the entrance lounges to the cedar drawing room, where Van Dyck family portraits hung and a crystal candelabra provided a focal point to the elaborate white and gold ceiling. Herr Wurm's White Viennese Orchestra, dressed in white and gold period costumes, played on throughout the evening, as guests danced before retreating to the Great Hall for a sumptuous sit-down supper at tables decorated with white lilies of the valley, orchids and hyacinths. 'The assembly was undoubtedly one of the most brilliant which has ever been gathered together within the wall of the historic Castle,'[13] said the *Morning Post* in its report of the event the day after the ball.

The young Duke of Marlborough, nicknamed Sunny, had also occupied pride of place in Minnie's thoughts lately, as she contemplated how she could advance the prospects of a match with her friend Alva's daughter, Consuelo Vanderbilt. The dinner party at Belgrave Square last summer had witnessed such a promising first encounter, but since then there had been no developments of consequence. Sunny was probably embroiled in an intoxicating web of love affairs, as gentlemen of his age and position often were, but in all likelihood he was becoming increasingly aware of his precarious finances and would soon reach a point where he needed to find a remedy. The solution to his woes was obvious: Consuelo Vanderbilt and the Vanderbilt fortune. It was just a matter of Minnie bringing the two parties together. She had been in contact with Alva several times during the intervening period, keen to offer advice and assistance on the matter, but Alva was proving difficult to pin down.

After consulting her own mother, Minnie had discovered that all of New York society was rife with gossip that Alva's marriage to Willie K was experiencing difficulties and Minnie's own contacts in Paris had commented on Willie K's presence in the French capital in recent months, accompanied by a woman of dubious moral character. Perhaps Alva was biding her time and waiting for the fuss to dissipate before she made a decision on Consuelo's future. Or maybe she had changed her mind about an English husband for her daughter; after all, she had married an American plutocrat, affording her the kind of fortune that had enabled her to become one of the most powerful ladies in New York society. If Minnie had considered the differing fates of herself and one of her oldest friends, she may have felt a familiar pang of jealousy. For Alva did not have to concern herself with the social promotion of others. Free from financial restrictions, she lived in a world where money wasn't a consideration and self-promotion was the only objective. Minnie might have escaped the stifling tedium of New York society for the lively diversions of a life in England, but was she really any better off? A cartoon published in *Town Topics* the previous year, drew parallels to Minnie's life. It was of a lady and gentleman discussing the business of marriage brokers. The text read:

She – 'The Countess is in the business of marrying off young American heiresses to titled Englishmen. She was one herself once.'

He – 'What a revenge.'[14]

Perhaps watching the innocent Consuelo Vanderbilt navigate her way through the ruthless English aristocracy would make up for her past struggles.

For now, she would continue on her chosen course when it came to Sunny and the Vanderbilts. It was quite a simple process, which she had been quietly honing and mastering over many years. It was easy to position oneself at occasions where one might accidentally encounter a person of interest and it was this tactic that Minnie had been employing with the Duke. The previous month she had found herself at a select dinner at the Savoy Hotel, which later in the evening had turned into a rather delightful skating party at Niagara Hall. Sunny had attended, along with her dear friend Consuelo Manchester, who also acted as a conduit for Anglo-American relations. Minnie had taken her opportunity to consult the Duchess, who was rather usefully Consuelo's godmother – indeed the young Consuelo Vanderbilt had been named after her mother's friend. She also used the event to present Consuelo's case to Sunny once again and had further pressed the subject at the Warwick Bal Poudré. Of course, she had to be careful not to be too forceful: she had learned that English gentlemen liked to feel in control of their destiny at all times. Yet a little gentle reminder of the Vanderbilt millions, the beautiful young debutante and the responsibilities of Blenheim could be relied upon to ensure the subject elicited the serious consideration it deserved.

In the meantime, she would contact her mother to learn more about the Vanderbilt situation. Marietta would be sure to discover Alva's thoughts on a move for Consuelo from the Fifth Avenue new-money mansion to an ancient family seat in the bosom of the English countryside. She would also gently remind her that she almost certainly needed Minnie's assistance, as the Vanderbilts had no other real connections in England. Minnie knew if she could ensure a Vanderbilt became a duchess, her place would be assured as society's greatest hostess for years to come. Such a match at the very pinnacle of the English aristocracy would be worth a great deal indeed to all the parties involved.

Protégés and Plans

February 1895, London

*'After her debut, Mrs Chamberlain took her
daughter to England, and presented herself with a
letter of introduction to Lady Paget, who at once
arranged a dinner to meet the Prince of Wales.'*
– FREDERICK TOWNSEND MARTIN

Minnie Paget's unmistakable Brougham carriage pulled up slowly
outside the Naylor-Leyland mansion at Albert Gate. The liveried
coachman descended from his commanding position surveying the
streets ahead to assist his mistress out of the carriage. The mansion in
front of them enjoyed one of the best views in London, overlooking
Hyde Park, and its magnificent five-storey façade was a testament to
the vision and deep pockets of Captain Thomas Leyland, who had
commissioned the palatial residence in 1852. It was now occupied
by his grandson, Captain Herbert Naylor-Leyland, and his American
wife, Jennie. Number 3 Albert Gate represented all that was great

about the English aristocracy and had established itself as a bustling centre for opulent entertainments during the Season. Jennie had been instrumental in this transformation of the house from just another grand building to a dynamic political and social salon. Her success ensured that her husband's career remained on course, despite his consistent attempts to sabotage it with unwise political decisions, and she maintained her beneficial links to Bertie by having the space and means to entertain grandly. From Minnie's point of view, Jennie was one of her most successful protégés; now they just had to ensure that her sister Josephine continued the family tradition.

Both Jennie and Herbert had been dangerously ill with typhoid fever for some time, causing London society to speculate on whether they would survive. It was believed that the disease had taken hold after they had eaten oysters, and it had raged violently with no signs of retreating. But eventually they had begun to recover and, with diligent care and attention, appeared to be over the worst. Minnie had been in close contact with Jennie's parents, Mr and Mrs W S Chamberlain, asking for regular updates on Jennie's health, as had Consuelo Manchester. They had both known the Chamberlains for over a decade, after Jennie had stunned the aristocracy by capturing the attentions of Bertie and therefore compelling the whole of society immediately to accept her into its circle.

Jennie's impact had been part of Minnie's plan, of course, which she had formulated the moment her mother had written informing her of the Chamberlains' arrival in London in 1882 and appraising her of the details of Jennie Chamberlain's background. Jennie was a nineteen-year-old debutante from Cleveland, Ohio, whose father had become an influential judge after a successful career as a lawyer. Although this profession afforded the Chamberlains a comfortable existence, the family had been thrust into the realms of the *nouveaux riches* when they inherited a large fortune from Jennie's uncle, Selah Chamberlain, who had derived his wealth from Minnesota state bonds and Cleveland's booming real estate. The family's wealth and standing in the community immediately afforded them the position of leaders of Cleveland's provincial society, yet this failed to satisfy the Chamberlains. Hoping to conquer the highest society that America could offer, they headed to Newport, where Mrs Astor and the most elite members of the New York upper classes spent their summers. Marietta told Minnie that Jennie's debut in Newport had been a triumph. The *New York Sun* described her as having eyes that were 'liquid blue shaded by dark lashes'[1] and features of a 'classic Grecian cast'[2].

Despite this success, New York's drawing-room doors would not open so easily for the Chamberlains and a trip to Europe to cement their social credentials was considered prudent if they didn't want to fall into the trap of attempting an assault on New York without the proper preparation. Many Swells had unwittingly sabotaged their efforts to be accepted by the elite by making their move too early. Consequently, families would use less fashionable resorts than Newport, such as Saratoga Springs or Bar Harbor, as a practice ground and to establish connections before committing to a summer in Mrs Astor's backyard. The Chamberlains had received a warm initial welcome in Newport, but it was in no way certain that this would extend to a place on the influential guest lists during New York's winter Season. *Cosmopolitan* acknowledged that for the daughters of the *nouveaux riches* a period spent abroad would enhance their marital prospects: 'Had she lived in America, the chances of her marrying into the real society of this country would have been small.'[3]

Those society matrons with experience, such as Marietta, agreed and would advise ambitious families like the Chamberlains to be patient, as such manoeuvres could not be rushed. Far better to head to Europe to experience the culture, learn finesse and have the chance to build alliances with the French, Italian or English nobility before attempting a calculated move on New York. Many families had been ostracised for having the audacity to assume they had been accepted when they had been merely tolerated, and once they had been shunned by society it was almost impossible to claw their way back in.

Frederick Townsend Martin remembered in his memoirs Jennie Chamberlain's trip to Europe, where she presented herself to Minnie: 'After her debut, Mrs Chamberlain took her daughter to England, and presented herself with a letter of introduction to Lady Paget, who at once arranged a dinner to meet the Prince of Wales.'[4] The beautiful and flirtatious Jennie had been a conscientious student, filing away in her pretty little head every piece of advice that Minnie bestowed upon her, ready to spring into action as soon as an opportunity presented itself. She proved so successful that many started to whisper that she must have had help. Speculation of this kind with regard to all American heiresses endured for many years, with one reporter for *Harper's Magazine* writing, 'One is almost tempted at times to believe that there must somewhere be a school in existence given up to teaching American women how to be English, and to coaching them in all the subjects required for social honours.'[5]

Minnie had perhaps underestimated just how successful Jennie would be at charming Bertie, and became concerned by worrying rumours of his infatuation with her. Jennie quickly gained a reputation and was variously known as 'American Beauty' or 'Morning Glory'. Bertie and the Chamberlains were spotted at fashionable European holiday resorts such as Homburg and Cannes and there were reports of a rendezvous between the pair in Paris at the Hotel Balmoral. The flirtation appeared to progress apace and, although the Chamberlains continued to chaperone their daughter when she was invited to Sandringham in Norfolk, the normally impassive Princess Alexandra, who made a habit of ignoring her husband's dalliances, showed her displeasure at the situation when she nicknamed Jennie 'Miss Chamberpots'. The rumours surrounding Jennie gained her notoriety but not the virtuous, respectable reputation that was vital for acceptance into high society on either side of the Atlantic. For a time it looked as if Minnie's meticulous planning had been in vain.

When the Chamberlains retreated back to America in 1883, a number of shops were selling portraits of Jennie, along with Bertie's longstanding mistress, Lillie Langtry, to the general public. Realising the gravity of the situation and the implications of Jennie's portrait being sold alongside Lillie, Jennie's father took action. He informed the newspapers that any business caught selling Jennie's picture would almost certainly face prosecution. Her behaviour had been reckless and had almost derailed the family's plans for social acceptance. They briefly abandoned their plans to infiltrate New York society and instead spent time in Cleveland and on extended tours of Europe. They had made great inroads there before and it was certainly true that Europeans had a less puritanical view of morality than their American contemporaries. They requested help to rebuild their social position from their American friends in England, but it would be another six years before Jennie would finally marry.

In 1889, Captain Herbert Naylor-Leyland and Jennie Chamberlain of Cleveland, Ohio, were married, with Jennie's sister Josephine as one of their bridesmaids. In June 1889, Mrs Chamberlain and Josephine were presented at the Queen's Drawing Room, their journey to the upper echelons of the nobility complete. The Chamberlains, now gloriously content with their new status, abandoned all attempts to be accepted by Mrs Astor and her associates and instead made a permanent move to England. When Minnie moved on from her first marital home at Halkin Street, London, it was the Chamberlains who quickly moved in.

In contrast with the mansion that Jennie now occupied, with its large drawing room, impressive ballroom and gallery housing paintings by Brueghel, Gainsborough, Rubens, Tintoretto and Van Dyck, 35 Belgrave Square paled into insignificance. Minnie must have found it hard to believe how far her young apprentice had come, but she could be proud of her own achievements as well as basking in the light of her protégé's, and the money she earned would always be hers. Never would she have to rely on the whims and mood of her husband to secure a paltry amount of pin money. Now that divorce was becoming more acceptable, marriage was ever more precarious. If a gentleman found himself in possession of an errant or inferior wife, he could simply divorce her, rescinding her position, money and access to ancestral seats. Minnie had been party to negative rumours about the Naylor-Leylands' marriage, which had been heightened by Herbert's sudden resignation from the Conservative party owing to his sympathies with the Liberal cause, triggering a by-election. Minnie had predicted a bumpy ride for the Naylor-Leylands while they navigated their way through those two scandals, which were being played out in the press for all of England to comment on. Then she had heard that Herbert and Jennie had contracted typhoid fever, which she had to admit was not awful timing, if such a thing was destined your way. The *Evening Telegram* reported on their progress speculating that: '…the resignation was due to other than political reasons, and that it was in some way or other connected with divorce proceedings against his wife, which proceedings have been the gossip of clubs and papers for some time past. Rumour has it that Captain Leyland even went so far as to direct his solicitors to prepare to serve a citation. While this was supposed to be going on, the Captain and Mrs Leyland fell ill with typhoid fever, and both were nursed to convalescence at the Naylor-Leyland mansion, Albert Gate. It was during the wearisome days of this disease, said to have been occasioned in their case by eating oysters, that a reconciliation was effected, and with complete convalescence came domestic peace.'[6]

Minnie was pleased that common sense had prevailed and harmony had been restored. Divorce was bad for business and Minnie had been anxious to enquire about Jennie's sister Josephine's progress in the matrimonial market. She was now twenty-five years old and generally considered plainer than her ravishing sister. Minnie had heard rather concerning stories about Josephine's lack of deportment or elegance and her unflattering features.

'She has been carefully kept in the background and will never make such a furor as did her handsome sister. Josephine was known long ago as the "flamingo", because of her length of limb and her unvarying scarlet frocks. The "flamingo" was at that time a source of immense entertainment at a late dinner… and she used to skip into the dining room, a haggard, careworn expression on her childish face, contrasting so eloquently with the madly mirthful motion of her feet.'[7]

What she lacked in beauty, Josephine more than made up for in experience. She had grown up in her sister's shadow, but during the whole period she had made a careful study of the British aristocracy and had attended endless occasions where royalty were present, standing her in good stead for duties as a wife of a viscount or lord. In 1894, a reporter for the *New York Evening Post* described Josephine as looking girlishly sweet at a reception held by Queen Victoria. They continued describing her toilette: a white crêpe-de-chine Empire-style gown, trimmed with small fringed ruching, which was evidently very becoming.

Minnie had met Josephine many times and found her perfectly charming, as she should be, given the influences she had had. Everything was a bit less about Josephine than her sister. She was quieter than Jennie, less fair, less charming, less interesting, but she would still make a good wife for any gentleman and Minnie knew the Chamberlains were determined to procure her a good match. Jennie, who had been on a rollercoaster of fortune, seemed to be on the rise again, and her younger sister was riding, as usual, on her coat-tails. This visit to Albert Gate would be a good opportunity for Minnie to counsel Jennie in the ways of the aristocracy once more and to remind her gently that she was always there whenever the Chamberlains needed assistance.

An Impassioned Proposal

March 1895, New York

*'Nature will have her way among any group of young
people thrown together.'* – ALVA VANDERBILT

A single American Beauty rose sat perfectly wrapped in a box on
Consuelo Vanderbilt's dressing table. The young woman stared
dreamily at it. There had been no card with the delivery, but of course
a card wasn't necessary. The sender was obvious. It was 2 March 1895,
the day of Consuelo's eighteenth birthday. She knew she was bound
to receive many ostentatious gifts, perhaps some jewellery from her
father and an antique fan from her mother, but none would be more
cherished than the rose that lay before her. Consuelo, no doubt, felt a
rising excitement within her, the growing intrepidness of a young lady
on the brink of her first experience of love, the sense that this could be
her chance to escape.

Winthrop Rutherfurd was the man on whom she was pinning all
of her hopes. Older, dashing, handsome and from an Old New York

family that had long been integral to society, he represented everything that Consuelo dreamed about in a future husband. It was just a pity she had neglected to tell her mother about her plans. Alva Vanderbilt was certainly not in favour of the match and so the courtship had been conducted in secret, with the young couple snatching anxious, feverish moments together when they could, but always with enough discretion not to arouse too much suspicion. However, Alva noticed everything when it came to her children and so had now taken to observing her daughter's movements even more carefully than she had before. It left little opportunity for the debutante to emerge from her domineering mother's shadow and presented her with a very real problem of how to influence the question mark that hung over her future.

For this year would mark the culmination of a power struggle which mother and daughter had been locked in for many years. While Consuelo had been raised to respect her parents' wishes and to make decisions based on seeking their approval, she also had an inner belief that when it came to marriage, she, like most American heiresses, should be able to choose her own husband. Whether that decision was based on love or money or status or a combination of those factors, it would still be her decision to make, for better or for worse. Unfortunately for Consuelo, Alva completely disagreed with her daughter and was determined to mastermind her transformation from naive debutante to one of the most influential women in society. Consuelo must continue on the trail that Alva had blazed before her and ensure that the Vanderbilt name and place was maintained, no matter what it took.

Despite years of watching her mother's calculated social manoeuvres from the sidelines, Consuelo was completely unsuited for the role. Certainly she was beautiful, intelligent and cultured, everything a Vanderbilt heiress should be and more – Alva had made sure of it – but she lacked the natural flair for entertaining and the naked ambition that her mother had so skilfully employed to assume her position within the establishment. The truth that Alva did not want to accept was that any spark Consuelo might have shown for the game of society had been extinguished by a life spent being drilled on the right way to behave. A childhood that had included relentless study in order to become an accomplished linguist, talented musician and knowledgeable companion. Not only was Consuelo expected to excel and frequently asked to recite long passages of prose to her mother, but she also had to endure her lessons attached to a metal back brace to ensure perfect posture. While Alva was confident, formidable and determined, Consuelo was shy, demure and a romantic. Faced with a daughter who seldom vocalised what she wanted, it is little wonder that Alva, so used to being in charge, attempted to lay the foundations for her future.

Towards the end of her life, Alva shared her views on her children's marriages, telling her biographer Sara Bard Field, 'You cannot help your children to advantages through sentimental romance but through money which alone has power.'[1] Perhaps she was reflecting on her own marriage to Willie K, which had afforded her power and status but little personal happiness. However, despite her experiences of a union more reminiscent of a business arrangement than a partnership based on love, she still believed that this sacrifice was worthwhile and advocated it to her daughter. In a Gilded Age when men were the rulers of Wall Street and women were discouraged from asserting themselves in business or politics, marriage was their only route to power. The domestic sphere provided an opportunity for real influence and the domination of society was an extension of that. Alva had understood that as a young woman, and was determined Consuelo would carve out her own place. Given recent developments in her own marriage, she knew this would be difficult. Winthrop Rutherfurd, despite his good name and family connections, would not be enough to secure Consuelo's position as her mother's eventual successor.

The Vanderbilts' divorce had once more put the family in a precarious social position. After more than a decade of dominating New York's upper classes enveloped in a cloak of perfect propriety, their personal desires threatened to unmask them as society pretenders. Alva's lawyer had pleaded with her to reconsider the divorce; after all, the couple had been leading separate lives for some time, they had the money to travel and entertain independently, and the scandal of the separation would deal an irreparable blow to their status. Their situation was far from unique, and within the upper classes there were many unwritten rules about how to successfully navigate a marriage, particularly an unhappy one. Mrs Astor had endured many years tied to an errant husband, but never let it engulf her position as the moral compass of the establishment. In the Vanderbilts' New York, marriages were generally not expected to be happy and if they were, it was certainly a lucky accident. Edith Wharton encapsulated the reality of society marriages in the *Age of Innocence*, when Newland Archer ruminates on his own impending nuptials:

'… with a shiver of foreboding he saw his marriage becoming what most of the other marriages about him were: a dull association of material and social interests held together by ignorance on the one side and hypocrisy on the other.'[2]

Alva Vanderbilt had decided that in her marriage she would not keep up the charade any longer. Divorce was the only option and she would not relent for fear of what lay before her. She was confident that she could ride out the inevitable media storm and face down the society matrons who chose to shun her. She had taken on society before and outwitted them all, and she could do it again, because this time the prize was her freedom and the chance to marry Oliver Belmont for love.

Unfortunately for Consuelo, her mother's happiness would come at the cost of her own. Since the divorce news had broken, she had endured several social occasions where her parents' marriage was the main topic of conversation. While long-standing supporters such as Marietta Stevens had been kind and ensured that she was invited to dinner parties and balls, the mild-mannered debutante had felt the eyes of New York burning through her as she attempted to move effortlessly from one engagement to another while the Season continued relentlessly. On 27 February 1895, a dinner in the style of Napoleon's First Empire had been given by John W Murray Jr in

Consuelo's honour, with great attention paid to ensure every element was historically accurate, an honour afforded to only the most highly regarded debutantes. So Consuelo Vanderbilt's Season was not a disaster – but it wasn't the heady success Alva had been dreaming of either, particularly now that the family of Cornelius Vanderbilt, Willie K's brother, had closed ranks and publicly disowned Alva. For Alva, who took the combative view that you were either with her or against her, this proved an irresistible challenge. She would have to find another way for Consuelo to stun society, and once again she looked to old friends for help. Consuelo must secure a match that would capture the imagination and the loyalty of American society.

In the summer of 1894, Alva had taken Consuelo to England with the idea of a foreign marriage for her daughter slowly crystallising in her mind. After consulting Minnie Paget, her old friend from Paris and the daughter of Marietta Stevens, on the subject, they had together started to formulate a plan for Consuelo's introduction to the British aristocracy. Minnie had suggested possible suitors and had arranged the fateful dinner party where they had first met Sunny, the Duke of Marlborough. They had spent the rest of the London Season attending the most fashionable occasions and ensuring Consuelo was seen by those who mattered, as Minnie had suggested, and then in August had retired to a house on the Thames, so Alva could consider her next move. She knew divorce from Willie K was inevitable and that Consuelo's prospects would be affected by the fallout, but was an aristocratic match the answer? Since the divorce announcement, Alva had felt the chill of New York society's reaction and was incensed that not all of the elite were falling into line behind her. 'During the following months I was to suffer a perpetual denial of friendships and pleasures, since my mother resented seeing anyone whose loyalties were not completely hers,' Consuelo remembered. 'I had moreover to render a strict account of the few parties I was allowed to attend without her, and if I danced too often with a partner he immediately became the butt of her displeasure.'[3]

If Alva had doubts before about the merits of a transatlantic marriage, they now disappeared. They would go to England, Consuelo would become a duchess and Alva's friends, who were now masters in engineering such marriages, were going to help them.

For the time being, Consuelo remained delightfully unaware of her mother's plans. She did as she was told, diligently approaching the monotony of society: paying calls, attending the opera, taking tea with acquaintances, all while quietly remaining detached from the undercurrent of gossip and intrigue that permeated her world. She had spent years perfecting a distant quality for which she would become known throughout her life. An artist visiting the United States commented that Consuelo had 'the grace and elusiveness of a swan, and the painter who could adequately transfer her movements to canvas would make his name, and go down to posterity'[4]. The skill of remaining aloof would work to her advantage, allowing her to remain above the whispers and to imagine an entirely different existence – a life with Winthrop Rutherfurd. In many ways Consuelo was more like her father, Willie K, than her mother. She was charming, gentle and genuinely likeable, all characteristics that she had witnessed in her father. She also disliked conflict and carried with her an air of melancholy that would cause one reporter to remark on her 'subdued sadness'.[5] Willie K's inability to confront Alva's forceful personality had led to him abandoning Consuelo for Europe at this crucial time and would see him consistently fail to intervene in the question of her marriage in the months to come. While he spent most of his life indulging his passions for women and sailing, travelling extensively on his yacht courtesy of his grandfather's millions, the money did not seem to bring with it contentment. Rather tellingly, he was once reported as saying, 'My life was never destined to be quite happy… inherited wealth is a real handicap to happiness. It is a certain death to ambition as cocaine is to morality.'[6]

His daughter shared this predilection for melancholy and would spend years trying to find the courage to abandon her sense of duty to others in favour of her own happiness. However, on this day, as a young woman on the cusp of adulthood, she could dream about a future that she had created for herself. A future that paid no heed to her mother, her father or the Vanderbilt fortune, a future based on love.

It's clear that Consuelo had fallen for the older Winthrop, as was probably to be expected. He had been negotiating society for a number of years and was probably well versed in courting young debutantes. He was tall, athletic and was described by Edith Wharton as 'the prototype of my first novels'[7]. From Consuelo's own recollections of the period, Winthrop seems to have returned her feelings. In her memoirs she does not refer to him by name, instead describing him as 'an older man who by his outstanding looks, his distinction and his charm had gained a marked ascendancy in my affections'[8]. A cycling outing had been arranged where Consuelo and Winthrop could indulge in the new craze that was taking New York by storm and hopefully steal some time alone. Alva was of course present, as she always was, and was determined to ensure that didn't happen.

'Nature will have her way among any group of young people thrown together. I was careful that my daughter should not meet men for whom she might have a youthful and passing fancy,'[9] Alva remembered in her memoirs, and she was true to her word. After Consuelo was introduced to society, Alva was omnipresent, never risking her daughter's reputation or heart for one moment, except when *she* deemed it acceptable.

On 2 March 1895, Consuelo was to enjoy a small victory over her mother. During their ride on Riverside Drive, Consuelo and Winthrop used their evident youth and skill to surge ahead from the rest of the party, including Alva. As they sped along together, further and further away from the constraints of family and duty, the couple, a sense of freedom and bravery engendered in them, sought to reclaim their future. They stopped to catch their breath and Winthrop proposed. With Alva and the others in pursuit, they had only moments to talk: '… as they strained to reach us he pressed me to agree to a secret engagement, for I was leaving for Europe the next day. He added that he would follow me, but that I must not tell my mother since she would most certainly withhold her consent to our engagement. On my return to America we might plan an elopement.'[10]

When Alva finally caught up with the couple, Consuelo knew that she had guessed their secret. 'I have never succeeded in hiding my feelings and my mother must have guessed the cause of my new radiance,'[11] she said.

With events rapidly engulfing Alva's plans for her daughter, she took the only course of action available to her. She ploughed on with her plans for an English titled match for Consuelo. The foundations had already been laid the previous summer and she had enough contacts to ensure that it would become a reality. Marietta had assured Alva that Minnie was in place and ready to guide the Vanderbilts through the complex world of British etiquette. But they must work quickly. Unquestionably, Consuelo had a large dowry that would attract the highest calibre of suitor, and Willie K had assured Alva that this would be unaffected by their divorce. After all, the Vanderbilts would all surely benefit from Consuelo securing an advantageous marriage. However, the scandal surrounding the separation was not only taking its toll on Alva's reputation in New York, and in a world where the upper classes travelled frequently and widely, the tales of impropriety would almost certainly make their way across the ocean. Would such assaults on their character be enough to put off the British nobility, who already had preconceived ideas about the suitability of American wives? Minnie Paget was confident that, with her assistance, certain members of the aristocracy would quickly see the benefits of an alliance with the Vanderbilts. And so, as Consuelo mused about Withrop and his dramatic and impassioned proposal, the women packed for Europe.

A Most Superior Person

March 1895, Washington DC

*'I think London wonderfully delightful, although
I know so little of its people. Everything is in
full swing, and we read long accounts of balls
we don't go to!'* – MARY CURZON

From her bedroom window on the top floor of the family's mansion on Dupont Circle, Mary Leiter would have had a perfect view. The wide tree-lined avenues that converged on the circle bustled all day long with carriages, carrying politicians to meetings and ladies to afternoon appointments. Mary would have looked down on this scene every day, noting the contrast between the clatter of horse's hooves and the peaceful tranquillity of the circle itself, filled with exotic flowers and ornamental trees that enveloped the imposing statue of Samuel Francis Du Pont, a widely respected rear admiral during the Civil War. Would she miss the daily ritual when she left America for England, indeed would she ever look down on this view again? She had spent a great deal of time away from Washington over the past five years, yet the journey she was about to make was more permanent. Her marriage to George Curzon would mark the beginning of a new era, one that would take her a long way away from her birthplace and family, and for Mary that was a serious concern.

She looked once more at her copy of *Town Topics*. She knew that she should be wildly happy and excited at the prospect of the engagement announcement. After five long years, George Curzon had finally succumbed to the inevitable and they had declared to the world their intention to be married. There had been a flurry of congratulations, with favourable articles in the newspapers, naming George 'a very promising politician, who has much of the quality of a statesman'.[1] Mary had been simply inundated with letters and gifts to mark the announcement of the coming together of the brilliant young couple, but one disturbing comment in a tawdry gossip rag had permeated her giddy mood, replacing it with an anxiety that now loomed large over her. The article read, '… the engagement has also revived a discussion of the characteristics of the fair fiancée's family, and the almost numberless malapropisms that are attributed… to Mrs Leiter.'[2]

The accusation illuminated a problem that had plagued Mary since her debut into society. The charge was nothing new and had been levelled at the *nouveaux riches* many times before: that they lacked the refinement and cultural superiority of their more socially established contemporaries. Often it was an accusation that had no merit, a rumour largely put about to subdue the threat from *arrivistes* who had grown too ambitious, too hungry for the acceptance of society leaders. In this case, however, Mary knew that *Town Topics* was right. Her mother was a hindrance to her aspirations, one she had been trying to control unsuccessfully for many Seasons. Mary had been confident that, apart from a few unfortunate moments she had not been able to prevent, the impeccable performance she had managed to maintain at all times, never putting a foot wrong in society, had been enough to make up for Mrs Leiter, but now she wasn't sure. Her mother wasn't terribly vulgar, of course, just not quite up to the standards that Washington society demanded. She had spent the majority of her life supporting her husband, Levi Ziegler Leiter, in his business endeavours and raising their three daughters, Mary, Daisy and Nancy. Levi Leiter had made his fortune after establishing Field and Leiter, a store in Chicago, known later as Marshall Field, in 1865. He quickly became a multi-millionaire, sold his share to his business partner and moved to Washington with his family. The Leiters then embarked on the familiar routine of the American upper class, following the social Seasons in America while also travelling the world in an effort to broaden their education and acclimatise themselves to European culture. It was Mrs Leiter's remarks when asked about a recent trip to the Orient that had prompted rumours of her lack of refinement. Her inquisitor asked if she had seen the Dardanelles, to which Mrs Leiter had replied, 'Oh dear, yes. We dined with them.' Much to Mary's embarrassment, this story was retold again and again and had now been revived by *Town Topics* at the very moment she should have been revelling in her happiness. She just hoped the gossip didn't reach George.

George Curzon was a perfectionist and he demanded the same of Mary. Throughout their long courtship, which had lasted years and had mainly been conducted through correspondence, he had consistently advised Mary on every aspect of her appearance and demeanour, telling her, 'You must learn to think and spell as an Englishwoman, my child,'[3] when she used American spellings in her letters, and imploring her to learn some simple songs for him even though she was an accomplished musician and had far more knowledge of the piano than he did. On receiving a photograph of Mary, when he might have been expected to exalt her beauty, he instead criticised her expression, saying it made her look stern, contemplative and severe, and impressed upon her the need to adopt a softer, gentler demeanour. He even commented on the way she wore her hair and on her linguistic abilities, even though she was fluent in French and German, skills he had failed to master. There really was nothing that George would not give his opinion on.

It must have come as a relief to Mary that George did not reserve his pomposity and vanity for her. As the eldest son of Lord Scarsdale, hailing from the Curzon family who had an aristocratic lineage that could be traced back for generations, George was supremely confident of his position and superiority. He had been educated at Eton and then Oxford, where he had proved himself to be highly intelligent and had demonstrated an aptitude for literature and an obsessive interest in the East; this led to his becoming an authority on the region, writing many books on the subject. In 1886, when he was only twenty-seven, he became Conservative MP for Southport, beginning a journey that would propel him to the upper echelons of British politics. His arrogance was so ingrained that he became infamous in British society, inspiring the poem:

> My name is George Nathaniel Curzon,
> I am a most superior person.
> My cheeks are pink, my hair is sleek,
> I dine at Blenheim once a week.[4]

While George demanded much of his future bride, in some ways it was nothing more than he demanded of himself. When he was writing, he subjected himself to a punishing schedule, often isolating himself for long periods until he was content with his efforts. He also suffered from incurable curvature of the spine, which he resolved to keep hidden from all but his closest confidantes. The condition meant that he was forced to wear a padded leather corset and was often in excruciating pain, particularly when he embarked on long, laborious and perilous research trips to Persia and India. George emanated an inner strength, intelligence and sense of entitlement and he was determined that his wife would have the same qualities. She would be a mirror image of himself, ensuring that, together, the Curzons would make an unfaltering partnership.

When George met the twenty-year-old Mary at the Duchess of Westminster's ball on 17 July 1890, he couldn't possibly have predicted how such a thoroughly American heiress, brought up in the midst of a confident and thriving democracy, would adapt to become the perfect embodiment of an aristocratic wife. She was exceptionally beautiful, with an oval-shaped face, deep grey eyes and long hazel hair pulled back into a love-knot at the nape of her neck. She was tall and slim and carried herself with a practised poise and elegance that fascinated George from the moment he first laid eyes on her.

It wasn't just George whom Mary entranced: she had been making waves on the social scene for two years in America, after coming out in 1888. Ward McAllister expressed his unqualified admiration for her and invited her to a Patriarchs' Ball in New York, while she had already charmed the elite in Washington, establishing a friendship with Frances Cleveland, President Cleveland's wife, the youngest First Lady in history, who occupied the centre of Washington's social whirl. This friendship would be one of the few that Mary established outside of her immediate family circle, with some, such as Virginia Peacock, society editor of the *Washington Post*, speculating in her book *Famous American Belles of the 19th Century* that she had a natural shyness: 'She formed but few close friendships, the natural reserve of her temperament rendering it impossible for her to respond easily to those intimacies which enter into the lives of so many girls.'[5] Others ventured that Mary's tendency to be aloof was the root cause of her lack of friends, noting that she snubbed acquaintances when they failed to be useful to her, as her biographer Nicolson explains: 'It was said that she dropped friends, that she was cold, that she formed few intimacies, that she alarmed people, that she made them aware of the social category in which she placed them.'[6]

This appears not to have applied to Frances Cleveland, who was endlessly helpful in establishing the Leiters as stalwarts of Washington society, introducing them to Henry Adams, Theodore Roosevelt and other prominent politicians. Such associations led to the family being accepted in New York, where Mary would have encountered Marietta Stevens and other influential hostesses. She was also a frequent visitor to Newport, where she dazzled society with her sweetness of character, innate dignity and intelligence – cultivated by tutors paid for by her indulgent parents and comprehensive trips to Europe, where she had been afforded sojourns to Paris and London but had also travelled more widely to Norway and Sweden.

By the time the Leiters were in Paris again in the Spring of 1890, Mary was an experienced social operator, used to admiring glances from ladies and gentlemen and adept at remaining aloof from the vicious whispers that branded her family nothing more than simple shopkeepers. The romantic novelist Elinor Glyn, who would go on to become George Curzon's mistress, remembered in her memoirs seeing Mary for the first time at a ball in the French capital: 'Opposite to me in the cotillion, I remember, was the beautiful Mary Leiter, afterwards Lady Curzon. Her Aphrodite type was a great joy to my Greek-loving eye.'[7]

Marietta Stevens was also in Paris at this time and had already encountered the Leiters on several occasions in New York and Newport. Mary and her mother were now intent on finding a suitable match for the popular debutante and after Mary branded the French 'self centred' and 'snobs'[8], their attention turned to England. From Mary's recollections it seems that, although they had spent a great deal of time in London, they had failed to make any connections of consequence: 'I think London wonderfully delightful, although I know so little of its people. Everything is in full swing, and we read long accounts of balls we don't go to!'[9]

Mary's growing frustration at sitting on the sidelines of the London Season is palpable, but then suddenly everything changed. Mary produced a letter of introduction to Sir Lyon Playfair, a Member of Parliament, whose wife happened to be American. He promptly took her to a high-profile luncheon at the Royal Naval Schools, Greenwich, where the Prince and Princess of Wales were due to watch a demonstration by cadets and award prizes to the most promising. Widely attended by society and described by one newspaper as 'one of the most attractive of the al fresco gatherings of the Season'[10], it was the perfect opportunity for Mary to make her mark on London society. Rather unexpectedly, Mary was presented to the royal guests by the Duchess of St Albans, who, Mary's biographer Nigel Nicolson suggests, had 'heard of her from an American friend'[11]. It therefore appears possible that, by using their American and British contacts, Minnie and Marietta may have had a hand in launching Mary onto the social scene. After her triumph at Greenwich, Mary's life was transformed: she was suddenly in vogue and invited to a dizzying array of events in just one week, including lunching at the House of Commons where she was introduced to Gladstone and Austen Chamberlain, an appearance at a society wedding and attending a country house party in Oxfordshire. The contrast with her life on the fringes of London society just the week before was distinct and culminated in her attendance at the Duchess of Westminster's Ball, which she opened by dancing the first quadrille with the Prince of Wales. If Mary was unsure whether she had arrived, then Bertie's decision to choose her as his dance partner would have convinced her. She had been accepted, and the accomplishment was made all the sweeter when she discovered that an aristocrat named George Curzon had been watching the entire display with great interest.

Like many gentlemen of the aristocracy, George Curzon had an enduring interest in women and idealised the romantic notion of love affairs. He was part of a select group called the Souls, so named because of their sensitive and enigmatic natures. This rather earnest band, which included Margot Asquith, Ettie Grenfell, George Wyndham and Arthur Balfour, was created after the death of their close friend Laura Lyttleton. Their overwhelming grief after her death bound them together tightly, causing them to restrict their company to one another and reject wider society. Before long, Arthur Paget's friend and fellow racing enthusiast Lord Charles Beresford had christened the group the Souls, a moniker which caught on and spread throughout the aristocracy, marking the Souls out as intellectual, elite and mysterious. Minnie, who avidly followed their activities, as she did the whole of society, declared Curzon the 'captain of the Souls'[12], reflecting her keen interest in the eligible bachelor and his activities.

Of course, among a group of romantics such as them, infatuations and affairs were rife, and George often found himself at the centre of such intrigues. In 1886, he had declared himself madly in love with Sibell Grosvenor and ardently pursued her, only to find that she had chosen to marry his friend George Wyndham. He continued to hurtle from one love affair to the next, causing one of the subjects of his affections, the novelist and socialite Pearl Craigie, to observe that he was 'madly reckless with women'[13].

Perhaps it was inevitable that George would immediately become infatuated with Mary. After meeting her at the ball, he sought her out again at a house party given by Lady Brownlow at her country estate, Ashridge in Hertfordshire. He wrote to Mary later that when she had taken him into the rose garden, he had 'a strong inclination to kiss you, with difficulty restrained'.[14] In the ten days that followed before the Leiters departed for Europe, George and Mary corresponded daily, exchanging small presents and photographs. There was no doubt that Mary was intoxicated with the enigmatic George and he was certainly charmed by the graceful American who had captured his attention when she seemingly floated around the ballroom with Bertie; however, if Mary was at this stage confident of a smooth courtship that could perhaps lead to marriage, she would be proved wrong. George would be an elusive and unconvincing suitor, yet Mary's regard for him endured throughout five long years of sporadic and uncertain contact.

George's ambition for an important political position in government would always be his top priority. Engaging in romantic entanglements would come second, and Mary was just one of a number of ladies to receive his attentions. In 1891, he wrote to the now married Sibell Grosvenor, 'I loved you earliest and I have loved you longest; and the joy and treasure you have been to me, although we have never been married, has been as great as most wives can give their husbands.'[15]

In the same year, he asked George Wyndham to act as his intermediary with an anonymous mistress who had taken to blackmailing George Curzon when he tried to end their affair, threatening to expose him to members of the cabinet and sabotage his political career. When

Wyndham finally brokered a meeting between the pair, Curzon's mistress spitefully informed him that she had previously slept with another man on one of the many occasions George had left England a research trip. George, horrified, wrote to Wyndham, 'Treachery, betrayal, anger, abuse, revenge – all I have forgiven but coarse and vulgar sin never – no, not till I die.' Despite his own dubious morals, George was quick to denounce others.

Meanwhile, back in America, Mary was basking in the success of her London trip. The *Chicago Tribune* was full of praise for a young lady who had won over the British nobility with consummate ease: '… only very occasionally do American girls make their way in this hedged-about, over sensitive, very suspicious class. It takes a woman of limitless tact, dignity, money and culture to make any impression… yet this is precisely what Miss Leiter has done.'[16]

She continued to write to George, seemingly unaware of his other liaisons, and made another trip over to England in 1891 for the Season, again proving popular. She seemed to secure the tacit approval of the Souls, receiving invitations to several gatherings, and was even presented at the Queen's Drawing Room. Mary's regard for George was unchanged, yet he continued to blow hot and cold. He attended a small party given at Claridge's for Mary's twenty-first birthday and invited her to Norwood, his country retreat, where he preferred to isolate himself from friends and acquaintances, rarely extending an invitation to anyone. To Mary and the Leiters, it appeared that George's affection was growing and they were hopeful that a proposal might be forthcoming, but when she returned to America it was as though the previous few weeks had not happened. Having recently secured the post of Under-Secretary of State for India, George immediately began again to concentrate on his career rather than occupying himself with thoughts of romance. He understood that as one of the few gentlemen to travel extensively through Asia and the Middle East, his knowledge of the region would prove invaluable to the government. Feeling certain that this expertise would be the key to his eventual success, he redoubled his efforts and continued to immerse himself in his studies, working obsessively on his mammoth tome *Persia and the Persian Question*.

Mary, who had returned to America still unsure of George's feelings, wrote to him. It would be six long months before she would receive a reply. In 1892, he embarked on a round-the-world trip, which included the USA. His letters continued to be sporadic and, although he spent a large amount of time in the country and even visited Washington, he neglected to inform Mary or try to arrange a meeting with her. Instead he began a flirtation with a young Virginian lady named Amelie Rives while he was staying with her family. It appeared that George's interest in Mary was waning, although he did maintain occasional contact. It was just enough to leave Mary with hope and, despite having many suitors of her own, she had fallen in love with George and refused to entertain the possibility that they would not share a life together, writing to a friend, 'I will have him, because I believe he needs me. I have no shame.'[17]

Inherently George did not approve of Americans, calling them 'the least attractive species of the human genus'[18], but Mary Leiter presented an interesting opportunity. She was respectable, elegant and kind, all of the attributes he admired in a woman, and she was able to provide him with the funds to pursue his political ambitions. George was certain of Mary's devotion but continued to debate her place in his future. Finally, in March 1893, George and Mary found themselves both in Paris and, after having dinner with the Leiters at the Hotel Vendôme, the couple were left alone.

'I had entered the hotel without the slightest anticipation that this would be the issue. After dinner, when we were alone, this beautiful, sweet and faithful woman told me her story... was there not something wonderful in this long trial, in the uncomplaining and faithful devotion of this darling girl?'[19] George wrote when he recalled the evening years later. He proposed on the spot and then quickly insisted that the engagement remain a secret until he had taken another trip to the Pamirs and Afghanistan and could be sure of his father's response to the idea of an American daughter-in-law.

George's romantic retelling of the proposal fails to illuminate the long years of uncertainty he had forced Mary to endure. Perhaps he was overwhelmed by the sight of this beautiful, cultured, wealthy young woman declaring her utter devotion to him and realised this was his chance for personal happiness. Or perhaps he calculated that after years spent pursuing his political ambitions, he would need Levi Leiter's financial assistance to progress any further. While George's intentions aren't certain and his behaviour was certainly erratic during their courtship, it is clear that the couple were well suited. Virginia Peacock described Mary as 'serious and earnest rather than scintillating, with a reserve and dignity of manner tempered by a sweetness that admitted no suggestion of austerity'.[20] These characteristics were all highly valued by George and gained added appeal when combined with the prospect of a large dowry.

Chauncey Depew could have been writing about George and Mary when he wrote in *Titled Americans*: 'As a rule he belongs to an old and historic family, is well educated, traveled and polished, but poor. He knows nothing of business, and to support his estate requires an increased income. The American girl whòm he gets acquainted with has that income, so in marrying her he goes to heaven and gets – the earth.'[21]

Mary returned to America and the couple met only once more in London in 1894 for two days, when George finally agreed that she could share the news of their engagement with her parents. After that, they did not plan to meet until the eve of their wedding.

After years of tentative, painstaking courtship, Mary must have wondered whether the malicious gossip that magazines such as *Town Topics* insisted on peddling would alienate George. She had an innate understanding of his need for appearances to be maintained at all times and his suspicion that the admittance of frightful Americans to the English upper classes would only damage it. And now he was marrying one, a decision that seemed at odds with these long-held beliefs. Mary could only hope that her own impeccable behaviour and the promise of a healthy income would help George to ignore any doubts he and others had about the Leiters' pedigree. It would be easier to keep her mother at arm's length when she was in England, although it might pain her to even think about leaving her close-knit family. It was here in the capital that she had taken her first tentative steps into society and here that she had befriended the President's wife, ensuring Washington's elite were at her feet. Now, she had her own wedding to look forward to, at St John's Church opposite the White House, where she would look luminous in the Scarsdale family diamonds and a gown from Charles Worth. As Mary Leiter she had achieved so much, but as Mary Curzon the possibilities were endless.

Faith, Figures and Francs

March 1895, Paris

*'Like an automaton I tried on the clothes she
ordered for me.'* – CONSUELO VANDERBILT

Alva Vanderbilt was unquestionably irritated. She clasped her
hands tightly in her lap and sat up even straighter than usual, her
jaw tightening into a forced expression of interest that belied her
displeasure. A cursory glance at Consuelo could only engender a
sense of disappointment. True, she was a beautiful, elegant young
woman, educated and intelligent – the epitome of the new American
aristocracy – and had dutifully complied with all of her mother's careful
directions to become a lady of substance, yet there was something
missing. Alva would have known, as she observed Consuelo, sitting on
a chaise longue in a posture of flawless grace, that her daughter lacked
spirit and must have wondered whether this model of a perfect bride
would actually be enough to get the job done. No matter, she would
carry on regardless with the plan, which could not be fully executed if

Consuelo's wardrobe was not carefully prepared and fitted while they were in Paris. London would never accept the Americans if they could not compete sartorially. And that was the source of today's irritation. The news had reached them as they arrived in Paris; Charles Frederick Worth was dead. The renowned couturier and widely accepted oracle of fashion had passed away on 10 March 1895, meaning the Vanderbilt women had missed him by only a few days. It was inconvenient, to say the least. Apart from the fact that the designer's workroom would likely be in a state of mourning, which really was not the best environment for a debutante to be excitedly planning a summer wardrobe, it also placed a question mark over the quality of the clothes themselves: could the grand master's sons really continue his great work? This year, Alva could leave nothing to chance. Consuelo's wardrobe simply had to be the most elaborate, intricate, modern and beautifully crafted that London and Newport had ever seen and of course, as the mother of the most popular debutante of the Season, Alva herself needed to take her rightful place in the limelight too. The stakes were high and, despite the awkward timing, she had to ensure the House of Worth lived up to expectations.

Charles Frederick Worth had long been considered the leading couturier for women of fortune. He was the son of a country solicitor, born in Lincolnshire in England before moving to London to work in a draper's shop at the age of twelve. After years of training, he made the bold decision to move to Paris and, without any money or connections, he slowly began to build up a loyal following of clients. He pioneered several unique design elements, including slightly shorter skirts to enable easier walking, a skirt with no crinoline or hoop but a bustle, and fashionable clothes for pregnancy and mourning; he was also the first designer to put his name on labels inside his clothes and to use live models to show off his designs. When the Empress Eugénie discovered his creations and championed him to the French court, his establishment as the designer of choice for fashionable society was complete and a twice-yearly pilgrimage to his chic salon to choose a stunning array of outfits for the Season ahead became *de rigueur*.

'For a generation M Worth has been supreme in his own domain. He has known how to dress woman as nobody else knew how to dress her,"[1] *The Times* wrote in its obituary of Worth on 12 March 1895. *Town Topics* told its readers that Worth's death meant the removal of 'one of the striking personalities of fashionable Paris'.[2] Now that the great man was gone, society on both sides of the Atlantic held its breath to see if Worth would maintain its flawless workmanship and inventive design and whether it could continue to attract the most exclusive clientele. Everything about the fashion house had come from Worth himself. Known far and wide for his temperamental and autocratic style, he ruled his workshop of over three hundred seamstresses with a rod of iron, ensuring that every gown received the utmost care and the immaculate finish his vision demanded. He had an innate understanding of his clients, knowing almost instantly which colours would flatter their skin tone and the particular cut of gown to enhance their figure. That was his brilliance and the wealthy were hooked.

Worth attracted clients from around the world, not just from France, but he once declared that his favourite clients were Americans because they had 'faith, figures and francs'[3]. Whether his faithful *nouveaux-riches* clients who travelled across the ocean to spend their fortunes on Worth gowns did so because they were confident in his ability to drape them in the most appropriate gowns for any and all occasions, or whether they came because they had heard it was the fashionable thing to do, isn't clear; however, dressed in an armour of Worth, the wives and daughters of Wall Street plutocrats marched into social functions in the heart of Belgravia and Fifth Avenue with confidence and that, they reasoned, was worth the thousands of dollars that his designs commanded. An endless round of fittings would usually accompany a shopping trip to Paris for a Season's wardrobe. An array of gowns and outfits would need to be chosen and fitted, from intricate beaded ball gowns to simpler tea gowns, riding habits and bathing costumes, all with a bewildering choice of fabrics and adornments to choose from. As Edith Saunders noted in her biography of Worth: 'The distinctive dress of the 'nineties was extravagantly elegant; the class of immensely rich people in the world was now considerable, and the women belonging to it demanded costly workmanship in their dresses as well as an imposing style.'[4]

This rapid development of clothes as an indication of social status was something that designers like Worth had encouraged, shored up by wealthy clients desperate to secure a position in the most exclusive circles. Intelligent Swells like Marietta Stevens had quickly ascertained the value of the right wardrobe by the right designer and had slavishly followed the dictates of Parisian designers for the past thirty years. As early as 1867, *Harper's Magazine* had denounced the growing trend when it wrote: 'Why should American women so strenuously endeavour to follow out the Paris fashions, which are invented by capricious women of rank and wealth, or by the dress-makers, who, with the intention of inciting their customers to inordinate expenditure, rack their imaginations for the purpose of producing something new?'[5] Despite such criticism, by 1895 a visit to Paris for dress fittings had become so much a part of the social year for American heiresses that to be without an array of Worth dresses would elicit comments from fellow members of society keen to speculate on the family's financial situation.

For Alva Vanderbilt, who had fled the scandal of her divorce and her daughter's burgeoning relationship with Winthrop Rutherfurd in New York to journey to Paris for Consuelo's new wardrobe, Worth's death threatened to derail her plans for her daughter's polished presentation in London. Luckily, however, so far all appeared to be in order at the couturier's. The Vanderbilts had been offered their usual fitting room, which was luxuriously furnished and tastefully decorated, as one would expect. They had been provided with their usual plate of *foie gras* and glass of Sauternes and had been given the exacting attention that their status demanded. The Vanderbilts were likely to spend around twenty thousand dollars[6] on this trip and would be ensuring that every dime was accounted for in the service and apparel they received.

Consuelo seemed distracted, and had been quieter than usual since they had arrived in Europe. She was very different from the last time they had travelled to Paris, during the previous spring for Consuelo's debut. Alva had used Paris as a training ground for the more demanding London Season that began in earnest in June. After spending so much time in the French capital herself when she was growing up, she knew the city well and, from their suite at the Hotel Continental, set about filling Consuelo's days with walks under the flowering chestnuts of the Champs Elysées and drives in the Bois de Boulogne. Consuelo had immediately been enthralled by the fabric of the city, using her daily walks to observe its inhabitants, enchanted by the wide boulevards that opened up the frenetic activity of the city's daily life to inquisitive tourists.

Alva also continued Consuelo's cultural education, arranging visits to museums and churches, lectures at the Sorbonne and matinees at the Théâtre Français. When Consuelo finally made her debut at the Duc de Grammont's ball at a hotel on the Rue de Chaillot, she made an enviable impression. She was wearing a white tulle dress, custom-made from Worth of course, with a long, full skirt that lightly skimmed the ground and a tightly laced bodice. Her dark hair was curled and piled high on her head and a long narrow ribbon was tied round her neck, which, as Alva had predicted, caused onlookers to comment on its swan-like and regal quality. The finishing touch was long white gloves that almost reached her slender shoulders. Like most debutantes, Consuelo had been terrified that she would not be asked to dance by the young French gentlemen drafted in to populate the ball and would instead be destined to spend the night standing against the wall with the lady chaperones, desperately waiting for an invitation. But she need not have worried. All of French society knew who she was. Consuelo Vanderbilt, the rich American heiress, would not be without a partner for long.

Alva had been pleased with Consuelo's performance and was especially gratified when rumours began to swirl around the city and beyond that Consuelo had received several proposals of marriage from members of the European aristocracy. Of course, Alva would not be entertaining any such offers until they had been to England, for England was the ultimate prize. In the complex web that characterised the European nobility, English titles were the most revered among Americans. Most were well travelled enough to have regularly come into contact with the so-called aristocracy of many countries, yet England alone appeared to hold tightest to its traditions and lineage. In Italy or France there seemed to be a baffling number of old and newly created titles that had no real heritage to accompany them. In England, there were titles and family seats that could trace their history back hundreds of years, and what truly interested competitive mothers like Alva Vanderbilt was that British titles were limited. It was immensely difficult to capture a duke, as there were only thirty dukedoms in the country. She knew that if Consuelo could successfully marry one, her status as an integral part of the British aristocracy and the Vanderbilts' place in the inner sanctum of New York society would be assured, no matter what kind of scandal followed them around the globe. After spending large swathes of 1893 and 1894 travelling as a family on Willie K's yacht, attempting to repair the W K Vanderbilts' marriage and failing miserably, Alva knew that the scandal of divorce had the potential to signal the downfall of them all.

It was July 1894 when Consuelo found herself in a fashionable London hotel, with strict instructions from her mother to impress Minnie Paget at all costs. Her first impressions were not good, as she recalled their modest hotel, a far cry from the luxurious surroundings of Fifth Avenue's modern establishments. 'The rooms were frowsty in the true English sense and contained a bewildering medley of the rubbish of centuries... Over the windows hung heavy plush curtains and the meagre light was still further dimmed by the heavy lace window-curtains.'[7]

When Consuelo and Alva finally made the journey to call on Minnie at 35 Belgrave Square, Consuelo found herself feeling 'like a gawky, graceless child under her scrutiny'.[8] Alva listened carefully to the appraisal of her daughter by Minnie, who had received them with 'the affection due to an old friend and the condescension that seemed to infect the habitués of the inner circles of London society'.[9] She agreed to Minnie's plan to bring Consuelo and Sunny together at a small dinner party. Something intimate, something effective, and there was no one better than Minnie to achieve it. She was adept at being endlessly creative in social situations on behalf of American clients, seeming instinctively to know the best way of achieving the desired result. The romantic novelist Elinor Glyn once said of Minnie, 'She knew how to entertain and mix people better than anyone I have ever met, and her house in Belgrave Square was the centre of all that was most chic in English and Anglo-American society.'[10]

Alva was counting on Minnie's social prowess and, although she hadn't yet decided whether a titled marriage was the right path for Consuelo, she knew that if she did plump for an aristocratic son-in-law, no less than a duke would do. She would not be content with an untitled son from an aristocratic family such as Minnie had settled for. Minnie, who had spent years trying to attract suitors, never quite making up her mind, until it was too late and she had been forced to accept a marriage without a title, the one thing she had been coveting for so long. Nor would a lowly lord or viscount do for Consuelo. No, if she decreed it, the Vanderbilt millions would purchase a duke for her daughter. That was the least they could do.

Minnie delivered, as she always did, and the dinner party was a success. Sunny had seemed intrigued by the young American and had obviously been appraised of Consuelo's beauty before their meeting, writing to a friend, 'I hear that she is quite good looking.'[11] For her part, Consuelo had seemed to receive his attention with genuine interest and grace. 'I thought him good-looking and intelligent,' she would later write of her first impression of Sunny in her memoirs. 'He had a small aristocratic face with a large nose and rather prominent blue eyes. His hands, which he used in a fastidious manner, were well shaped and he seemed inordinately proud of them.'[12]

Minnie's efforts did not go unnoticed by the rest of society. The Dowager Duchess of Marlborough, the Duke's grandmother, wrote to her daughter-in-law, Jennie Churchill, in July 1894, commenting, 'Mrs Paget has been very busy introducing him to Miss Vanderbilt and telling everybody she meant to arrange a marriage between them....'[13]

Consuelo had no idea of the plan that was beginning to take shape on her behalf and was relieved when Alva took a house on the Thames for the rest of the summer. Away from the prying eyes of London, she could be herself once more and return to her studies, diligently working for the Oxford University entrance exams, which she would later pass with flying colours. She knew she would never go to university, but she savoured the fleeting moment of success anyway, a singular flash of accomplishment that was hers and hers alone.

Now, just a few months later, Consuelo looked back on those idyllic days spent by the river with her brother, Willie, and the family's friends from New York, Mrs William Jay and her daughters, who had idled the time away with them, and wished for that life again. A life full of simple pleasures and simple problems. The most drastic of these was the ill-conceived party that Alva had thrown for the local village children, which had included well-known American treats such as ice cream. Despite the generosity of the visitors, the children, not familiar with such rich tastes, had all complained about stomach ache and pleaded for hot tea. Such mis-steps by Alva were few and far between, and to be relished on the rare occasions they presented themselves.

Consuelo still longed to see Winthrop or hear from him. On the voyage to Europe she had been preoccupied by thoughts of their last meeting, when he had asked for her hand in marriage and implored her to elope with him on her return. She had made up her mind there and then that she would, and throughout her journey her resolve had not wavered, but now that she was in Paris and she had not received any contact from Winthrop, she began to question her decision. Consuelo wrote in her memoirs, 'I never laid eyes on Mr X, nor did I hear from him'[14] during her time in Paris. What she was unaware of was that Winthrop did in fact follow her to Europe, but Alva had given strict instructions to her staff and the hotel that he was not to be admitted under any circumstances. She ensured that any letters he sent to Consuelo were intercepted and reminded her servants that, should Consuelo make any furtive attempts to contact her beau, these notes were to find their way to Alva. The lovers had been thwarted, but Consuelo remained unaware of her mother's actions.

Consuelo earnestly continued her daily routine in Paris, including regular trips to Worth on the Rue de la Paix for fittings. 'Like an automaton I tried on the clothes she ordered for me,'[15] she remembered. Her mother seemed steadfastly committed to another Season in London, with Consuelo at the heart of her plans to charm certain members of the aristocracy and so, dutifully, Consuelo complied with all Alva's requests to ensure she was fully equipped for the social functions that lay ahead. Alva casually began to mention Minnie Paget, increasingly peppering their conversations with references to Minnie's far-reaching social network and connections to Bertie, the Prince of Wales. Every time Consuelo heard Minnie's name it evoked an involuntary reaction that made her want to shrink away from the conversation, back into the elegant wooden panelling that embellished Worth's salon walls. There was something about Minnie's terse appraisal of the young debutante the year before that alarmed Consuelo, but she couldn't quite understand why it filled with her such concern. However, Consuelo was right to be worried: London was the Vanderbilts' next stop and a duke, as well as society, awaited her. As she later recalled: 'Then we moved to London, where events began to move rapidly and I felt I was being steered into a vortex that was to engulf me.'[16]

Roguey Poguey Stories

March 1895, Civitavecchia, Italy

*'There is not a day that I do not think of you and
long to see you and the children and I talk of you.'*
– CONSUELO, DUCHESS OF MANCHESTER

Consuelo Manchester would have looked out across the sea from her position on the yacht, the *Valiant*. It was a clear, still day and if she continued to look out to the horizon, she might be able to forget for just one moment what lay on board. Her recollection of the events of the past few days would have grown vague, days where she had barely slept as she nursed, then kept vigil and finally was forced to let go of one of her twin girls, Mary. Now, she found herself sailing from Civitavecchia in Italy to Marseilles on board Willie K Vanderbilt's prize possession, trying to bring the remains of her daughter back home to England.

Lady Mary Montagu was sixteen years old when she died of pneumonia at the Grand Hotel in Rome on 14 March 1895. Consuelo

Manchester now doubted the decision she had made to bring her daughters to the Continent in search of a warmer climate and the chance to immerse themselves in the ancient culture. It was the kind of pilgrimage the aristocracy had been partaking in for centuries and Consuelo herself had grown used to the rhythmic quality of her year, which included a trip to Europe in the winter, London for the Season and then a retreat to the Manchesters' country estate. There had been nothing new about this trip, yet everything had changed. Now she found herself, on this return journey, a mother of two to her eighteen-year-old son and heir to the dukedom, Little Kim, and Lady Alice Montagu, Lady Mary's twin. She was fleeing gossip and grief and, of course, the ghost of her husband Kim.

Kim had died in 1892, nearly three years ago, yet Consuelo hadn't stopped tormenting herself as she had throughout their marriage with thoughts about where it had gone wrong. She knew that socially she was at her peak. She enjoyed the freedom that being a widow afforded, as well as the financial independence she had long craved while married, thanks to her enterprise in ensuring a smooth passage for new-money Americans into English society. It afforded her a lifestyle that the title of duchess had not been able to provide and she had felt a brimming sense of hope as to the limitless possibilities of the venture. This year was supposed to mark a new beginning, a time when *she* could choose her destiny, forge a life for her children and a place for herself, and now suddenly everything was different. The warm Mediterranean breeze hinted at days past, yet she seemed so very far away from that summer in Saratoga when she had met Kim, the man who would one day become the Duke of Manchester.

Kim had first noticed Consuelo Yznaga on the veranda of the United States Hotel in Saratoga Springs, New York. He had watched as she walked slowly and skilfully up and down with her sister Natica, fully aware of the effect she was having on the young gentlemen lounging against the railings that enclosed the hotel's gardens. She walked gracefully, purposefully, her lace parasol protecting her delicate features from the sun's harsh rays, incessantly chatting to her companion, pausing only to throw her head backwards and laugh, before continuing on her parade. Kim could hear the remnants of her laughter float over to where he stood, rendered languid by the summer's humidity. His fleeting fascination with Consuelo may have been just that, as it often had been before, for he found boredom quickly set in, especially when faced with numerous opportunities to observe young debutantes; however, as he regarded this young lady, she did something that piqued his interest. After a further conspiratorial whisper with her sister, she proudly took off her gloves, rolled them into a ball and proceeded with her walk. Kim observed the matrons sipping iced tea at their tables, straightening their backs and looking aghast at this young pretender. Who was she? Where did she come from? And had nobody instructed her on the etiquette of dress here? Consuelo Yznaga took note of their expressions, smiled sweetly, turned on her heel and went inside, giggling with Natica all the way.

After this first encounter, Kim ensured that he discovered everything there was to know about Consuelo and her family. He was pleasantly surprised to hear that her father owned a cotton plantation, Ravenswood, in Louisiana, which spanned three thousand acres and had three hundred slaves working the land. Consuelo's mother, Ellen Yznaga, who had inherited the property from her father, Captain Samuel Clement, was tasked with managing the plantation while her husband, Antonio, who was of Cuban descent and was the Spanish Consul in New Orleans, split his time between that city and New York, where he had a business importing Cuban produce. Kim paid no heed to the stories that the Yznagas' fortunes were unpredictable and that the family seemed to be poorly regarded in polite society. There were rumours they were free spirits, with Ellen often to be found smoking, reclined on a chaise longue in her smart hotel room, while her three daughters enjoyed the freedom their indulgent parents afforded them. For Kim and Consuelo that meant unchaperoned walks together in the Saratoga deer park and long drives in a rented phaeton to the lake before sauntering home. Consuelo's evident beauty and soft Southern drawl was intoxicating to the twenty-three-year-old Kim, who found her a delightful contrast to the rather solemn and stuffy marital prospects that awaited him back in England. Consuelo Yznaga was said to attract 'rich and poor alike, solely through her fascinating personality'.[1]

However, her unique temperament did not suit everyone's tastes, as a letter from Consuelo's friend and fellow American heiress, Jennie Jerome, to her future husband Lord Randolph Churchill in 1874 illuminates: 'I am sorry I quarrelled with you about Consuelo as *entre nous* – I am changing my opinion of her – but then poor girl – one must make allowances for her wretched education. I really think she would have been a very nice girl if it had not been for her bad bringing up.'[2]

As the summer went on, the temperature and humidity increased, and reflected the inseparability of Kim and Consuelo, who luxuriated in each other's company and the first flush of love. Saratoga Springs was well known as a destination for ambitious mothers keen to marry off their daughters. Granted, it did not attract the calibre of beau of Newport in Rhode Island but, for those families still trying to penetrate the elite social circles, Saratoga Springs was an acceptable alternative where they could polish their skills and plan their next move. Some would never be accepted into the ultra-exclusive Newport set, where New York's Four Hundred retreated to spend their summers. Others would simply need to bide their time, while they established themselves in society. The Yznagas may well have resigned themselves to being in the former group, had it not been for the evident success of Consuelo. While Ellen Yznaga appears to have been industrious in her efforts on behalf of her daughters, she never attempted the all-out assault on society that Marietta Stevens committed to on behalf of Minnie or that Alva was embarking on for her daughter Consuelo Vanderbilt. Along with Jennie Churchill's family, the Jeromes, and Alva Vanderbilt's family, the Smiths, Ellen often retreated abroad when the Yznaga fortune was floundering and the pressure of trying to assimilate herself into New York society became too much. By her nature, she was indulgent when it came to her children and much more comfortable singing while Consuelo played the piano and Emily played the banjo at their simple plantation home than in the stuffy drawing rooms of a New York brownstone.

It was Ellen's beautiful mezzo-soprano voice that became the Yznagas' passport to Empress Eugénie's court in Paris when the family visited in 1866. Here, the Yznagas' exuberant and seductive personalities were celebrated by the vivacious Empress and Ellen's singing impressed Eugénie so much that the family were invited to participate in court functions. Along with other Americans, who were virtual outcasts in their own society, like the Stevenses and the Smiths, the Yznagas found a home in France and acceptance. Consuelo was a young girl during their time in Paris and was still only twelve years old when they headed back to Ravenswood in 1870. However, her experiences of the excesses and gaiety of the French court would have a profound effect on her. Her observations of the beautiful and frivolous Eugénie, who insisted nobody at court wore the same dress twice, and the way that Princess Pauline Metternich, the wife of the Austrian Ambassador, delighted visitors to her salon with witty repartee, would all affect the way that Consuelo herself would evolve into an enticing young woman. Like Minnie and Alva, her friends and conspirators, Consuelo Yznaga's sojourn in Paris and her experiences of European nobility would define her social path for the rest of her life.

The United States Hotel in Saratoga Springs was well known for its weekly dances, where pretty debutantes and dapper young gentlemen would congregate to indulge in harmless flirtations under the watchful eyes of their chaperones. The hotel's ballroom was one hundred feet long with a parquet floor and sparkling chandeliers. An orchestra would play while champagne flowed with ice cream and blancmange also served to the clammy participants. It was on one such occasion in the summer of 1875 that Kim took his chance to advance his attachment to Consuelo. High on champagne and a winning streak at the gaming tables of Saratoga's Club House, he was even more confident in his position as an eminently eligible member of the British aristocracy. He was all too aware of the effect that having a viscount in their midst had on American society and how the Saratoga matrons had been clamouring for his attention since his arrival. Of course that had been his purpose all along, to find and secure an American heiress as a wife and then bring her millions home to shore up the coffers of the Manchester estate. After all, the law decreed that all of his wife's money should pass to him. In many ways he considered himself a trailblazer and congratulated himself on being one of the first English gentlemen to identify this prime marriage market. Finding a bride with beauty, charm and wealth would see him return to the good graces of his parents, the Duke and Duchess of Manchester, as relations had been somewhat strained in recent years. Kim's penchant for gambling, drinking and pretty women had meant that he was heavily in debt and his lax morality was being questioned in aristocratic circles. The gossips had said that his family had banished him to America to ensure an end to his relationship with an Italian countess, but whatever the reason, he found himself in Saratoga Springs, conversely enjoying the very same intoxicating combination of vices that he had been charged with avoiding. With a spring in his step and his well-known 'winning friendliness'[3], Kim asked the seventeen-year-old Consuelo to dance, and as they spun around the ballroom, he held her very tightly indeed.

In the spring of 1876, Kim visited the Yznagas' plantation, Ravenswood, in Louisiana. The double-storey wooden house that stood at the heart of the property was painted canary yellow instead of the more traditional white typical of the region, a nod to the Yznagas' unconventional tendencies. There were ten rooms, simply furnished with mahogany beds and wardrobes and an obligatory rocking chair. A large veranda encircled the entire house, perfect for lazy afternoons watching the chickens and turkeys running through the wild undergrowth that surrounded the house and stretched out to the cotton fields beyond. For Kim, Ravenswood was like stepping into a completely different world, far away from the cold, imposing Manchester seats of Kimbolton Castle in Cambridgeshire and Tandragee Castle in Ireland. He continued his courtship of Consuelo, but just as the couple were reacquainting themselves, Kim contracted typhoid and was immediately bedridden. This potentially dangerous turn of events – typhoid was often deadly at that time – was actually fortuitous for Consuelo, who now nursed the young viscount through his illness. As he slowly began to recover, she entertained him with playful anecdotes and her musical talents, slowly re-establishing the intimacy they had enjoyed in Saratoga.

Now confident of the blossoming relationship between the viscount and his daughter, Antonio Yznaga took his opportunity to visit Kim's bedside and assured him that a dowry of £200,000 would accompany Consuelo when she was married. Soon afterwards, Kim proposed, and the now eighteen-year-old Consuelo was ecstatic, knowing that one day she would become a duchess. Although it is clear that Consuelo and Kim both had practical reasons for their marriage, it is also evident that they had genuinely fallen in love. Mrs Carter H Harrison, a neighbour and friend of the Yznagas, remembered Kim's undeniable contentment in her memoirs, *Strange to Say*: 'He sat beneath the flowering magnolias, breathing in the delicious perfume of the cape jasmine hedges and listening to the mockingbirds, and declared himself radiantly happy with his bride.'[4]

Kim and Consuelo were married at New York's fashionable Grace Church at 3.30pm on 22 May 1876. Kim had delayed informing his family of the engagement for fear they would not approve of the bride's family connections but news had reached the 7th Duke of Manchester in England anyway. During March 1876 he briefly referred to the engagement several times in his diary with increasing frustration:

> *Monday, 13 March*
> *Louise [his wife] heard from Augusta I.W. of*
> *Kim's intended marriage to Miss Yznaga.*

> *Saturday, 18 March*
> *At dinner telegram from Dufferin [then Governor-General of*
> *Canada, resident in Ottawa]. Kim to be married on 8 April.*
> *Answer: 'Try to prevent it.'*

Sunday, 19 March
Wrote Mrs Yznaga. Kim extravagant and weak.

Monday, 27 March
Telegram from Kim. 'Mind made up. Telegraph consent.'

Tuesday 28 March
Letter from Kim affectionate and dutiful. Louise wrote
and telegraphed him. Self wrote to Mrs Yznaga.

Tuesday, 4 April
Telegram from Mrs Yznaga. No answer.[5]

The New York Times reported that at the wedding, 'The crowd was so dense that it was impossible to get near the rail, and a person was accounted fortunate who was able to catch a glimpse of the bridal party as they came up the centre aisle of the church.'[6] The five bridesmaids were dressed in white tulle with satin sashes and carried posies of white lilac. They included Consuelo's two sisters, Emily and Natica, Miss Mary Bright, Miss Kate Kernochan and of course, Miss Minnie Stevens, whose mother Marietta was also in attendance, along with the newly married Alva Vanderbilt and Jennie Churchill's father, Leonard Jerome.

There was a moment of concern when Kim and his best man, Colonel William Jay, a fashionable and rakish New York lawyer who enjoyed similar pursuits to the viscount, failed to arrive on time, as was noted by *Town Topics*. They wrote that guests began to speculate on whether Kim had jilted Consuelo, until a flustered-looking Kim finally appeared, apparently having been delayed by a broken-down carriage. If Consuelo was worried that Kim had changed his mind, she didn't show it. She enchanted her guests in a dress of white satin damask trimmed with lace and wore sparkling diamond stars in her hair and a dramatic white point lace veil. She played the part of a society bride to perfection while the New York matrons that represented the more exclusive parts of Old New York gritted their teeth and congratulated the Southern *arriviste* who had managed to acquire a title. The bridal party and their guests made their way through the crowds to the Yznagas' New York house on Third Avenue to admire Consuelo's bevy of beautiful presents, including priceless point lace from Alva and Minnie, a diamond and ruby bracelet, a diamond solitaire ring and a silver tea set, which the bride had excitedly been unwrapping for the past few days and Ellen Yznaga had gladly put on show for all of society to see.

After an indulgent wedding breakfast, the new Viscount and Lady Mandeville spent the next two months enjoying the conviviality their marriage had afforded them among New York's high society and luxuriated in the generous hospitality of their friends, including Marietta Stevens, who gave a decadent afternoon tea in their honour. There were rumours that Kim had left his hotel with his bride for England after only paying half of his outstanding bill, but such rumours were swept aside amid the romance of a titled marriage. Like Jennie Jerome before her, another American heiress was on her way to England. This one would eventually become a duchess, a title that was only exceeded by a princess and so eclipsed Jennie and most of the aristocratic ladies that Consuelo would be associating with over the coming months. The American press were delighted to see one of their own invested with one of the highest positions available in the English aristocracy and showed none of the cynicism and hostility that would characterise their reports of later titled marriages. By 1905, when Marie Corelli wrote *Free Opinions Freely Expressed*, the optimism over such marriages had disappeared: 'There is always a British title going a-begging, always some decayed or degenerate or semi-drunken peer, whose fortunes are on the verge of black ruin, ready and willing to devour, monster-like, the holocaust of an American virgin, provided bags of bullion are flung with her into his capacious maw.'[7]

The young couple arrived in England on 22 July 1876 and headed straight for the mansion that the Duke and Duchess of Manchester occupied in Great Stanhope Street in London. Consuelo had been forewarned by Kim that she faced a herculean task to win his parents' affections. Kim's mother, Duchess Lottie, was known for being a formidable character who loved gambling and was engaged in a long-term affair with Lord Hartington. An affair that would eventually see her become the Duchess of Devonshire when she married Hartington after her husband the Duke of Manchester's death. Forever after she would be known as the 'Double Duchess', following the rare feat of acquiring two dukes in matrimony. Her reputation as a leading member of the 'fast set' ensured that Queen Victoria refused to invite the Duchess to the Prince of Wales's wedding in 1863, surmising that Lottie had 'done more harm to Society from her tone, her love of admiration and "fast" style than almost anyone.'[8]

The Duke of Manchester owed much of his son's behaviour to the example he had set. A sprendthrift, with a wandering eye, Kim's father was a perfect role model for an aristocratic rake. Nevertheless, the Duke, entrenched in the Manchesters' perceived position as stalwarts of the aristocracy, expected and demanded more from his son and was not impressed with Kim's choice of bride, despite the promise of money she brought with her. He icily wrote in his diary, without further comment, on 22 July 1876, the day of their arrival, 'Kim and wife arrived from USA.'[9]

However, if Consuelo Manchester faced a battle for the approval of her in-laws, it would be a battle that she would relish and would ultimately provide a useful training ground for the rest of British society, which had yet to be convinced of the merits of transatlantic marriages. Indeed, Jennie Churchill had faced extreme prejudice when she had married into that family two years previously, and Consuelo Manchester knew she would have to prove herself worthy of the aristocracy to ensure her place as an acceptable society hostess. She immediately set to work and, following the advice of her friend Minnie, who had already become popular among the Marlborough House Set, attempted to beguile the Prince of Wales with her unique brand of Southern charm and amiability. Typically, she was an immediate success among the nobility, even though Jennie Churchill remained unconvinced of her particular combination of refined social graces and risqué storytelling. In a letter to her sister Leonie, Jennie described a dinner party at which Consuelo Manchester shocked her guests with her bohemian tendencies: 'Consuelo proposed herself to dinner the other night. We had old Chancellor Ball and Lord Portarlington and she being *envirée* [inebriated] insisted on telling "roguey poguey" stories, which I think astonished them, they did me; quite between ourselves I think it *du plus mauvais goût* [in the worst taste] to talk like that before men.'[10]

But despite committing the odd social faux pas, Consuelo Manchester quickly became very popular. She used the same lively, candid and witty repartee that had so charmed Kim to ingratiate herself with the hedonistic circle that surrounded the Prince of Wales. They were captivated by the wide-eyed young American novelty who was always ready with an amusing tale, inventive practical joke or entertaining musical interlude. Lillie Langtry, who was at that time occupying the demanding role of Bertie's mistress, described Consuelo in her autobiography: 'Lady Mandeville [Consuelo Manchester], fair and ethereal, was of so merry and witty a disposition that she was a general favourite and always welcome at Marlborough House.'[11]

By 1878, it was clear that Consuelo had conquered the aristocracy, with one British newspaper commenting:

'Lady Mandeville [Consuelo Manchester] presents a Southern type of beauty, embellished as it were with Northern accents. She has a very refined face, with small features, a fine transparent complexion, deep brown eyes, and a wealth of light hair, in which her face is set like a jewel. Both at Cowes and in London she has necessarily become very popular, and there are few of the better kind of entertainments of which she does not form a principal ornament.'[12]

Even Queen Victoria wrote in her diary of Consuelo Manchester: 'Ly Mandeville [Consuelo Manchester] is very attractive, fine features, a lovely creamy complexion, & quantities of fair hair.'[13]

It should have been a source of great pride to Kim that his American bride had triumphed so spectacularly, against such odds, but he was barely around to accompany Consuelo to her many social engagements, never mind bask in her social success. As soon as the Mandevilles had arrived in England, the honeymoon was abruptly over. Kim returned to the typical behaviour of a young aristocratic gentleman. Barely modifying his activities from his bachelor days, he indulged in drinking heavily at his club, frequenting London's night-houses in search of prostitutes and courtesans to satiate his sexual appetite and gambling away large amounts of Consuelo's dowry at the card tables. Her fantasy born out of a dream-like Saratoga summer of a fairytale marriage as part of the English nobility, were quickly dashed and at only eighteen she quickly had to adapt to her new life, alone in a foreign country. The 7th Duke of Manchester, who had hoped marriage to Consuelo would curb his son's debauchery and enable him to grow into the responsibilities presented by his position as the future duke, grew tired of Kim's high jinks in London and decided to banish the newlyweds for a year to the rundown Manchester family seat in Ireland, Tandragee Castle. Isolated and alone with a husband more interested in shooting game on the estate and partaking in protracted drinking sessions with his select circle of like-minded friends, Baron de Clifford, Derry Westenra, the 5th Earl of Rossmore and Lord Newry, the now pregnant Consuelo Manchester felt very far away from the idyllic peace of her plantation home.

The following year, in 1877, after giving birth to the requisite male heir, William Angus Drogo, forever to be known as Little Kim, Consuelo found herself again at Tandagree, but this time she invited her friend, Minnie Stevens, herself still on the hunt for a titled husband, for company. Little Kim had been born on 3 March 1877, one day after Alva Vanderbilt had given birth to her daughter Consuelo, named after her friend in England. The two friends decided that Willie K Vanderbilt would act as Little Kim's godfather and Consuelo Manchester would be her namesake's godmother, ensuring the ties between the families remained for years to come.

Cornelia Adair, another American heiress, who had married English landowner John Adair, accompanied Minnie on her visit to Tandragee and wrote to her friend Lady Waldegrave about their stay:

'We have just been staying up at Tandragree with Lord and Lady Mandeville – poor little thing, she is so delicate – so utterly helpless – and *most* charming. She cannot endure a country life and is quite miserable at Tandragee, although she has Miss Stevens with her who is the brightest, cheeriest companion. The more I see of her the more I like her. I hope she will marry an Englishman; she is suited to life in this country which poor little Consuelo Mandeville is not.'[14]

Increasingly, Consuelo Manchester was finding it difficult to keep track of her husband. Consuelo wrote to Lady Waldegrave in 1878 in reply to an invitation, informing her that Kim was 'yachting with the Gosfords and his movements are so erratic that I think I had better say he won't come with me on Sunday. He so often disappoints me that I generally make up my mind to go without him.'[15]

It appears that Kim returned to the family home long enough for Consuelo to become pregnant and give birth to twin girls, Lady Mary Alva Montagu and Lady Alice Eleanor Montagu in 1879, but his visits were a rarity, leaving Consuelo alone and adrift, unsure of how to deal with her errant husband. Still young, still beautiful, she decided to consolidate her position as one of Bertie's favourites, even though financial problems began to dominate her daily existence.

'I remember how she used to laugh over incidents in her early married life when she was excessively hard-up,' Frederick Martin remembered in his memoirs. 'Consuelo told me that on one occasion when the late King dined with her, the dinner was practically provided by her friends, who contributed *plats* [dishes] for the occasion. HRH expressed himself as delighted with the dinner. "And what is more," he added, with a smile, "I know exactly where all the dishes came from, for each lady has sent the one I always like served when I dine at her house."'[16]

Years later, when Consuelo had discovered her own means of earning money, she could poke fun at this period, but in truth she was desperately unhappy and continually implored Kim to return to her. She often knew so little about his whereabouts that she was forced to send her letters to his friends or to his club. In an undated letter to Kim, which Consuelo sent to the short-lived Pelican Club, known for its wild antics and bare-knuckle boxing fights arranged for its members' amusement, she indicates his slide into increasingly volatile behaviour and her desperation to bring her husband back from the brink of financial and social ruin.

> Dear Kim
>
> *Although I feel it is quite useless to write to you and effect an answer yet I cannot bear to let month after month go by without hearing anything of you. There is not a day that I do not think of you and long to see you and the children and I talk of you. I want them to love you and remember you though they can see so little of you. I will [two words missing] in the hope that when you get tired of your present life you will come back to those who love you sincerely.... If you would like me to send the children to see you at any time I can do so if you don't wish to come here.*
>
> *Your loving wife*
> *Consuelo[17]*

Consuelo's love for her husband appears undiminished through her correspondence, although his callous treatment of her must have caused her to re-evaluate her feelings. Still, one Christmas Day during this period, Kim was again upmost in her thoughts.

> *Darling Kim,*
>
> *This is Xmas day and I cannot let it go by without writing you a few words of love. I hope you are happy… please give me one little thought.*
>
> *Your loving wife*[18]

Consuelo's pleas did not sway Kim into reconsidering his behaviour. Instead, he continued his decadent lifestyle unabated, becoming less and less discreet as the years went on. The Manchester family motto had long been *Disponendo me non mutant me*, which meant 'By disposing of me, not by changing me' and Kim wore it like a badge of honour. Consuelo, along with the Duke and Duchess, had tried to encourage him to reduce his drinking and gambling and forgo the courtesans and rakish crowd that had become his constant companions, but Kim had steadfastly refused and had instead disappeared from the Manchester family altogether into a maze of London streets, only appearing occasionally when he needed money. Consuelo was devastated when Kim's relationship with the music-hall singer Bessie Bellwood became public knowledge. Bellwood had hit a hansom-cab driver on the nose when he tried to collect a debt from Kim, and Kim was called to court as a witness. When the 7th Duke of Manchester died of peritonitis and dysentery in Naples on 21 March 1890, the *Cincinnati Enquirer* reported that Kim's eyes had 'lit up'[19] for a moment when he heard of his father's death while drinking champagne and gambling with Bessie Bellwood.

Taking matters into her own hands, Consuelo, now the Duchess of Manchester, wrote to Bellwood requesting that she give Kim up, promising to pay his debts and give him an allowance of twenty pounds a week. The reply from Bellwood read: 'Miss Bessie Bellwood presents her compliments to the Duchess of Manchester, and begs to state that she is now working The Pavilion, The Met and The South

London at £20 a turn so she can allow the Duke £30 a week and he is better off as he is.'[20]

Despite this acerbic refusal to end her relationship with Kim, it appears that the Duke severed all relations with Bellwood in 1890 and attempted a reconciliation with Consuelo. Bellwood in turn sued Kim for money she had lent him, but the legal proceedings came to nothing and, apart from the obvious embarrassment, the Manchesters appeared to ride out the storm.

If Consuelo was pleased to finally get her husband back, her happiness would not last for long. She had for some time been concerned about his influence on Little Kim and, despite her desire for Kim to visit the children at Kimbolton or Tandragee, there had been incidents when his particular style of parenting had bordered on cruelty. When Little Kim was only four, his father had chosen to teach the little boy to ride. His method was to simply put him on an unsaddled pony and slap it hard to make it gallop. Of course, Little Kim kept falling off and his father kept repeating the practice, until the boy learnt to cling on with all his might. Similarly, he had tried to teach Little Kim to swim by throwing him in a lake until he managed to splutter to safety. Kim's possible masochistic tendencies are implied by a story that Little Kim remembered in his memoirs. He recalls an incident when, having run to catch a train to Tandragee from Portadown, his father's finger had been accidentally trapped in the door by the porter in the frantic commotion. Little Kim was too small to pull the emergency cord, yet Kim chose not to ask his son to alert another passenger or the guard. 'My father made no fuss whatever, but sat down and told me to open his newspaper. Then, holding it with one hand, he read aloud calmly until the train reached Tandragee, but his forefinger was crushed for the rest of his life.'[21]

In 1891, Consuelo was visiting Paris with Marietta Stevens, while Kim appears to have opted for an extended trip to Australia, but by August 1892 they were both back at Tandragee, Kim lying prostrate, dying, with Consuelo the ever-dutiful wife by his side. He died on 18 August 1892, at only thirty-nine years old, his years of debauchery and excess finally having caught up with him. Kim's death brought a new freedom for Consuelo Manchester. Although she was still plagued by debts and determined to preserve the Manchester estates for the benefit of her son, she could embark on a new phase of her life, one of independence, free from the constant worry of what trouble her husband would plunge the Manchesters into next. Now she could forge her own way as a dowager duchess within the English aristocracy, and she was still young and beautiful enough to even find love. 'There are many… that read with surprise that Mrs Yznaga, the mother of the Duchess of Manchester, had asked Mr "Willie K" Vanderbilt to have the *Valiant* transport the remains of the dead Lady Alva from Civitavecchia to Marseilles, and that not only Mrs Yznaga, but Miss Emily and Mr Fernando Yznaga accompanied the Duchess and her surviving daughter on the sad journey,'[22] reported *Town Topics* to its readers on 21 March 1895. Although the scandal sheet could not always be relied upon for its accuracy (here referring to Lady Mary Alva as Lady Alva), its report hinted at another rumour that was being increasingly repeated in the most exclusive social circles. The report alluded to gossip that Consuelo Manchester and Alva Vanderbilt, lifelong friends since childhood, had quarrelled, referring to 'those happy days when the mothers were friends and before they had parted and ceased to remain on even speaking terms'.[23]

For those who followed such stories, there was great public interest in what could have caused the rift. Why would the two friends who had masterminded Alva's social coup over Mrs Astor just over a decade ago suddenly cease contact, while the Duchess's apparent friendship with Willie K blossomed? For months during 1894, US newspapers and gossip columnists had been faithfully reporting Willie K's appearances with the *demi-mondaine* Nellie Neustretter around Europe, but now people began to question whether this relationship had ever really existed or whether it was a decoy to distract attention from an affair between Consuelo Manchester and Willie K. On 7 March 1895, the *New York World* had printed a story about the affair, calling into question the conduct of Consuelo Manchester, who was in Rome with her daughters, regarding her old friend's husband. *Town Topics* eventually asserted that 'Mr Vanderbilt would have become the husband of the Duchess of Manchester had it not been for her bereavement....'[24]

The mystery surrounding the disintegration of Consuelo Manchester and Alva's friendship was never openly discussed by either party and continued to baffle journalists and society commentators alike. The previous summer, in July 1894, *Town Topics* was happily reporting: 'London has received Mr and Mrs "Willie K" thanks to the good offices of the Duchess of Manchester, with a cordiality that the wealthy couple could hardly have anticipated.'[25] However, after 1894 Consuelo Manchester seems to have disappeared from Alva's life altogether, while her friendship with Willie K continued, with him even being named a trustee in her will. For a pair of Southern girls who had risen to the top and conquered society side by side to suddenly turn their backs on each other, many surmised that only the ultimate betrayal could be at the heart of it. Alva told her biographer, Sara Bard Field, many years later, that Willie K 'had brought his mistresses right into the home'[26], including 'poor women of the nobility of England'.[27] Whether one of those mistresses was Consuelo Manchester, society could only speculate.

For Consuelo, who now faced the task of burying her beloved daughter in the family vault at Kimbolton, tales of affairs and intrigue were a world away. She was surely grateful for Willie K's help and for his foresight in not personally accompanying the yacht. That would have attracted far too much attention. After almost twenty years managing the expectations of society while creating a veil of secrecy over her own complex personal affairs, she couldn't allow herself to be embroiled in the messy entanglements of the Vanderbilts' divorce. Consuelo Manchester needed to summon all her courage to bring Mary on her final journey behind a familiar mask of dignity and grace. She knew it was time to go home to England.

The Changing Guard

April 1895, New York

'You know, I am a fighter, and I will fight this case
if it costs $20,000.' – MARIETTA STEVENS

As she placed her copy of *The New York Times* on the bedside table, Marietta Stevens sighed. The paper had covered the strike in detail, ensuring all of New York knew the Victoria Hotel was in trouble. The reporter chronicled how its opulent entrances had been besieged by chambermaids and scullery help, desperate for information on their future, increasingly despondent over whether they would secure the wages that were owed to them. It all seemed a far cry from the intoxicating and glamorous days that the hotel, situated on 27th Street and Fifth Avenue, had enjoyed just a few years earlier. Known for the very best service, the most accomplished food and lavish interiors, it had played host to opera star Christine Nilsson and President Cleveland, but now it stood on the brink of bankruptcy after failing to keep up with fierce competition from the newly opened Waldorf Hotel.

'A lot of lampblack daubed on rough brown paper, such as one might have expected to see in the windows of a defunct grocery in payback junction, informed promenaders in Broadway and Fifth Avenue yesterday that the Victoria Hotel was "closed",' *The New York Times* informed readers on 2 April 1895. The news came after a week of feverish speculation about the hotel's future when every detail of its finances had been pored over by New Yorkers keen to ascertain whether this iconic building would survive the year. It had been reported that the Victoria's management owed $75,000[1] in rent arrears to the Stevenses' estate and, after many months of wrangling over lines of credit, the trustees' patience had finally run out.

Since the whole unpleasant business had begun, Marietta had not left her home on 57th Street and Fifth Avenue. The official reason for her seclusion from society was that she had caught a severe cold but the press also speculated that she was 'completely prostrated' with worry over the Victoria and that the anxiety over her own financial situation, which was so closely linked to the hotel's, had caused an 'apoplectic fit and a consequent mental depression'[2].

It was true Marietta was worried, perhaps more than at any time in her life. She had known difficult times before, and since her husband's death she had endured the financial ups and downs that accompanied a widow with a limited income who had to maintain a certain status in society. However, she knew the hotel business, and the fact that the Victoria, one of the Stevenses' most prominent acquisitions, was now facing a very public downfall uncovered the indignant side of her personality, the side she usually kept hidden, quietly bubbling along beneath the surface. It was actually the facet of her character that drove all others and she had used this burning rage against the inequitableness of society, ironically, to lead her to its pinnacle. The newspaper had consulted an anonymous prominent local hotel manager on the reasons for the Victoria's position. He had said: 'There is not a better location in this city for a magnificent hotel than the

Victoria.... But it is out of date. It has been allowed to run to seed. Any manager with modern ideas, who is willing to spend $250,000 in improving it and making it what a hotel in that location and with that prestige really ought to be, could make money.' [3]

Marietta had to agree; the hotel had failed to keep pace with the extraordinary rate of change that was sweeping the city. She thought about the days when Paran had been intimately involved in all of his businesses, how together they had planned the details of using their hospitality to make their hotels stand out from the crowd. Indeed, Marietta had made a living out of anticipating what New York society wanted, and now it rankled her that she had let the situation get this far out of control. Of course she blamed the trustees of Paran's estate, her brother-in-law Charles G Stevens and her son-in-law John L Melcher, who was the husband of Paran's daughter from his first marriage. The three of them had been engaged in a legal war of words since Paran had died in 1872, with Stevens and Melcher repeatedly disagreeing with Marietta's handling of the hotel magnate's fortune. Whether Paran thought that Marietta, ambitious for social success and lacking in business acumen, needed the steadying hand of two distant relatives to preserve the family's millions for the next generation isn't clear, but it's unlikely he anticipated the ferocious fallout that his decision would have. His death signalled the beginning of years of legal wrangling over the estate, with Marietta keen to have more control over the fortune and the trustees continually blocking such moves. In October 1887, the *New York Tribune* gleefully laid bare the rifts between the Stevenses when it reported on a number of incidents between John Melcher and Marietta when the matriarch had allegedly attacked her son-in-law. 'She had repeatedly pummelled him – once beating him over the head with an umbrella, another time striking him in the chest and breaking all the cigars in his waistcoat pockets, and on a third occasion seizing an ink bottle with intent to throw it at him, but repenting of this design and hurling strong language at him instead.'

This was not the first time Marietta had failed to keep her temper in check. In 1887, she was sued by a Miss Sallie Gibbons, the owner of a gallery who rented her store from the Stevens estate, for trespass and assault. According to Miss Gibbons, Marietta had used abusive language when she had visited the gallery and threatened to evict her, before assaulting her. Marietta had finally been forced to leave by the police. In court Marietta maintained that she had only entered the premises to enquire about making improvements to the property; however, the jury favoured Miss Gibbons's account and awarded her fifty dollars plus costs.

Marietta found herself in court again in 1891 when her French chef, Desiré Schmitt, sued her for wrongful dismissal, accusing Marietta of swearing at him and telling him, 'Go! Leave this house at once and never darken its doors again.'[4] Again, she fought the case, blaming Schmitt's drinking for his dismissal. She told the press, 'You know, I am a fighter, and I will fight this case if it costs $20,000.'[5]

She was right. Despite the adverse publicity that these court cases generated, Marietta never shied away from them. She waged a two-decade war on the trustees of Paran's estate because she believed that she knew best when it came to managing her family's finances. Time and again her pleas were rejected in court. It appears that the justice system did not share Marietta's views that the trustees were mismanaging the estate and withholding funds from her. It is impossible to tell whether her blind belief in fighting the trustees or the defamation of her character as propagated by Gibbons and Schmitt was because she believed herself to be on the side of the truth or whether she had to fight such accusations or they would almost certainly be considered fact, endangering the carefully crafted image she presented to society. For Marietta Stevens, her first line of defence was attack and attack she did, with utter conviction.

Such public battles would have usually rendered a lady impotent in New York society but Marietta's complex character saved her from obscurity. *Town Topics* observed:

'Whatever may be Mrs Stevens's faults of temperament, no one can doubt either her intelligence or her courage. She has recognised for some time past that the time has arrived for New York society to be less narrow and less provincial and that the ruling out of any presentable person from fashionable gatherings, simply because he or she did not happen to be numbered with the elect... was depriving herself and friends of much perfectly lawful amusement and entertainment, which could be contributed by artists and people of intellect.'[6]

Marietta knew how to use her talents well, so in the face of scandal and gossip, she could maintain her hard-won place as a society matron by keeping the establishment interested and entertained. Her ability for reinvention and anticipating what the elite needed was a trick she had been using since her days in the hotel trade. It had served her well when she introduced her Sunday night *musicales* onto the social scene and it did so again when she delighted society with unique entertainments in her palatial residences. She invited the opera sensation, Nellie Melba as a guest of honour to a dance at a time when performers were considered not presentable enough for New York society occasions, and entertained guests at her Newport villa with a hypnotist, creating geniune excitement as to what she would dream up next. The *Sunday Herald* said of one occasion that it was 'exclusively and excruciatingly select. Many have called but few were chosen to be the recipients of cards or invitations.'[7]However, that is not to say that Marietta had conquered all of society. There were still elements of Old New York who would never truly accept her presence among them and although they were now forced to tolerate her, every indiscretion that appeared in the newspapers only served to solidify their opinion. She would never be one of them.

In Edith Wharton's *The Age of Innocence*, the character of Mrs Lemuel Struthers, the rather brash shoe-polish queen, is based on Marietta. When Madame Olenska is introduced to Mrs Struthers, it becomes obvious where Wharton discovered her inspiration:

'"Of course I want to know you, my dear," cried Mrs Struthers in a round rolling voice that matched her bold feathers and her brazen wig. "I want to know everybody who's young and interesting and charming and the Duke tells me you like music... Well, do you want to hear Sarasate play tomorrow evening at my house? You know I've something going on every Sunday evening at my house – it's the day when New York doesn't know what to do with itself, and so I say to it: 'Come and be amused!'"[8]

Of course Wharton knew Marietta very well indeed, as Marietta's only son, Harry, had been engaged to Edith in 1882. In many ways, Harry Stevens was a catch. He was attractive, sporty, charismatic, 'one of the most popular men in society'[9] and due to inherit a large fortune that Paran Stevens had left when he died. Edith Jones, as she was then, began her courtship with Harry Stevens in 1880 and an engagement was announced in the *Newport Daily News* on 19 August 1882. Unusually, the groom's name appeared in the announcement before the bride's, perhaps indicating Marietta's hand in the engagement notice. By now, as an expert in managing the newspapers, she knew the value of the Stevens name taking prime position. Harry was said to be 'desperately in love' with the intelligent and quick-witted Edith, who, as a Jones, came from the kind of Old New York stock that would render the Stevenses' transfer from *nouveau riche* to part of the establishment complete. From society's point of view, it appeared to be the perfect match, but it seems that not all of the respective families were in agreement.

There are conflicting accounts of who was to blame when the engagement was eventually broken off a few months later. Edith's family accused Marietta of being behind it all, surmising that she was looking for a bride with more attractive prospects than Edith for her only son. Helen Rhinelander, Edith's cousin, wrote in a letter to her brother Tom, 'It is evidently Mrs S's fault, or rather she is the cause… I doubt Pussy [Edith] and H have changed in their feeling for one another, but that Mrs S is at the bottom of it all.'[10]

For their part the Joneses let it be known that they thought that Marietta would make an 'impossible mother-in-law' and still harboured suspicions that the social-climbing Stevenses were not quite good enough to be associated with their name. Indeed, the friction between the two families could be traced back to Marietta's first foray into entertaining, when the matriarch of the family and Edith's great-aunt, Mary Mason Jones, had categorically refused ever to entertain Marietta in her house on account of her Sunday-night *musicales*. The influential society leader had steadfastly clung to her view of Marietta as unworthy of the inner sanctum of New York society, so it is unlikely she would have supported the match. *Town Topics* had its own opinion on why the engagement had been broken off, citing 'an alleged preponderance of intellectuality on the part of the intended bride. Miss Jones is an ambitious authoress and, it is said that, in the eyes of Mr Stevens, ambition is a grievous fault.'[11]

Marietta may have had her own reasons for not supporting Harry's choice. According to the terms of Paran Stevens's will, she controlled her children's inheritance until they were twenty-five or married and, with Harry only twenty-three years old, Marietta may have been keen to hold on to her financial control for as long as possible. Another possible explanation is that she knew what everyone else did not. Harry Stevens had tuberculosis and, despite attempts to improve his health with lengthy trips abroad, she knew that he would almost certainly not be the husband that Edith had imagined for herself. Is it possible that Marietta was simply trying to protect Miss Jones from life as a young widow?

Whatever the causes of the split, Edith retreated to Europe with her mother before returning to New York anxiously for the Season the following year, braced for the inevitable stares from society's matrons. In her autobiography, *A Backward Glance*, Edith Wharton doesn't mention her engagement to Harry Stevens, airbrushing it out of her own personal history. Two years later, she would be married to Teddy Wharton. During the summer of the same year, 1885, Harry Stevens died in Newport. In a decision that illuminates just how intrinsically linked the press had become with the Stevens family's fate, Marietta made public the results of an autopsy conducted by three prominent New York doctors that she had ordered. *The New York Times* had reported the arrival of Harry and his mother at Newport the previous month, noting that his condition was serious but the reason was unknown. Whether Marietta genuinely didn't know the cause of her son's death or whether she wanted to silence speculation over its links to Edith's recent marriage is unclear, but the publication of Harry's cause of death as being from a cancerous stomach tumour provoked by too violent exercise at athletics was highly unusual and seems unlikely, given his previous tubercular diagnosis.

Now, as Marietta sat in her sumptuous bedroom, surrounded by a riotous assortment of antiques, in the very house that used to belong to Edith's great-aunt, she must have reflected on the whole sorry business with the Jones family. Everyone's reputations had been damaged by the affair, and of course there was poor Harry, who had never really recovered. Still, she had weathered the storm, as she had always done, and had moved onwards and upwards despite the challenges. Perhaps the Joneses' had been right all along, she was an ambitious upstart; she had a temper and an unconventionality that meant she created drama and complications for herself, which forced her to be equally creative to smooth them over. This was perhaps her most useful skill: she could adapt, she could identify and capitalise on opportunities – hadn't that been her greatest asset? And then there was Minnie. Dear Minnie. Her greatest accomplishment. How she had travelled so much further, armed with the drive and intelligence her mother had engendered in her, bolstered by wit, culture and an innate sense of knowing her rightful destiny. Together they had passed the daughters of the *nouveaux riches* through their hands and positioned them in the most influential places of society. Biographer Joan Hardwick noted that Marietta was 'well known for arranging marriages between wealthy young American girls and European titled aristocracy',[12] before emphasising that 'any girl she took on had to have money'.[13]

Marietta thought about Ward McAllister. They had helped each other, he understood her and she understood him. In many ways they were cut from the same cloth, both outsiders employing all their guts and guile to get into society and using the fortunes of the more desperate *arrivistes* to stay there. She felt unnerved when she thought about how his life had ended. He'd died from an attack of flu only two weeks after his glittering last Patriarchs' Ball on 31 January 1895 at the age of sixty-eight, never fully regaining the trust of the elite he had betrayed.

McAllister would have expected a large funeral with the pomp and ceremony that a stalwart of New York's social scene demanded. However, although the Vanderbilts turned out in force for their most loyal social sponsor and Marietta Stevens was of course in attendance, the inner sanctum stayed away. Only a handful of the Patriarchs attended. There was no Mrs Astor, who was busy preparing for a dinner party she was giving that evening. At Grace Church the crowds came, but it was a crowd of ordinary New Yorkers desperate to see the last journey of a notorious figure once so elevated but lately, in many quarters, lampooned and ridiculed. Afterwards, the crowd wrestled the police for floral mementoes of the great man, but the leaves were already wilting and, like McAllister's sweeping proclamations on the Four Hundred, would soon fade away completely.

Now, the same New Yorkers walked past the Victoria Hotel, some reading the closed notices on the doors with interest, some picketing the streets outside, hoping that the woman who owned this vestige of Old New York hospitality would do the right thing by the common people. Was she Marietta the chambermaid, the grocer's assistant, the Lowell girl done good or Mrs Paran Stevens, the money-grabbing social climber, who discharged every threat in her path? Marietta herself didn't know. In this ever-evolving New York it was difficult to know where you belonged. All she knew, was that for the first time she didn't want to fight any more.

On 5 April 1895, the Waldorf Hotel gave a *musicale*. The venue had been changed at the last minute due to the untimely death from heart failure on 4 April 1895 of Mrs Marietta Stevens, the occasion's social sponsor. In the obituary section of *The New York Times* two days later, a reporter wrote of Marietta: 'When… she knocked on the door of exclusive fashion, there was much rolling up of the eyes and much whispering within. Admittance was denied. Stories, creations of gossiping old women were circulated… but undaunted, socially ambitious, she pursued her course until those who had rolled their eyes and spoken in whispers felt themselves honoured to be invited to her house.'

For Minnie, who was on the way to New York on the *Lucania*, there could be no greater tribute to her mother. New York had seen Marietta Stevens for what she was and through her guile had been forced to accept her anyway. Society had been transformed from the days of McAllister, Mrs Astor and the Four Hundred and the pace of change continued, an unstoppable force, reminiscent of Marietta herself. There was a creeping sense among the elite that the guard was changing. Who would be next to step into the breach, because it was simply unthinkable that new leaders wouldn't take their long-awaited places and fill the vacuum? Society would continue to march on as it always had.

'What struck me so much was that these deaths seemed hardly to leave any impression upon society, although the dead had slaved and devoted themselves to its service,' wrote socialite Frederick Martin. 'Everything went on as usual; one heard parrot cries of condolence, the stereotyped remarks suitable to the occasion and then the world smiled again.'[14]

As for Marietta's beloved Victoria Hotel, it too underwent a transformation. It was soon remodelled and redecorated and opened its doors once more, but this time under new ownership and without its fiercest champion.

Love is Bourgeois

April 1895, New York

> *'The diamond-like glitter of her wit was a tangible*
> *thing and she wore it like a jewel; it glowed*
> *round her like an aura round the moon, pale and*
> *phosphorescent, as exhilarating as the cold air of*
> *a frosty night.'* – RODERICK CAMERON

The small party who occupied the Buckingham Hotel's lounge, drinking champagne and exchanging stories, would not have attracted much comment had it not been for the beautiful young lady at the centre of the group. Fellow guests speculated that the pretty blonde was a visitor from out of town, an acquaintance of the Belmonts perhaps, as that well-known couple, fully-fledged members of the Four Hundred, had joined the gathering some time before. They certainly seemed in high spirits, with the young lady the most enamoured with the company. She was particularly attentive to an older gentleman who sat, mesmerised, to her right throughout, hanging off her every word, occasionally scanning the faces of his companions to ensure they were as beguiled as he clearly was.

'The diamond-like glitter of her wit was a tangible thing and she wore it like a jewel; it glowed round her like an aura round the moon, pale and phosphorescent, as exhilarating as the cold air of a frosty night,'[1] her friend Roderick Cameron said of Maud Burke. And as she held court at the Buckingham, it was clear that she had her companions firmly under her spell.

Maud could see the pride in Sir Bache Cunard's face as she regaled the assembled party with tale after amusing tale. She had seen it many times before in the faces of different men, for she was an expert at knowing how to keep middle-aged men entertained. Her skills had served her well so far, and today she had gained her highest position yet. From now on, she would be known as Lady Maud Cunard.

The ceremony had been arranged for four o'clock in the afternoon on 17 April 1895 in the front drawing room of Mr Horace Carpentier's fine house at 108 East 37th Street. The Reverend Doctor William S Raynsford had married the effervescent Maud and the eager Cunard in front of around half a dozen guests. Behind her mandatory smile, Maud was a little disappointed with the plain and pedestrian quality of the day. There were no bridesmaids to escort her down the aisle, no ushers to show reams of guests to their places, no cascading flowers, or tuneful hymns sung to the strains of a fashionable orchestra, no exquisite gown and no elaborate wedding breakfast. Instead, she had worn a simple white satin dress trimmed with old Limerick lace, a veil and a single ornament: a jewelled pendant, given to her as a token of the groom's affection. In lots of ways it was a day to forget and a very different prospect to the occasion she had in mind when she accepted the proposal of the heavy-set English gentleman with the drooping moustache, who had so earnestly asked for her hand in marriage only a few weeks before. Maud must have imagined a June wedding, on a scale of opulence befitting the marriage of one of the most popular and vivacious debutantes San Francisco society had ever seen to a Cunard, heir to the steamship fortune and member of the English aristocracy, but it quickly became apparent that this would not be possible.

Almost immediately after sending out the engagement announcement to a blindsided press, which quickly began making enquiries as to the social pedigree of Miss Maud Burke, Cunard had gently told his ebullient fiancée that his family would not be making the journey to New York for the wedding. The best he could muster was a cousin, Mr Bache McEvers Whitlock, as his best man. Maud had considered the news carefully, swiftly trying to decipher whether his family's non-attendance was a sign of their hostility and desire to halt the nuptials or simply a question of distance. In any case she decided not to react in the slightest, having already realised that what Cunard admired most about her was her light, breezy temperament, which seemed to balance his tendency for melancholy. He already looked to Maud to quietly solve trifling problems in an uncomplicated manner, and here she was doing it once more. She kindly suggested that a quick wedding would be perfectly acceptable and proper, considering the poor health of her so-called 'uncle', Horace Carpentier, a convenient detail that had just come to light. Cunard agreed and, while the *New York Herald* dutifully explained in their report that the wedding was a small affair, 'owing to illness in the family of the bride's guardian'[2], the irrepressible *Town Topics* raised its suspicions that it was Maud's desire to secure a title that had been the cause of such haste: 'I hear much comment upon the fact that none of the immediate family of Sir Bache Cunard... came over to his wedding. Miss Burke... elected to be married very quickly and quietly.'[3]

Maud was all too aware that theirs was not a love story, but she was pragmatic when it came to love; she had had to be. She shared the view of Edith Blackwell, a leading character in the play *The Title-Mart*, which was a satire of Anglo-American marriages of the period. In Act Three, Edith declares: 'Love is bourgeois; only the lower classes and fools marry for love. We are learning better in America – nowadays our marriages are arranged.'[4] These were Edith's words but they so easily could have been Maud's. She had told the press before her marriage, 'I like Sir Bache better than any man I know,'[5] and, given her past record, she had meant it. However, it wasn't love she felt for her husband, who was twenty years older than twenty-three-year-old Maud, it was affection and nothing more.

Until now, Maud's life had been characterised by a reliance on Horace Carpentier, her protector and guardian, who had indulged her with money and access to the finest cultural experiences, including opera, taking her to her first Wagnerian opera at the Metropolitan in New York when she was just twelve. He also introduced her to Shakespeare's plays, Balzac, and Greek and Latin poetry and encouraged her musical talents. But at what price did this attention come for Maud? Her introduction to opera clearly made a lasting impression on her, as she later wrote: 'It was as if a new role had opened out, revealing a race of men and women, very Titans of humanity, endowed with superb gifts…'[6]

The former Civil War general was a wealthy man, having built up an enviable real-estate portfolio, and was notorious in San Francisco, Maud's home city, for taking an interest in young women. As Maud's biographer Daphne Fielding suggests, Carpentier was a 'collector of young girls… in mint condition'[7]. Historian Brian Masters agrees that Carpentier's 'hobby was to educate and advise pretty adolescent girls, whom he called his "nieces", the favourite among them was the obviously intelligent Maud Burke.'[8] It's unclear how far this interest in Maud went but Carpentier was the impressionable young woman's guide and teacher for a number of years and provided her dowry of two million dollars[9] that went with her to Nevill Holt, Cunard's country seat in England.

Carpentier had been introduced to Maud through her mother, whom he had courted after her husband, James Burke, had died during Maud's childhood. Maud had always brushed off the rumours that she was not Burke's daughter. Many thought her real father was William O'Brien, the infamous part-owner of a Nevada silver mine, and many years later his 'family believed he left her a large sum of money'.[10] What is clear is that her childhood was chaotic and something she rarely talked about. The San Francisco of the 1880s was a young city that lived at a frenetic pace, morally questionable undesirables rubbing shoulders with affluent newcomers keen to establish a formal society. While Maud's family were wealthy, easily affording the Chinese servants who had flooded the city, the suitability of their background was in doubt and, seeing that Maud needed help to establish herself socially, Carpentier paid for extended trips to New York, Washington and Europe to enhance her education.

It was during one of these trips to Europe with her mother in June 1894 that she met the English author George Moore. Carpentier, with his large and impressive library back in America, had encouraged Maud's interest in literature. Perhaps unsurprisingly, Samuel Richardson's *Pamela*, the tale of a vulnerable girl skilfully warding off the unwanted advances of her older employer, became her favourite novel. She also ensured she was up to date with new authors of note and was therefore excited to hear that Moore, who was one of the darlings of the London literary scene, was due to attend a large luncheon at the Savoy in London to which Maud had also been invited. Determined to meet Moore, she stole into the restaurant and adjusted the place cards to ensure that he would be sitting next to her. It was to be the beginning of a lifelong relationship that would change Moore's life forever. Over lunch as the angelic Maud listened entranced to the passionate Moore declare his admiration for the French realist writer Emile Zola, one of own her favourite authors, she couldn't prevent her hand from reaching forward and clasping his arm. 'George Moore,' she declared, 'you have a soul of fire!'[11] From that moment, the hopelessly-in-love Moore was a constant visitor to Maud's rented house in Park Lane, where they would spend hours debating their most cherished literature or lines of poetry, luxuriating in each other's company. They would take trips to the country, whiling away hours walking under the hot summer sun. Moore described one such encounter:

'Her sensuality was so serene and so sure of its divine character that it never seemed to become trivial or foolish. While walking in the woods with one, she would say: "Let us sit here," and after looking steadily at one for a few seconds, her pale marmoreal eyes glowing, she would say, "You can make love to me now, if you like."[12]

Given the strict rules regarding the chaperoning of young ladies, it at first seems unlikely that George and Maud would be able to find this amount of time alone together. However, Maud's mother, who was accompanying her on the trip, was a rare breed. She had allowed her daughter to set up house with Carpentier when she was only eighteen and had given her consent for her to travel extensively with him. Therefore it seems perfectly possible that Maud was given the freedom to ensnare the enraptured Moore, ensuring that he was completely in love with the young American.

When Maud announced that she was returning to America, Moore was heartbroken. Maud was resolute in her course of action. She was twenty-two years old and her experiences with Moore had confirmed that her feminine charms were at their peak. It was time to find a husband and Maud was aiming high. Of course there was that unfortunate business with Prince André Poniatowski to contend with, but she was confident that it had been handled correctly. In fact it had probably only made her more determined to attract a better calibre of gentleman than a third-rate Polish prince and everyone knew that, therefore, her future husband would have to be English.

In Maud's eyes, Prince Poniatowski had pursued her. On his first visit to San Francisco, she did what she did best, flirting outrageously with the Prince, impressing him with her keen intelligence and vast cultural knowledge and bonding over their shared experiences touring the capitals of Europe. When Poniatowski wrote to her on his return to Europe she was convinced her strategy had been a success and when he told her of his plans to return to America in early 1894, she felt confident that it was to propose marriage. She confided in her friends about their imminent engagement and may have even surreptitiously informed the press, as the newspapers began to report the story. Indeed, Poniatowski's intentions did include marriage but, unfortunately for Maud, his intended was not her. The object of his affection was one of San Francisco's most coveted belles. Miss Beth Sperry was the sister of

Mrs Harry Crocker, one of the leaders of San Francisco society, who regarded Maud Burke as a social upstart of questionable character. Therefore, when the rumours reached Poniatowski of his 'engagement' to Maud he was quick to confront her and demand a public denial. Maud had made a disastrous miscalculation and now turned to her mother and stockbroker stepfather, James Tichenor, to help smooth things over. Tichenor quickly made it known that he had forbidden Maud to accept Poniatowski, saving Maud's reputation and thereby removing all barriers for Poniatowski and Miss Sperry. For the betrothed it wasn't an ideal situation for, as their engagement was announced, Maud was still front and centre of the story and 'the rumour had already gone about that Miss Burke's mamma and stepfather had interposed their parental authority, and entirely disapproved of her alliance with the Prince'.[13]

However, Maud would not be around to see if she could withstand the indignity of it all. She had already moved on to her next project and had fled to Europe in search of a husband better suited to her ambitions, someone who would surpass Miss Sperry's efforts. Maud's flirtation with Moore in 1894 was a tantalising diversion, an intellectually stimulating flirtation, but it was not love. Maud was very fond of Moore and would remain so for many years, despite his increasingly obsessive attempts to garner her attention in the future. She viewed him as a harmless practice ground for her talents, a study to observe the idiosyncrasies and expectations of an English gentleman. For she had decided, after long years of travelling the world with Carpentier, that England was where she wanted to be. England presented an opportunity that did not exist in San Francisco, New York or any of the other large cities in America. While America was an exciting and energetic place to make money if you were a gentleman on the rise, as a lady, trying to establish herself among the smart set, Maud had observed, it offered very little of the lively repartee and genuine influence that was readily available in London society. Even if Maud was able to capture the heart of a wealthy plutocrat and climb the social ranks despite her new-money background, what did she have to look forward to? Days and nights spent in the stagnant drawing rooms and dreary dining rooms of The Four Hundred, instructed by her husband to restrict her comments to acceptable subjects such as philanthropy and social engagements. In New York, the political intrigues and the pace of Wall Street were the domain of men and men alone, whereas she had seen in London that married women were much more visible in the corridors of power. Women like Jennie Churchill, who had influenced her husband Randolph's career by hosting political salons and quietly nudging the status quo while moving from country houses to court to her grand town house in London. Granted, after his death in January 1895, it was unclear what would become of Jennie, but her undoubtable influence had convinced Maud of what was possible in Britain; as a woman it was all there for the taking.

She had followed avidly the movements of the original American heiresses who had married into the English aristocracy and now turned to them for advice on how to secure her own successful passage into British society. Marietta Stevens had spent some time in San Francisco and, as Cunard was a close friend of the Manchesters, having been an usher at their wedding in 1876, it seems likely that Consuelo Manchester, Minnie and Marietta may have had a hand in their courtship. Maud certainly visited London and New York frequently in the years leading up to her marriage and, as an enterprising and ambitious young heiress, was keen to place herself at all the right social occasions in both countries. Although little is documented about Maud's previous life, it's clear that after her marriage she was considered good friends with both Minnie Paget and Consuelo Manchester. In a letter to Maud, George Moore thanks her for introducing him to Minnie, a sign of their growing closeness: 'Minnie Paget I saw once again, she sent for me. I am obliged to you for the introduction, for I think I shall always see her with pleasure; she is of our kin and one must keep to one's kin.'[14]

The man on whom she settled, Bache Cunard, was well known among the country set for being an excellent horseman and had been credited as one of the first to bring polo to England. He was a simple, uncomplicated man, who had spent most of his life ensconced in his stately home, pursuing his sporting passions. His mother had been American and the family had spent several years living in Staten Island, which meant that Cunard made regular journeys back to New York. His trusting nature was to become his biggest downfall, as an American cousin, Charles Francklyn, whom he had charged with overseeing his investments in the United States, appears to have mismanaged the fund or pocketed the proceeds: in 1887, Cunard alleged in court documents that Franklin owed him some three million dollars and had ruined him. It began a long period of litigation that was to lay bare Cunard's dwindling fortune as he battled to restore what was rightfully his. Maud presented an opportunity not only to install a young and lively woman as mistress of Nevill Holt but also to rejuvenate the Cunard fortune with her substantial dowry.

Although the swiftness of Maud's engagement to Cunard surprised many in society, the *New York Herald* countered that it had been well known within Maud's circle for a number of weeks. 'The formal announcement of the engagement, which has just been made, will scarcely be news to some of the friends of Miss Burke, who were some time ago informed by the young woman herself that she was soon to become the wife of the titled and wealthy Englishman.'

However, society insiders could see how ill-suited the quiet, middle-aged Cunard and the perky, glamorous Maud were. Maud herself was fully aware of their differences and there were even rumours that some of Cunard's relatives had pleaded with the bride to break off the engagement. Perhaps they saw what Cunard did not, that this modern woman would never suit his English sensibilities and wouldn't be happy living a life filled with country pursuits in Leicestershire, the life that the confirmed bachelor had been living for many years. Frederick Martin encapsulated Maud's attributes when he wrote about American heiresses in his memoir, *Things I Remember.*

'The American woman… takes people as she finds them – not on the valuation of their ancestors; she is a person of spirit, she has her own ideas, and she is worldly to the tips of her fingers. She realises her own value; she knows what she wants in exchange of it, and she makes up her mind that once she has obtained her ambition she will play her part to perfection. The heiress makes no secret of her admiration for a title; she knows that her money will work wonders… they spend their money lavishly… and if their manner of doing so is occasionally a little blatant surely, as the saying has it, much can be forgiven those who give much.'[15]

Despite their differences, Cunard, blinded by the possibilities that the high-spirited, flirtatious and wealthy Maud represented, proceeded, undeterred, and confident that once he brought his bride back to Nevill Holt he could integrate her into his life in the countryside. Little did he know that as the assembled group toasted the future happiness of the newlyweds, Maud had a very different idea of the life that lay before her. Marriage meant a title and freedom, and that freedom started in London.

A Rare Miscalculation

April 1895, New York

> '*I must say I think this business very cruel, but at the same time I can't help thinking she deserved a snubbing as she told me she had £20,000 a year and would have more....*' – LADY WALDEGRAVE

Minnie Paget would have digested the news of the recent abundance of transatlantic marriages over breakfast in New York, where she had been busy attending to aspects of her mother's affairs. Sir Bache Cunard's hasty marriage to Maud Burke garnered a knowing smile from Minnie, for she would have recognised an enterprising nature when she saw one. Little, sprightly, young Maud had shown hers when she encouraged Cunard to make it official before he had any chance to change his mind. Minnie wondered what the future held for the newlyweds. They seemed wildly unsuited, but it was now up to Maud to carve her place out in England, as those who had come before her had had to do.

The wedding of Mary Leiter to George Curzon on 22 April was more interesting. The newspaper had reported on the crush of spectators on the sidewalks of Lafayette Square, Washington DC, outside the church, all keen to see their most popular belle married into the aristocracy. The peach and apple trees had been in full bloom and the fine weather provided a beautiful spring day for the bride to arrive in an open carriage, poised, smiling at the crowds. The regal overtones were not lost on Minnie, something she knew George would have directed. She had heard that he had been immensely involved in the preparations, no doubt keen to display Mary's ample fortune. Until now, George hadn't had the luxury of spending money without the ever-present shadow of guilt looming over him. Minnie knew he would be enjoying the loosening of the purse strings, so that he could put on a display befitting the Curzon name. She wondered whether Mary, a rather sweet and deferential girl, was really ready for a life spent living up to George Curzon's high expectations. Tracking the progress of her compatriots would provide a useful diversion for Minnie while she decided what to do with her mother's Newport and New York properties and concluded her affairs as quickly as possible.

It had been a couple of weeks since Marietta's death and the visceral pain she felt whenever she thought about her still plagued Minnie's days and nights. It was a loss she wasn't sure she could recover from, for Marietta had almost been more than her mother. She had been her friend, co-conspirator, fiercest champion and harshest critic, and a life without her unique and incisive observations was unthinkable – yet here it was. New York society had continued unabated by the absence of one of its most influential matrons. The social whirl forged ahead, the press reported the latest gossip and of course there were the weddings. So long a source of preoccupation for Marietta and Minnie, it almost seemed improper for the spring wedding season to have begun in earnest without Marietta being at the top of every guest list in town.

For many years Marietta had been a constant presence at the churches on Fifth Avenue during the spring and autumn, which in society were considered the most advantageous times to schedule any nuptials. To Minnie, who had by now attended more weddings than she cared to remember, it made perfect sense. Prominent New York families always based their decisions on the accepted routine of society as a whole, ensuring that entertainments and celebrations coincided with the most practical time of year for extended family and associates to attend. It was now accepted that marrying off a son or daughter or two provided the perfect opportunity to highlight social prominence. Balls and dinner parties were given every Season, as standard, by elite members of The Four Hundred, but a wedding and the chance to parade a family's wealth while the rest of society was forced to extol the merits of the union was something the residents of Fifth Avenue could not resist.

Before Marietta's death, Minnie had consulted her on the potential matches due to come to fruition in New York in the spring. Marietta had been confident of a particularly busy round of events and anticipated her dominant role in proceedings. For the Stevenses a wedding didn't just provide the opportunity to bask in the victory of a job well done, it was also a productive platform for eliciting further business, since much could be gleaned from a whispered conversation here and an innocent comment there. Now that Marietta had gone so unexpectedly, Minnie felt adrift. The usual method whereby Marietta identified heiresses hungry for an English title, assessed their capabilities and mettle for such an enterprise and then handed them over to Minnie, had been successful and had created a healthy income which allowed them the financial freedom from men they had always craved.

It had seemed that 1895 was shaping up to be their most promising year, but now she wasn't sure how to proceed. She had the Vanderbilt project quietly bubbling away, which could be her greatest triumph yet, and there was no doubt that her husband's brother Almeric was looking like an attractive prospect for young New York heiress Pauline Whitney. Minnie knew that Marietta had always been fond of Almeric and had also seen it as her duty to find a gentleman suitable for Pauline when Flora, Pauline's mother and Marietta's close friend, had died. So Minnie now focused her efforts on Pauline's behalf, because that was a marriage that simply had to go ahead. Beyond the Vanderbilts and the Whitneys, it felt almost unseemly to make further plans; besides, it was Marietta who had always been the unstoppable force propelling her and the matchmaking enterprise forwards.

When Paran Stevens had died in 1872, it was Minnie's mother who had made the fateful decision to leave New York. Despite years knocking on the door of Mrs Astor's high society, Marietta had been barred from the most exclusive drawing rooms. The high priestess of Old New York had decreed that the Stevens family, with their dreadfully vulgar chain of hotels, were simply not refined enough for polite society. They were unconventional and outwardly ambitious, and Marietta had only made her task more problematic when she had introduced her Sunday-night *musicales*. Marietta had known that, despite her successes with their husbands, society's matrons would never receive her if she didn't do something drastic. She would need to force them into acceptance and it occurred to her that Minnie might be her passport to Mrs Astor.

Minnie had been a willing student. She had a core of steel like her mother and had watched from the sidelines as her parents had been cast aside by society because they lacked good breeding. This treatment had fuelled her desire for more – more connections, more money and more respect – and she had used this objective to galvanise herself into becoming a model student at Madame Coulon's school, where she met the rebellious and tenacious Alva Smith and the beautiful Consuelo Yznaga. Minnie's most pressing task had been to acquire a husband with a title, as instructed by her mother. A title, something not obtainable in America, would place her in an enviable position. Marietta knew that her compatriots couldn't resist a viscount or preferably a duke. She had witnessed the fervour that had been created by the Prince of Wales's visit in 1860 and how all of New York had clamoured for just a glimpse of Bertie. If she could manage to acquire just a pinch of that social gold dust then victory would be hers. After a lengthy stay in Paris, Minnie and Marietta had made their way to London, where Minnie was presented at court by Lady Suffield and Marietta quickly re-established contact with the Prince of Wales, who had been so impressed by the hospitality he had received at the Fifth Avenue Hotel over a decade earlier.

The irrepressible Bertie was immediately charmed by the articulate and engaging Minnie and began inviting her to Marlborough House and the Prince and Princess of Wales's country estate, Sandringham in Norfolk.

'We are staying in this charming house where I always think the host and hostess shine in their brightest light,' Minnie wrote in a letter to a friend about a Christmas visit to Sandringham. 'Wednesday we went out hunting, it poured in torrents from ten to four in the afternoon, and yet we remained out the whole day... Thursday, there was a servants' ball when we danced reel and jigs until five in the morning... Friday was the Xmas tree, the Prince and Princess gave me the most lovely presents, afterwards we had the loving cup and the mistletoe which occasioned many jokes and laughter.'[1]

Minnie had quickly established herself at the heart of the Marlborough House Set, and was confident that her position and obvious charms were likely to attract aristocratic gentlemen keen to secure a wealthy wife. 'That Lady Paget, while still Miss Stevens, should have succeeded in becoming a member of the most exclusive section of this brilliant and "cliquey" society, must be attributed entirely to her intelligence and charm,'[2] Bertie's biographer, J P C Sewell, wrote when recalling Minnie's swift rise to the top.

Initially, the strategy seemed to work, and Minnie received plenty of attention from aristocratic gentlemen, with possible suitors including Lord Rossmore, Lord Newry and Lord Hay. However, Minnie and Marietta were convinced she could do better. Given time, they would surely cross paths with a gentleman of greater social standing than a lord. Jennie Jerome, Minnie's friend from Paris and fellow heiress, had secured Lord Randolph Churchill in 1874 and Marietta felt certain that Minnie, with the right kind of direction, could be counted on to supersede her friend. And of course there were the rumours about Consuelo Yznaga having captured the heart of Kim, Viscount Mandeville. If she married him, she would become the Duchess of Manchester one day. Minnie simply had to do better.

However, the seasons moved on. Minnie travelled from country estates to town houses, sparkled at balls and entertained at dinners, yet a proposal of note wasn't forthcoming. After returning to New York for Consuelo's wedding to Kim in 1876 and successfully navigating a summer in Newport, Rhode Island, Marietta and Minnie recognised that time was running out.

Minnie was exceedingly popular with eligible bachelors in America. 'All the handsomest men adored her,'[3] remembered Frederick Martin. But, having tasted the glamour and distinction that London society offered, Marietta was determined to find a titled gentleman for Minnie and quickly 'intimated to him that she had other views for her daughter'.[4]

It was usual practice for a debutante to be 'out' in society for only a couple of Seasons before marrying. Now in her early twenties, Minnie increasingly appeared to have been left on the shelf. Marietta decided to travel to France and use her connections there – after all, her sister Fanny Reed was now resident in the French capital and her musical talents ensured that the very best of Parisian society flocked to her concerts, just as they had in New York. The Duc de Guiche, son of the influential Duc de Grammont, looked like an intriguing prospect for Minnie and immediately she went to work, winning him over with her flirtatious and lively conversation. The couple began spending time together and it began to look as if Marietta might get her titled son-in-law after all. To hasten a decision, she skilfully put it about that Minnie's dowry was considerable. She knew how the French aristocracy were suffering after the Franco-Prussian war of 1870 and felt certain that if the Duc de Grammont thought that Minnie's large fortune would regenerate the ailing family finances, he would cajole his son into a proposal.

Marietta was right: the attraction of an American heiress proved too much of a temptation for the Duc and he encouraged the courtship. However, she had underestimated the French aristocrat and did not foresee him dispatching one of his business associates to New York to ascertain just how much of a fortune the young lady known as the 'Great Heiress' would provide. Marie Corelli wrote about the position European aristocrats found themselves in when faced with an heiress who claimed she could furnish them with a large fortune:

'… the American girl arrives as more or less of a financial mystery. She may have thousands – she may have millions – he can never be quite sure. And he does all he can to ingratiate himself with her and give her a good time "on spec". To begin with, while he makes cautious and diplomatic enquiries. If his hopes rest on a firm basis, his attentions are redoubled – if, on the contrary, they are built on shifting sand, he gradually diminishes his ardour… and "fizzles" away.'[5]

When the Duc de Grammont mounted a shrewd and covert investigation into her fortune it was discovered that the Stevenses had overestimated Minnie's dowry. The Duc immediately withdrew his support for the union and the Duc de Guiche's daily calls on Minnie ceased. The rumour mill on both sides of the Atlantic went into overdrive, with Mrs Adair writing to Lady Waldegrave on the subject: 'Did you hear of the Duc de Grammont having a man of business in New York to go thoroughly through her affairs, and finding out she has really only £5000 a year which he did not consider sufficient for the Duc de Guiche… her mother must have mismanaged her property dreadfully to have reduced it so much.'[6]

It didn't happen often to the Stevens women, but this time they had gambled on the gullibility of one man who had proved them wrong, with disastrous consequences for Minnie's future. It was a miscalculation that would haunt her for the next few Seasons, as she was forced to hold her head high and ignore the gossips who prevailed at every occasion she attended. In a letter to Lady Strachey, Lady Waldegrave wrote, 'I must say I think this business very cruel, but at the same time I can't help thinking she deserved a snubbing as she told me she had £20,000 a year and would have more.'[7]

The incident called into question Minnie's character and her reputation, which had been carefully constructed but easily swept away. It was a mistake she wouldn't make again. She was acutely aware that, among her American friends from Paris, she was the only one who remained unmarried. Alva Vanderbilt, while still on the fringes of New York society, now had unlimited wealth at her fingertips and Minnie knew it was only a matter of time before she was accepted into Mrs Astor's ranks. Consuelo Manchester had managed to snare her viscount and, despite the fact that her father's fortunes were plummeting and the Manchesters would not receive what they had been promised by her family, the Yznagas, Consuelo Manchester would become a duchess one day. For once Minnie was perplexed at the unfortunate turn of events. She was beautiful, clever and calculating enough to have manipulated her way to the heart of the Prince of Wales's set, yet she had overplayed her hand and been left with nothing.

The Paris Exposition of 1878 was billed as the greatest the world had ever seen. The city was keen to put memories of the Franco-Prussian war, which had reduced Paris to ashes, behind it and, although it was still recovering from the ravages of war, the Exposition was seen as its chance to resurrect its international reputation. After Queen Victoria and Prince Albert's Great Exhibition in London in 1851, Paris had staged two expositions in 1855 and 1867. The 1878 offering would be bigger and more impressive, covering a huge expanse of central Paris. It stretched from the Champ-de-Mars to a Moorish palace constructed on the Place du Trocadéro on the opposite side of the Seine via a bridge that was the result of an architectural competition to elicit the best design. It was full of innovations and curiosities, great works of sculpture such as the display of Bartholdi's head of the Statue of Liberty (where huge crowds queued to climb the steps to her crown) and a sparkling demonstration of electric lights that illuminated the main concourses and fascinated visitors more used to gas lighting. An impressive hot-air balloon stood proudly in the Tuileries Gardens.

Ward McAllister, self-appointed social arbiter of New York society and founder of the Patriarchs' Balls. An invitation to one such event signalled acceptance into America's elite.

Alva Vanderbilt dressed as a Venetian princess for her opulent costume ball in March 1883. The ball cemented her status as a leader of New York society.

The famous Delmonico's restaurant. Setting for many of Ward McAllister's entertainments and favourite haunt of the Four Hundred.

660 Fifth Avenue, home of Alva and Willie K Vanderbilt. Designed by the architect Richard Morris Hunt and occupying a huge block of land on Fifth Avenue, known as "Vanderbilt Alley," the French Neo-Gothic palace stood next to mansions belonging to Willie K's father, William Henry, and brother, Cornelius.

Consuelo Vanderbilt and Winston Churchill at Blenheim Palace in 1902. The pair would enjoy a lifelong friendship.

Sunny, the Duke of Marlborough (fourth from left) and Consuelo, Duchess of Marlborough (second from left) on board the P&O liner *Arabia* en route to the Delhi Durbar in 1902.

The interior of Marble House, Alva Vanderbilt's "cottage" on Bellevue Avenue in Newport, Rhode Island. Italian and French artisans worked with five hundred thousand cubic feet of marble to build the palatial residence. By completion it had cost Alva around eleven million dollars.

Young people on a picnic in Newport, Rhode Island in 1893. Consuelo Vanderbilt is sitting in the back row, fourth from the left.

Consuelo Vanderbilt getting into her horse-drawn carriage on her way to St Thomas Church to marry Sunny, the Duke of Marlborough.

Marietta Stevens' dining room in her mansion on 57th Street and Fifth Avenue in 1893.

Consuelo, Duchess of Manchester on the cover of *The Bystander*, 1906, painted by the artist Sir William Blake Richmond.

Minnie Paget dressed as Cleopatra for the famous Duchess of Devonshire's ball of 1897. After her death the celebrated and elaborate costume would raise only nine pounds at auction.

Washington heiress, Mary Curzon pictured in 1903. Mary became Vicerine of India in 1898 when George Curzon was named as Lord Elgin's replacement.

Two women on the shore at Bailey's Beach, one of the fashionable places for heiresses to be seen during the Season in Newport, Rhode Island.

The gatehouse at Kimbolton Castle, Cambridgeshire, the country estate of Consuelo, Duchess of Manchester.

Newport Casino in 1895 was a gathering place for New York's elite, after vacating Manhattan for the Rhode Island town during the hot summer months. The Casino was a hub of activity for the Four Hundred, playing host to tennis matches, bowls and dances, all in pursuit of keeping the wealthy entertained.

Crowds enjoying Cowes Week Regatta on the Isle of Wight, England in 1908. The Regatta was popular with Bertie, the Prince of Wales.

Spectators lining Fifth Avenue for the wedding of Pauline Whitney to Sir Almeric Paget in November 1895.

Fashionable riders in Rotten Row, Hyde Park, London from the *Illustrated London News,* 25 May 1889.

Safely moored to the ground, guests like the actress Sarah Bernhardt, who was a ballooning enthusiast, would delight in taking trips aboard and imagine themselves floating away in its wicker basket.

Prince Leopold, Queen Victoria's youngest son, was visiting the Exposition and Minnie used the opportunity to reacquaint herself with him. She had already established a friendship with Leopold through his brother, Bertie, the Prince of Wales, and now he wrote to Minnie from the chic Hotel Bristol to try and arrange a meeting: 'The best cafe is Bignon in the Avenue de l'Opera. There are very nice private rooms upstairs.'[8] On 9 June, Leopold wrote again to Minnie, thanking her for a gift she had sent him and imploring her to come to England. 'You must come to England, I have set my heart on the project we have talked about.'[9]

It is difficult to ascertain just how close the friendship between Leopold and Minnie was. In any case, Minnie would have known that any affection for her on Leopold's part would be meaningless, as Queen Victoria would never allow him to marry a commoner. However, it is a measure of how highly Minnie was regarded within the royal family that she received a constant stream of affectionate letters from Leopold, Bertie and other members for the duration of her life.

Prince Leopold and the Paris Exposition had provided a pleasant diversion from the heavy burden of marriage that was causing Minnie to become increasingly anxious. Her fate rested on her ability to attract a suitable gentleman but she remained adrift. Finally, she resolved to do what had been inconceivable when she had been a new debutante and the belle of London society. She turned her attention to an untitled suitor.

Captain Arthur Paget was the eldest son of General Lord Alfred Paget, chief equerry to Queen Victoria, clerk marshal of the Royal Household and Member of Parliament for Lichfield. The Paget family were certainly well connected and had been an integral part of court life for generations. Arthur's grandfather was the First Marquess of Anglesey and had been the commanding officer of the Cavalry Brigade at the Battle of Waterloo. While there was no doubting the family's aristocratic connections, Arthur's father had no hereditary title to pass down to his son. He wasn't what Minnie had imagined for a husband, but her ambition was quickly giving way to pragmatism and an innate understanding that at twenty-five years old, her time was running out.

In Edith Wharton's *House of Mirth*, the main character, Lily Bart, contemplates her future after several Seasons without securing a proposal of marriage, causing her friend Judy Tremor to speculate that her reputation for flirtations with several different suitors had hampered her efforts to attract a gentleman. 'She seemed to have raked up everything. Oh you know what I mean – of course there isn't anything, *really*; but I suppose she brought in Prince Varigliano – and Lord Hubert – and there was some story of your having borrowed money of old Ned Van Alstyne: did you ever?'[10] It was a situation that Minnie could well identify with.

Minnie had met Arthur through the Prince of Wales during one of her first forays into the Marlborough House Set in 1874. Arthur was handsome, intelligent and enterprising, all attributes that immediately attracted the opportunistic Minnie. He had been educated at Wellington School and purchased a commission into the Scots Guards in 1869, distinguishing himself on the battlefield in 1873 during the third Anglo-Ashanti war in West Africa. Afterwards, he settled down to a privileged life as one of Bertie's most trusted friends and, through his passion for horse racing, established himself as Bertie's unofficial bookmaker, placing bets for the Prince of Wales at race meetings so that the Prince's integrity would not be called into question. Arthur attended to this burgeoning enterprise under the pseudonym Mr Fitzroy, until in 1877 the *Glasgow Herald* revealed his true identity, writing: 'Mr Fitzroy, in whose name John Day runs, is a Captain Paget who is now one of our principal plungers.'[11]

He continued to buy thoroughbreds and together with Lord Marcus Beresford ensured a lucrative income for himself and a cordial relationship with the Prince of Wales that was to continue for many years. Minnie couldn't help but be impressed by Arthur, and his endeavours marked him out as different from many English aristocratic gentlemen of the period who, barred from traditional employment, were content to run up large debts while relying on diminishing family allowances to fund their extravagant lifestyles. Arthur was not wealthy by any means and Minnie's fortune had been exposed as much less than Marietta had purported, but the Captain had made an impression on the cosmopolitan heiress who found his industrious racing pursuits reminiscent of the business creativity of her father. Sometime between their meeting in 1874 and their marriage in 1878, Arthur proposed to Minnie and was refused. Minnie may have been convinced that she could make a titled match or perhaps Marietta's ambition for her daughter ensured that the offer was not properly considered, but by 1878, after five long years as an unmarried heiress, the Stevenses' resolve was crumbling. In June, Minnie's engagement to Arthur was announced.

'When I first asked you to marry me... my proposal came from my head. Now it comes from my heart,'[12] Arthur was reported to have told Minnie, and when she wrote to Prince Leopold soon after, she confessed that she had held Arthur in high regard since their first meeting. Leopold, writing from Windsor Castle, expressed his surprise and obvious disappointment at the news, alluding to an intimacy between them that Minnie had actively encouraged.

'But I am delighted that you are now going really to settle down in England. Arthur Paget is a most lucky fellow! And if you are fond of him & have been so as you say, for four years, I am sure that he is worthy of your choice – but what a shame to make a fool of me at Paris, as you did. All the Pagets are quite delighted... what does Mrs Stevens say? You know she told me at Paris I was to impress on you the necessity of choosing one... of your many admirers.... I shall send you a small token of friendship, which I trust you will accept, sometimes wear in remembrance of some of the happy hours we have spent together.'[13]

The Prince of Wales also expressed his delight upon hearing the news: 'Pray accept my most sincere congratulations, & as we are such old friends you may be convinced that my wishes for your happiness are not a mere *façon de parler* [manner of speech].'[14]

Whether Prince Leopold's relationship with Minnie was simply a close friendship or extended to a greater degree of attachment, it seems he was deeply affected by her impending wedding to Arthur. Two weeks after his letter of congratulations, Leopold, who was by now suffering from one of his frequent bouts of illness related to his haemophilia, again wrote to Minnie, this time enclosing a bracelet as a sign of his affection:

'My dear Stevens,

I write to tell you that I send you herewith a small bracelet, which I hope you will accept, sometimes wear in memory of "Auld Lang Syne" – I fear you never received from me a letter of good wishes about a fortnight ago – I daresay you have heard that I am & have been confined to my bed for the past fortnight, with much acute suffering…

With my very best good wishes.

Leopold'[15]

Prince Leopold would always hold Minnie in high esteem, and even after her marriage he still wrote to her frequently, his letters filled with compliments. 'You were much admired yesterday, I thought you looked better than anyone else. (Don't be offended at my saying so.)'[16]

The fashionable St Peter's Church in Eaton Square, London was the venue for Minnie and Arthur's marriage on 27 July 1878. Equally fashionable was the time of the wedding, 3.30pm (previous custom had led most marriages to be completed with little fuss before midday). Minnie and Marietta, who had witnessed the excitement surrounding Consuelo Yznaga's wedding, were keen to exploit the publicity potential of the big day and Marietta ensured that the New

York newspapers were sufficiently briefed with the minutest details. *The New York Times* breathlessly reported, 'The Anglo-American marriage which took place in London in Saturday will send a thrill of envy through some thousands of feminine breasts.'[17]

It was a testament to the interest the wedding had created that crowds of people turned out to catch a glimpse of the happy couple. No doubt they were also interested in the royal guests who graced the wedding with their presence. The Prince of Wales was of course in attendance, as were other members of the royal family: the Duke of Connaught, Prince Louis of Battenberg and Princess Louise. Minnie ensured that their presence was recorded for posterity when she asked the royal guests to sign the wedding register.

The bride drew gasps of appreciation from the largely aristocratic ensemble when she entered the church on the arm of her brother, Harry. She had been planning this moment for many years and was determined to savour it, as was Marietta, who could hardly believe the sequence of events that had taken them to this place and time in the company of the greatest royal family in the world. The meteoric rise of the Stevens family was not lost on the press either, which commented, 'The man or woman who, 15 years ago, should have predicted that the daughter of the late Paran Stevens would have been married under these conditions, and that his widow would, on the day of the wedding, receive a visit of congratulations from the Prince of Wales, would indeed have been deemed a visionary.'[18]

Minnie's magnificent robe of white satin trimmed with orange blossoms had been carefully chosen to accentuate all her greatest attributes and ensured she looked every inch a society bride with an impeccable pedigree. A delicate tulle veil fell over her elegant features, while six diamond stars glittered in her hair. Everything about the wedding highlighted the couple's aristocratic lineage and good taste. Arthur's best man was his old friend and fellow racehorse owner Lord Marcus Beresford and the Pagets had ensured the Dean of Windsor performed the service. The guests retired to the groom's parents' house on Queen Anne Street for the wedding breakfast and the pitch-perfect military band of the Scots Fusiliers played throughout. Marietta appraised the vast collection of wedding gifts, which lined the Pagets' drawing room. Some Dresden china from Consuelo Manchester, a Louis XIV clock and candelabra from Bertie and a gold serpent bracelet set with sapphires, diamonds and rubies from the Princess of Wales. She felt an immense sense of relief. They had done it. Minnie was firmly situated in the bosom of the English nobility and although she had failed to win a title, Marietta firmly believed that her position was now assured and she had played her part too, as *Harper's Magazine* observed some years later:

'It would have been against all the rules had not Mrs Paget with such a mother, been possessed of brains, for one thing, and a supreme capacity for the arts of social generalship, for another. These she has, and in London… she has used them not less strikingly than did Mrs Paran Stevens in New York, and on a far bigger and more attractive stage.'[19]

Marietta knew that money would remain a preoccupation but it was also recognised that a lack of fortune was a constant source of anxiety for much of the English aristocracy and she was certain they didn't have Minnie's natural drive and intelligence to create an income for herself. It was the position and the access to royalty that mattered and Minnie had managed both. Never again would either Marietta or Minnie feel the icy chill of an inhospitable New York drawing room.

Minnie had witnessed her friend Consuelo Manchester be cast aside by her husband Kim as soon as her honeymoon was over and after the long periods she had spent in London, she was well appraised of the repressed nature of English upper-class gentlemen combined with their penchant for debauchery. Arthur was not your typical aristocrat. He was a soldier and, although for a man of his station that meant long swathes of time enjoying his own leisure pursuits, he believed he was honour-bound to his duty as a soldier, gentleman and husband. Within the first ten years of their marriage they had four children, the first, a son and the requisite male heir, followed by a daughter and then, in 1888, twin boys. Minnie had married for Arthur's connections but also for love, and therefore their marriage was not characterised by the turbulence that plagued Consuelo and Kim. As historian Charles Jennings notes, '… the Paget relationship was, for all its workmanlike overtones, an advertisement for the apparently happy blending of American verve and finance with British caste superiority.'[20]

Now, alone in New York, Minnie longed to have Arthur by her side. Marietta had been very fond of her son-in-law and it pleased Minnie to see that she had left him five thousand a year in her will, as well as bequeathing the same amount to her sister Fanny. Naturally, Minnie was the main beneficiary of Marietta's fortune and, although it was substantial, she knew that she would have to be judicious to ensure it afforded her and Arthur a country home where they could host weekend parties, a goal they had long held. The inheritance was welcome but it would not prevent her from continuing with her business. She understood now that although money had been the driving force behind the enterprise, gradually as the years had gone by, it had become a growing source of self-satisfaction. There was a delicious sense of accomplishment in introducing a fledgling heiress to society. The effort it required to impart the wisdom she had accrued during her long journey to matrimony was worthwhile when she witnessed a protégé taking her first steps on the ballroom floor at Marlborough House. It had given her mother great pleasure too and she was never more proud than attending a wedding or reading about a marriage in the press, with the knowledge that Minnie had contrived the betrothal from behind the scenes. She may not have her mother's counsel to propel her endeavours forward in future, but she would still make her proud. The Vanderbilt and Whitney projects were already taking shape, but there were others to follow. Minnie just had to get back to work.

Lily of Troy

April 1895, London

*'Mrs Louis Hamersley is one of the handsomest women
in New York.... Add to this great beauty the fact that
she owns some five or six millions, and the natural result
is that her opera box is constantly filled with the most
attractive men in the town.' – THE BROOKLYN EAGLE*

Lily Beresford would have cast her eye around the large reception room
at Number 3 Carlton House Terrace. The room looked perfect, just
as she had imagined it. For once she had got the wedding breakfast of
her dreams, and she couldn't have been happier. This time she would
have been determined to leave nothing to chance. A young Winston
Churchill wrote to his mother, Jennie, that it was 'a most excellent
breakfast which must have cost a great deal'[1]. It had, but as a woman
of means, she could now afford to do things properly, and properly
she would, without the interference of her mean and eccentric first
husband or her second husband, an impoverished duke keen to make

as little fuss as possible. This time, her third as a bride, she would put on the occasion that everybody expected and she had longed for. Her marriage to Lord William Beresford would be different, of that there was no doubt.

The wedding had been set for ten o'clock on 30 April 1895 at the fashionable St George's Church on Hanover Square. The morning was clear and bright as the guests filed through the six vast stone Corinthian columns at the church's impressive entrance to take their seats. Awaiting them lay an interior festooned with Lily's trademark white orchids, a tradition she had established many years before when she became notorious for decorating her opera box with them. Today, they acknowledged her past life, as it would never be far away from her thoughts. She was conscious of the turbulent journey she had taken to arrive at St George's and she wouldn't be forgetting what she had learned along the way.

The wedding guests, including the Duke of Cambridge, the United States Ambassador and Winston Churchill, turned to look at the thirty-nine-year-old bride as she was slowly revealed at the rear of a procession headed by the choir and the Queen's chaplain, Reverend Edgar Shephard. She took slow, deliberate steps, arm-in-arm with her stepson, Sunny, the 9th Duke of Marlborough. Today, she would cease to be the Dowager Duchess, as she had been since 1892 on the death of Sunny's father, the 8th Duke. She wore a dress of satin brocade trimmed with point lace and finished with beautiful diamond buttons, and a small grey velvet bonnet trimmed with pearls, ostrich plumes and a flamboyant white aigrette. Ahead of her at the bottom of the chancel steps stood William with his best man and younger brother, Marcus. William represented everything her two former husbands had lacked: a future bright with possibility. He was popular, beloved by all those who met him, and Lily was hopelessly in love. His older brother Charles Beresford wrote that '… he had the most lovable nature, the most charming character, the pluckiest spirit and most generous mind that I ever met. He was always thinking of others and never of himself.'[2] William's friend Lord Cromer agreed: 'He was the cheeriest of companions and the most gallant of soldiers – in a word, one of the best fellows I have ever come across during a long life.'[3]

Lily felt sure that she had chosen well this time, although it had taken a long time and much heartache for her to find herself standing opposite a man she truly loved. Born Lilian Warren Price in Troy in New York State in 1854, she was the daughter of Cicero Price, a commodore in the United States navy. The Prices were decidedly middle-class and when they moved from the relatively sleepy Troy to the burgeoning New York, they lived simply and comfortably. They certainly could not have imagined that their daughter would capture the heart of one of the wealthiest men of the city. There was no doubt that Lily was beautiful, virtuous and good-natured, but nobody expected her to make a socially ambitious match. Elizabeth Drexel Lehr described her as 'Lily of Troy, with no money or social position, but a face as fair as the legendary Helen's'[4]. Perhaps Lily was underestimated by a New York society so concerned with position and family connections that it failed to notice the inroads she was making into the hearts of its young gentlemen. She had by now changed her name to Lily. Some suggested it was to reflect her pure, delicate flower-like beauty, others thought it was because Lilian rhymed with million and she wished to disguise her true intentions from potential suitors. She made a point of always wearing white, to ensure her porcelain skin looked alluring and was offset by her caramel-blonde hair. Gradually, Lily began to receive invitations to balls and dances and then, in 1877, she was invited to a Patriarchs' Ball, where her beauty and grace caused a sensation.

It wasn't long before she met and married Louis Carre Hamersley, who had made his money in bonds and real estate, in 1879. Louis was fourteen years older than Lily and lived at 257 Fifth Avenue with his father. The Hamersleys were considered peculiar by New York society and were largely shunned owing to the close bond between father and son, who never seemed to be seen apart. When Louis' father died in 1883, his son quickly followed four months later. Lily became a wealthy widow overnight, receiving over four million dollars from her husband's estate, although she would have to fight a long court battle with disgruntled relatives convinced they had been cheated out of their share by a wily gold-digger. This dispute persuaded Mrs Astor and her exclusive set that Lily's name should not be included on the guest list for the smartest events, but she remained undeterred. Aided by friends who were willing to accept her, like Marietta Stevens, and with a fortune that put almost limitless funds at her disposal, she gave elaborate dinner parties and *musicales* and attended the opera religiously. In May 1888, a reporter for *The Brooklyn Eagle* described Lily's opera excursions for its readers:

'Mrs Louis Hamersley is one of the handsomest women in New York, and is to be seen during the Season at her box in the opera calm, fair and beautiful, and generally in white, with heaps of snowy furs drawn about her and a huge fan of white curled ostrich plumes in her languid hand… Add to this great beauty the fact that she owns some five or six millions, and the natural result is that her opera box is constantly filled with the most attractive men in the town.'[5]

Lily's beauty and wealth were an enticing attraction for any eligible gentleman, but Lily wanted acceptance into society and therefore entertained another interesting proposition, the Duke of Marlborough. Widely known as the Marquess of Blandford, which had been his title until his father's death in 1883 (and formerly the Earl of Sunderland), the 8th Duke of Marlborough was perilously in debt. Blenheim Palace, the Marlboroughs' magnificent country seat in Woodstock, Oxfordshire, had been one of the most impressive stately homes in England for generations and a source of great pride to the family, but the sheer scale of the palace threatened to derail their future. It was outdated, uncomfortable and in desperate need of repairs, yet the income from the estate was dwindling as a result of declining rents from tenant farmers. Blandford's father had attempted to stop the rot in the late 1870s and early 1880s by selling off land, auctioning the Marlborough gems at Christie's and putting up for sale the priceless collection of books that formed the Sunderland library but his efforts weren't enough. When Blandford inherited the dukedom in 1883, he embarked on another sale, this time of the family's collection of paintings, including Raphael's *Ansidei Madonna* and Van Dyck's *Time Clipping the Wings of Cupid*. These paintings, along with other priceless canvases by Rubens, Titian and Rembrandt, enabled Blandford to purchase equipment for the tenant farms, as well as indulge his passion for orchids by installing hothouses at Blenheim, but again it proved insufficient to meet the needs of the great palatial residence. While the aristocratic system of primogeniture was designed to protect the family fortune, forever consolidating its wealth in the heir, it also put intolerable strain on the eldest son. The responsibility for dowries for numerous sisters and allowances for younger brothers and other family members could prove excessive, particularly in large families, which were common among the aristocracy. Blandford's duties as Duke were extensive and expensive, and he was increasingly desperate to find a way out of his financial difficulties.

In the summer of 1887, Blandford attended a house party thrown by Jennie Churchill's sister Clara Frewen at Lavington Park, with Minnie and Arthur Paget. Just a few weeks later he would be on his way to America, where his first stop would be Marietta's villa in Newport, Rhode Island. The play *The Title Mart*, which was produced on Broadway in 1906, features an aristocrat very like Blandford, who comes to America in search of a rich bride. In Act 1 he says: 'Well here I am in America, with fifteen thousand pounds' worth of debts, two country places, mortgaged up to the leads, – assets, a letter of introduction to Mrs Blackwell, stepmother to an heiress worth twenty millions.'[6]

Unfortunately, although Americans typically loved the aristocracy, the puritanical side of the American press won out in Blandford's case and, having heard lurid reports of his philandering throughout his first marriage, which had ended in divorce in 1883, it was in no mood to welcome him with open arms, reporting, 'Everything his Grace of Marlborough [*sic*] brought with him was clean, except his reputation.'[7] At first Newport society felt the same way, scuppering Blandford's plans to attract a rich heiress. Fortunately for him, the pragmatic Marietta Stevens felt differently, reasoning that making an alliance with any duke, no matter how debauched, was better than snubbing one altogether. Forewarned about about the Duke's visit and his dubious reputation by Minnie, nevertheless she was poised to extend an invitation for him to stay as her guest in Newport as soon as he stepped off the boat from England. She then began the familiar process of ensuring he was seen at the most exclusive events of the summer and identifying an American heiress who had the fortune and face to become the Duchess of Marlborough. It was a strategy Minnie and Marietta had been discussing and honing on Marietta's regular trips to visit her daughter in England. Establishing themselves as conduits for Anglo-American relations made sense and might prove to be lucrative. Now it began to bear fruit.

By the autumn of 1887, Marietta and Blandford were attending the Metropolitan Opera to see a production of *Tristan and Isolde*. As usual, Lily was there, as Marietta knew she would be, and for the first time she laid eyes on her future husband. Eventually the two were introduced, with both Marietta and Leonard Jerome, Jennie Churchill's father, playing their part in the courtship. Lily seemed particularly taken with Blandford's intelligence, as he was a keen inventor, often spending days at a time in a makeshift laboratory he had created at Blenheim. He even worked on an early communications system for the palace, installing Britain's first internal telephone system, and spent time with Alexander Bell when he was visiting America. Blandford was undoubtedly attracted to Lily's money, but he also appreciated her submissive nature and the way she indulged his ideas and fancies. They became engaged and, although her family opposed the marriage, telling her to break it off on the grounds of his divorce and commenting that Lily was 'as uncontrollable as a horse without a bit in his mouth'[8], the wedding went ahead on 29 June 1888.

Marietta was travelling in Europe when Lily and Blandford said their vows, rather unromantically at the mayor's office in City Hall. Blandford was careful to ensure that the legal papers regarding Lily's fortune were all in order before they began, and then insisted on a second ceremony at the tabernacle Baptist Church on Second Avenue afterwards, as divorcees were prevented from marrying in an Episcopalian church. The couple held a small dinner party with friends at Delmonico's that evening before sailing for England on the *Aurania* the next day. Once they arrived in London, Blandford escorted Lily to another wedding ceremony at the registry office on Mount Street. His determination to legally secure the marriage apparently knew no bounds. Two years later, *Cosmopolitan* would acknowledge the place money occupied in such unions, writing, 'They are married with few exceptions for their money or the money they are supposed to have – an ugly fact but nevertheless a fact. The charms so much talked about are thrown in and are appreciated… after marriage rather than before.'[9]

Awareness of the attraction of her fortune to Blandford did not prevent Lily pursuing the marriage. Even as a duke of dubious reputation, he was a duke all the same, and provided her with a position that would surely admit her to the most exclusive circles. The newlyweds travelled from London to Blenheim, where Marietta was one of their first visitors.

The new Duchess found the imposing and majestic Blenheim Palace impressive but uncomfortable. She was used to a palatial and modern mansion in the heart of the bustling city of New York, equipped with the newest technology to ensure the comfort of its occupants. Blenheim stood proud but isolated in the heart of the Oxfordshire countryside. It was vast and cold, with a labyrinth of passageways that saw servants bustling up and down, day and night, attending to the Duke and Duchess's every need. There were no convenient ensuite bathrooms – instead servants were forced to trek long distances with hot water to fill Lily's bath, which was positioned in front of her bedroom fire. Mealtimes were a problem too. There was no accomplished French chef to devise gluttonous menus at Blenheim, as Lily had been used to at home, and the dining room lay so far away from the kitchen that the basic food that made its way out of the kitchen was almost cold and inedible by the time it was served. Lily set about using some of her fortune to improve Blenheim, contributing to the repair of the three-acre roof, restoring the boathouse, repairing the family's chapel and crucially adding central heating and electricity, which greatly improved her comfort during the eternally long days and nights when the Duke and Duchess were in residence. She also had the Grand Willis organ installed, which bore the inscription:

> *In memory of happy days*
> *And as a tribute*
> *To this glorious home*
> *We leave thy voice*
> *To Speak within these walls*
> *In years to come*
> *When ours are still*
> *LM and MM*
> *1891*[10]

Remarkably, Lily and Blandford were happy together. Blandford had been finally released from the pressure of inevitable financial ruin into the arms of a woman who pandered to his whims and had the means to meet all his demands. Lily, as a duchess, had achieved an unassailable position that meant she would never again have to endure the humiliation of being left out of society. She made a triumphant journey back to New York, where Marietta held an ostentatious dinner in her honour and The Four Hundred inundated her with invitations to an array of occasions.

Lily still encountered obstacles, namely her failure to conceive a child and Blandford's stubborn continuation of an affair with Lady Colin Campbell, a passionate infatuation that saw him hang his mistress's portrait in his bedroom, much to Lily's embarrassment. The aristocracy also failed to accept her with open arms at first, the Churchill family making particularly cruel comments about her appearance. 'I don't think the Duchess Lily looking at all well in health and the moustache and beard are becoming serious,'[11] wrote Blandford's brother Lord Randolph Churchill to his mother. Whether these observations are true is difficult to ascertain, as many contemporary reports emphasise her beauty, although it is conceivable that by this time the middle-aged Lily's looks were fading.

Her attempts to win over the Churchills would not be unsuccessful for long. One morning November 1892, Blandford was unexpectedly found dead in his bedroom by his valet. Lily was devastated. Lord Randolph wrote to his wife, Jennie, 'I had a long talk with the poor Duchess while the post mortem was going on. You were really quite right about her and I quite wrong. Nothing could exceed her goodness and kindness of disposition, and my belief is that she means to do nothing but what is right, liberal and generous by the heir.'[12]

The Churchills were impressed by Lily's ability to maintain her composure faced with the gravest of circumstances, but it was a situation she had already experienced. A widow once more, after only five years of marriage, she would have known time was limited to carve out a new position for herself in English society and manage a smooth transition to the next generation, Blandford's son from his first marriage, Sunny, now the 9th Duke. She did allow herself one act of defiance, however, tearing to shreds the portrait of Lady Colin Campbell that had so tormented her throughout her marriage and posting every piece to her rival.

In December 1893, she took a twenty-one-year lease on Deepdene, a country estate in a valley at the foot of the North Downs, near Dorking in Surrey. Its highly likely that she was advised by her friends, including Consuelo Manchester and Minnie, to establish a visit to Deepdene as an essential part of the racing season. She scheduled a house party for June 1894 to coincide with the Derby at Epsom. Lily knew that the race always attracted high society, particularly elements of the Marlborough House Set who had an obsessive interest in horse racing, such as Arthur Paget and his crowd of gentlemen friends. Once more using the connections of her friends and acquaintances to draw up the guest list, she invited Lord William Beresford, who immediately impressed Lily with his impeccable military record, including the Victoria Cross for valour, and a reputation for being one of the most daring cross-country riders in England. He was warm and good-natured, and his blue eyes twinkled with humour, contrasting favourably with his silver-grey hair. He was completely different from Louis and Blandford, and Lily fell deeply in love. For William, who at forty-seven had resisted matrimony for many years, his introduction to Lily was a major turning point. The stability of her fortune must have been an attraction, but he was a man more used to primitive conditions after postings in Zululand and India than aristocratic country estates, so it appears there was much genuine affection on both sides. In 1895, Lord William Beresford proposed to Lily, once an American heiress, now a woman of means who had been widowed twice.

Maybe this time Lily would get everything she wanted. As her guests enjoyed the wedding breakfast she had always imagined, entertained by a groom who represented a life she had always desired but never quite achieved, the future showed potential to be different. The steps she had taken to become Lord William Beresford's wife had been necessary, educational and valuable, but she was older and wiser and now it was her chance to enjoy the spoils.

To Conquer the Season

June 1895, London

'When one came to London for the Season then, one came prepared for an orgy of parties and ivory cards fell like snowflakes.' – DUKE OF MANCHESTER

Rotten Row in the early morning was a good place to do one's thinking. Minnie Paget smoothed down the silk folds of her riding habit, carefully, meticulously, before giving the signal to her horse to walk on. The navy habit was tight-fitting, through necessity and design. Although she was now considered middle-aged, at forty-two Minnie's beauty endured and she was particularly fastidious at maintaining and showing off her lithe figure. As her exquisite horse, a present from Arthur after a particularly profitable few days at the races, began to trot purposefully down the rusty brown track that ran along the south side of Hyde Park, the day ahead looked promising. There was the wedding of Sir Charles Hartopp to Miss Millicent Wilson, daughter of the MP Mr C H Wilson, to attend, followed by a formal call from Alva Vanderbilt and then dinner and the opera.

It had been only a few days since she had returned from America but Minnie was approaching the Season with renewed vigour. She was all too aware that Marietta's death had left her languishing behind the social merry-go-round and she really did feel more comfortable when she was ahead of the game. Her trip had proved vexing at times. There seemed to be an ever-increasing pile of paperwork to go through with Marietta's lawyers and her trip to Newport to attempt to settle the fate of her mother's mansion and its contents had proved fruitless. Minnie was keen to get back to England, after all this was her busiest and most important time of year. So, after weeks of negotiations and very little movement on the sale, she booked her passage home.

Minnie had been thrilled to observe the familiar signs of the London Season springing into life on her return. All around her, the houses of Belgravia and Mayfair had undergone their annual facelift, giving them a smart sense of uniformity that delighted the crowds of visitors that the Season commanded. She could practically smell the freshly painted exteriors and marvelled at the beautifully planted window boxes groaning under the weight of vast collections of brightly coloured flowers. The royal standard flew over Buckingham Palace, acting as a reassuring beacon to the aristocracy, calling them home to the capital. Even now, after so many years on the treadmill of the London Season, she always felt a frisson of excitement when the gloomy London fog was finally swept away by the promise of spring. The upper classes began to make their way to town, a slow and steady drip, drip of familiar faces before the final flood of society descended on the capital by June.

'When one came to London for the Season then, one came prepared for an orgy of parties and ivory cards fell like snowflakes,'[1] remembered the 9th Duke of Manchester in his memoirs. June was when the Season was at its peak. It was then that Minnie was thrown into a never-ending whirl of garden parties, charity bazaars and balls. State dinners followed regimental banquets, with the opera and exclusive *musicales* filling every waking moment, along with annual events such as Henley Regatta, Royal Ascot, the Eton-versus-Harrow cricket match and shooting at Hurlingham. All of these occasions were short hops away from London but were eagerly frequented by the most fashionable set, and by default became simply unmissable events for ladies or gentlemen keen to make their face known. Minnie remembered how she had witnessed with wide-eyed incredulity the flurry of activity that accompanied those few weeks for the first time as a debutante. How her mother had ensured she barely slept, commanding her to dance at grand balls until the early hours of the morning and then instructing her to wake early to ride on Rotten Row, a habit she had retained during every Season since. By the end of her first Season she had been suffering from a delightful exhaustion that came from knowing she had grasped every opportunity possible. Twenty years later, she still felt the same about the Season. The hazy gauze of youthful innocence had been lifted, with the whole society scene crystal-clear to her now, yet none of that first flush of euphoria born from committing to and conquering London during the summer had disappeared.

Among the well-travelled upper classes, London was considered the pinnacle of all the social Seasons. While Paris was a perfectly acceptable training ground for young debutantes and a vital stopover to procure the latest fashions, its society was limited and suffered from the kind of immorality that encouraged Britain's aristocracy to partake in nefarious behaviour. Minnie considered Mrs Astor's bid to install New York and Newport society as the most well-regarded across the globe and felt a certain sense of satisfaction that this goal had floundered. Mrs Astor had simply put too many restrictions on the American aristocracy and so, while the lavish entertainments of The Four Hundred sometimes overshadowed European efforts, the rigidity of the behavioural code rendered the American upper classes stuffy and tiresome. London society struck a perfect balance between the two, representing a glorious confection of nationalities and talents. While maintaining its adherence to tradition, it had evolved by accepting those who could genuinely enhance its ranks. Bertie, the Prince of Wales, through his continuous bid to banish insufferable boredom, had encouraged wit and nurtured social talents and in so doing had discarded the formality of Queen Victoria's court and established his own, embracing all that was modern and provocative. It was an intoxicating mix and one that presented a myriad of opportunities for those willing to capitalise on them.

'The supremacy of the new English court, like that of its French predecessor, was based on the chief characteristic of the age – the trend towards internationalism, democracy's great ideal. The court of Tuileries had been exotic, that of the Prince of Wales was cosmopolitan. The difference was chiefly one of leadership,'[2] wrote W R H Trowbridge, Princess Alexandra's biographer, when describing the appeal of the Marlborough House Set and England for wealthy travellers. Edith Wharton also captured the lure of English society when one of the American heiresses in her novel *The Buccaneers* declares: 'Why, you dear little goose, I'd rather starve and freeze here than go back to all the warm houses and the hot baths, and the emptiness of everything – people and places… because London's London, and London life the most exciting and interesting in the world, and once you've got the soot and the fog in your veins you simply can't live without them…'[3]

Marriage was a constant preoccupation during the London Season. Minnie was perpetually conscious that, just as it was the most important time of the year for her, where all the careful foundations she had laid during the previous months would either come to fruition or evaporate to nothing, it was also considered a crucial time of year for other society hostesses. She had spent many years crafting her business, perfecting her techniques and establishing American contacts who would assist in the process, but there were other formidable ladies who sought to benefit from the same methods. English rivals, like the Duchess of Sutherland, who offered the same type of services for British debutantes. Lord Beaconsfield described the Duchess as a 'social fairy'[4] on account of her ability to procure sought-after invitations to costume balls or introductions to powerful aristocratic families. Lady Dorothy Nevill also commented on the practice: 'A curious development… is the system by which, for some financial consideration… well-known ladies of good social standing undertake to arrange entertainments for rich people anxious to attain a prominent place in London society.… I fancy some of those who organise entertainments for wealthy hosts or hostesses very often make something out of it directly or indirectly.'[5]

Lady Nevill was right: services related to the marriage market could be varied and lucrative for ladies like the Duchess of Sutherland, who was an integral part of elite society. However, other members of the upper classes could take advantage of the industry too. Adverts could often be found in newspapers or magazines, implicitly offering connections for money:

'A lady in the smartest society in London wishes to chaperone a young lady. Terms £1,000 for one year. Highest references given and required.'[6]

There was great emphasis placed on husband-hunting during the London Season, whether you were an English or American debutante, hence the rich pool of services the young ladies could draw on to help guarantee their success. Under the constant pressure of the ticking social clock, they had only perhaps two or three Seasons to secure a match, after which they were considered a failure. By the age of thirty, an upper-class lady who hadn't married was classed a spinster.

'Marriage was considered not so much an alliance between the sexes as an important social definition; serious for a man but imperative for a girl. It was part of her social duty to enlarge her sphere of influence through marriage,'[7] wrote the historian Leonore Davidoff in her book *The Best Circles*. The Season was a chance for debutantes to meet the widest selection possible of potential suitors, to make contacts, to impress influential society hostesses, all within the pressurised confines of a few precious months, forcibly pitted day after day against wealthier, better-connected or more beautiful competitors. It was no wonder that Minnie and her rivals were much in demand when so much was at stake.

Any heiress that Minnie was to take on had to have certain qualities. She could not be seen to be championing just any debutante, no matter how great her fortune. Minnie had spent many years as a young lady studying the social attributes that would be imperative for the rest of her life. She was described by a reporter for *Harper's Magazine* as having 'not only a natural grace in her movements and gestures, but she is also entirely mistress of herself… the same impression that Mrs Paget makes in a drawing room, that is, of a woman of the world, absolutely and with good reason sure of herself, and equal to any emergency that may come along'.[8]

Such skills had been mastered with great care and diligence, and she expected nothing less from any charges she agreed to take on. Her heiresses must be intelligent, charming, refined and possess a certain amount of fortitude, enough to get them through the Season and beyond. It was a characteristic she wasn't convinced Consuelo Vanderbilt possessed, although the girl had endured and survived a whole life in the presence of the domineering Alva, so perhaps she did have an inner resolve to draw upon that wasn't immediately apparent.

Minnie had made extensive enquiries about Alva Vanderbilt's position among New York society during her trip to America. She had been encouraged to hear that, despite the inevitable scandal the press coverage of her divorce had generated, there were those within the elite who were still prepared to support Alva. After her long trip to Europe, she would be cautiously welcomed back into the fold during the society's summer escape to Newport. Alva was just too powerful to cast aside, a position that Minnie both admired and envied. There was no doubting, though, that a proposal of marriage from Sunny, the Duke of Marlborough to Consuelo would help to silence Alva's critics permanently. She had turned to Minnie, as Minnie knew she would, to ensure the deal was done. Minnie had suggested that Alva and Consuelo attend a ball at Stafford House, where she had been pleased to see Sunny lay claim to several dances with the young debutante. The next step was a visit to Blenheim Palace, the Marlborough family seat, where Consuelo would unknowingly audition for the part of Duchess.

Minnie had been careful to advise Consuelo on the nature of English husbands, warning that it was best to compare them to a simple egg: 'So full of themselves that they are incapable of holding anything else!' She wanted Consuelo to see Marlborough for what he was, not some romantic notion of an aristocratic husband that was perpetuated by the novels and magazines of the day. Then they would all find out whether she had the heart and strength to commit to such a plan.

The morning spectators were gathering now, taking up their usual spot to observe the very best of London society. To be seen at Rotten Row wasn't just an opportunity to meet close acquaintances or engineer an encounter with those who were embracing the Season for the first time and so surreptitiously assess their fitness to be accepted. It was a chance to be seen by reporters, society watchers and the general public. An opportunity to be talked about, written about and remain a constant presence in public consciousness. For now that the newspapers reported every move of the aristocracy, the stakes of the Season were moved ever higher. This was the time the society game began in earnest, and Minnie galloped off down the track with her usual aplomb, always knowingly ahead of the chasing pack.

The Introductions Market

June 1895, Kimbolton, Cambridgeshire

*'So many Americans of means pursue her in
London for introductions to her titled acquaintances
that it simplifies matters for her to make it
a business.' – NEW YORK WORLD*

As she looked around the drawing room of Kimbolton, Consuelo Manchester noticed for the first time how worn it looked. The grand old house that had played host to the Manchesters for generations had lost its lustre: the deep, rich colour of its sumptuous furnishings now looked faded in the harsh daylight of the summer sun. Perhaps her surroundings had always been what they were in this moment, their luminous brilliance previously an illusion created by the warm envelope of family life. The stale air permeated her senses; everything seemed older now, lifeless somehow.

Consuelo had arrived back at Kimbolton after an extended stay at Compton Place, Eastbourne, a seaside retreat, loaned to her by the

Duke and Duchess of Devonshire. It was a kind gesture from Lottie, the 'Double Duchess', who had instantly known that her daughter-in-law would need a place to grieve and gather her thoughts, away from the memories of Kimbolton. Consuelo's remaining children, Little Kim and Lady Alice, had accompanied her to Eastbourne after she had brought Lady Mary back to England. Away from the prying eyes of society, she had been given time to think, time to plan her next move.

For the first time in many years she felt unsure of her place, and her daughter's death had shaken the very foundations of her life further. After Kim's death, she had ceased to be the Duchess of Manchester. She was, at only thirty-nine, a dowager duchess and, although the title was still recognised and respected, she knew it would only be a matter of time before she was expected to fade into the background, making way for a younger, more beautiful successor to take her place. To maintain her place in society, a place that she had fought for, won and paid for with streams of tears, she must continue to prove enticing, entertaining and useful to the rest of the aristocracy, and that is what she had affirmed to do. For the past three years, she had diligently worked all of her contacts, proving herself to be the perfect conduit for the parvenus striving for acceptance in England. This turn of events wasn't new to Consuelo Manchester: it was an arrangement she had been cultivating with the wealthy but unrefined for many years and she had come to an agreement with her old friend Minnie Paget, who also partook in a little social manoeuvring, to share their schemes and help each other where possible.

The question they had both been trying to answer for years was one of money. How was it possible to live among the aristocracy and convince them of the worth of an interloper, an American at that, without ready access to the one thing they needed? Their ostensible wealth was what had bought them their seat at countless aristocratic tables across the country, but the truth was that after financial mishaps, the fortune promised never materialised, their dowries a mere smokescreen swept away amidst the constant flow of champagne that characterised their first years in England. When Consuelo and Minnie had married, English law decreed that all of their money and property should automatically transfer to their husband. For Consuelo it meant witnessing a modest dowry and allowance being burned through at terrifying speed by a husband fond of gambling and heir to a family estate that was almost bankrupt. The agricultural depression had a devastating effect on the Manchester estates, seeing income drop from £95,000[1] a year to a deficit of £2,000[2]. However, the figures didn't seem to galvanise Kim into amending his spendthrift ways: he persistently pursued his extravagant lifestyle until the creditors finally caught up with him.

In 1888, the *St Louis Post* reported on rumours of Consuelo Manchester's financial limitations: 'Her entertainments are of a very modest kind because she has no money to make them otherwise. But Americans who have called on her in London say that her small out-of-the-way house is crowded by a more distinguished company than is to be found in any other house in the English metropolis. They take her cold bouillon and other unpretentious refections without any criticism whatever.'[3]

News of the gossip that had travelled across the Atlantic to her compatriots reached Consuelo and, although she was flattered by the kind comments on her abilities to attract the smartest set, she bitterly resented the humiliation that the questionable calibre of her hospitality attracted. After the *Married Women's Property Act* of 1882 offered a lifeline to women like her by allowing them to keep the money they earned, some embarked on their own money-making schemes and Consuelo chose one that used her amiable talents to their fullest.

'Lady Mandeville's [Consuelo Manchester's] plans were for Americans to provide themselves with letters of introduction from her ladyship's agents in the United States to present them in London and then be introduced to her Ladyship's bankers, modistes and circle of acquaintances. The Mandeville balance at the banks would be increased by gifts from the visitors and her bills at the milliner's regularly paid by her protégés,'[4] the *San Francisco Chronicle* told its readers in 1890 when writing about her activities in the introductions market. Whether Consuelo had failed to be discreet enough when making connections or reporters had discovered her profession from a careless acquaintance or servant isn't clear, but the scandal took pride of place in the society papers. The *New York World* reported: '… so many Americans of means pursue her in London for introductions to her titled acquaintances that it simplifies matters for her to make it a business.'[5]

Consuelo's venture was successful enough to be talked about widely in the newspapers and in society circles on both sides of the Atlantic; along with Minnie, she was gaining a reputation for being able to place American heiresses with titled husbands. The practice did not go unnoticed by the aristocracy, with many fearing that it destabilised the careful balance between historic tradition and cultural refinement, and vulgar and seemingly limitless wealth. Lady Dorothy Nevill commented, 'Society to-day and society as I formerly knew it are two entirely different things… wealth has usurped the place formerly held by wit and learning.'

Like Minnie, Consuelo had a unique insight into the motivations of the American heiresses and their families, and the practical obstacles that faced them if they were to assimilate themselves into the aristocracy. She had walked in their handcrafted shoes just a few years before and now used her experience to mentor others, as historian Marian Fowler notes in her book *In a Gilded Cage*:

'For a hefty fee, an American girl would be groomed and schooled by Consuelo, taught how to curtsy and comport herself in English society, presented at court and – if she measured up – invited to a select party where the Prince would be a guest. After that it was up to her to charm him… If she was looking for a peer, Consuelo would cast about for suitable ones and introduce her.'[6]

Bertie, as always, was the key to Consuelo Manchester's success. There were rumours that she was his one-time mistress, following the end of his relations with Lillie Langtry and before the start of his affair with Daisy, Countess of Warwick. It was Daisy who came between the long-time friends after Consuelo rather inadvisably circulated a satirical poem, 'Lady River', based on Daisy, whose nickname was 'Babbling Brooke' due to her inability to be discreet. Her actions caused Bertie to surmise that Consuelo may have been the author. She wasn't, but the damage had been done. Bertie, who hated disloyalty of any kind, made it known that Consuelo was not welcome at Marlborough House. It seems Minnie became embroiled in the quarrel too, although there is no evidence that she circulated the poem. Bertie wrote to his private secretary, Francis Knollys, in 1892, commenting, 'These American ladies talk too much… and their indiscretions and inaccuracies are most annoying. Those who profess to [be] Lady B's best friends have shown their friendship in a very doubtful manner.'[7] Bertie ostracised Consuelo from his guest lists, yet his brief irritation with Minnie did not seem to last. She retained her position within the Marlborough House Set and continued to wield influence with the Prince.

The stand-off between Consuelo and Bertie continued for some years and would only be resolved when Little Kim had a chance meeting with Bertie and begged him on bended knee to forgive his mother. Fortuitously, the ongoing tension between the two didn't seem to affect Consuelo's ability to introduce clients to the British nobility. Thanks to her success among the aristocracy, her sister Natica was by now married to Sir John Lister Kaye, and still enjoyed Bertie's favour. She 'was able to provide the second step in the royal conquest',[8] ensuring that any heiresses whom Consuelo was parading around town secured a pivotal encounter with Bertie.

Consuelo's talent for introductions was largely the result of her perceptive observations of British society. The novelist Robert Hichens wrote that he found her 'a mine of information about the London society of that time' and that she 'had a very shrewd judgment of both women and men'[9]. Throughout her troubled marriage to Kim, one of her only pleasures was to use her unique Southern charms to entertain large swathes of the aristocracy. Her effervescent and playful nature was something that placed her apart from many society hostesses, including Minnie, whose personality favoured intellectual stimulation. Consuelo Manchester's appeal was the easy brand of originality and practical jokes that made her deep brown eyes sparkle with mischief and brought laughter to Mayfair's drawing rooms. 'Looking back, I can still see everyone crowded round her at tea-time, all happily laughing at her continual flow of witty and amusing stories delivered in a charming soft Southern voice,'[10]recalled the Duke of Portland.

Her force of personality was so original that Edith Wharton immortalised her in her novel *The Buccaneers*, basing the character of Conchita Closson on Consuelo. The almost exotic allure of Conchita is palpable when she is described by Wharton: 'A warm fruity fragrance, as of peaches in golden sawdust, breathed from her soft plumpness, the tawny spirals of her hair, the smile which had a way of flickering between her lashes without descending to her lips.'[11]

Consuelo's ample attractions, which had first entranced Kim and then captivated London society, had served her well over the years. She had seen the quality and frequency of her introduction service increase, with ever more enticing compensations. So much so that in March 1895, before taking the fateful voyage to Italy, she had felt financially secure enough to purchase 17 Charles Street in Mayfair, where she had been living, renting from its owners. The house represented a new chapter, one in which she would establish a new role for herself in society, casting off the shackles of the Dowager Duchess and reinventing herself as a social doyenne, working with her network of friends and contacts to ensure she would never again be forced to endure the indignity of providing inferior dinner parties in an unfashionable part of town. Consuelo Manchester had been confident that 1895 brimmed with exciting opportunities.

At Kimbolton there was a sense of those possibilities slowly ebbing away. On a normal bright summer's day such as this, Consuelo would have rushed to open the tall windows that were swathed in long, sumptuous curtains, consumed with a desire to invite the warm breeze into the castle. Now she wanted nothing more than to draw them together, rejecting the day ahead. She knew that in London the

Season was in full swing, but who would wish to host her without the effervescent mask of vitality she was expected to assume for every occasion? For now she would remain at Kimbolton, secluded in the darkness, beyond the reach of them all.

Masters of Manipulation

June 1895, Oxfordshire

*'It is somewhat gratifying that American
heiresses are demanding a rather better article
of foreign title than was accepted a few years
ago.'* – THE *BALTIMORE AMERICAN*

Consuelo Vanderbilt sat straight beside Sunny, the Duke of
Marlborough, as he drove his horse-drawn carriage on a tour through
the Oxfordshire countryside. She was still perplexed that her mother
had declined to accompany them on their drive to survey the
Marlborough estate that surrounded Blenheim Palace, as she always
insisted on chaperoning Consuelo everywhere. She had become used
to Alva's ever-watchful eye, continually appraising her daughter's
performance and watching for any sign of inappropriate behaviour.
Today, she was conspicuous by her absence. Perhaps she hoped that,
left alone with Sunny, Consuelo's apparent reluctance to appreciate
his few redeeming qualities would disappear, melted away by the

bright summer sun. A chance to see all that could be hers if she was to become Duchess might prove irresistible and weaken her resolve. When she considered it in the light of her mother's behaviour back in New York, where she had pedalled furiously along Riverside Drive to prevent Consuelo and Winthrop from having a moment alone together, she was aware how much her mother's aversion to romantic trysts had altered. This unchaperoned jaunt around the countryside could only have been Minnie Paget's suggestion. Minnie, who thought she knew all the secrets to an aristocrat's heart. And maybe she did; Sunny certainly had an air of satisfaction about him as he negotiated the twists and turns of the road ahead, pausing periodically to point out a detail or landmark to Consuelo. He had an arrogance now, which seemed to give purpose to his small features, imbuing his face with a regal pride that screamed satisfaction at his possession of land and tenants.

'I realised that I had come to an old world with ancient traditions and that the villagers were still proud of their Duke and of their allegiance to his family,'[1] Consuelo wrote in her memoirs. England was a foreign land, entrenched in the seemingly immovable privileges of class and position, with very little opportunity for change. As a Vanderbilt, a family who had claimed their place in society through hard work and endeavour, it was a world she did not understand, an aristocracy far removed from the democratic principles of America.

Consuelo continued to perch as elegantly and dutifully as always, but looking around her, at the old women who curtsied and the farm labourers who touched their caps as the carriage sped by, she felt a pressing need rise within her. It was an overwhelming urge to take action, a desire to sabotage her mother's whole convoluted plan before it was too late. She spoke determinedly, questioning the Duke about his responsibilities as a landlord to his tenants. He had lofty ambitions for the future of Blenheim but surely his obligations must come first? 'Steeped as I then was in questions of political economy – in the theories of man, in the speeches of Gladstone and John Bright – it was not strange that such reflections should occur to me,'[2] she later reasoned.

In 1894, American newspapers had reported that Consuelo was a radical and a member of an elite society called 'The Downtrodden'. They alleged that she, along with other wealthy New York heiresses such as her cousin Gertrude Vanderbilt and her friend Pauline Whitney, met regularly to discuss their socialist values, including, rather surprisingly, the denouncement of the accumulation of wealth and the merits of heavy taxation on unearned money. Little is known about the group, but it seems an indication of just how far the Vanderbilts had risen that the granddaughter of the formidable Commodore, who had hauled his family out of poverty to become one of the wealthiest families in the United States through sheer hard work and ingenuity, would be calling for limits to be put on their fortune. It seems this new generation, completely secure in its position and wealth, had little concept of the perilous nature of the Wall Street stock market. Consuelo had never experienced the consequences of a fluctuating fortune that had plagued the adolescent years of her mother. Perhaps a lifetime of being surrounded by excess and opulence, and a growing awareness among wider society of the enormous gulf between rich and poor, mobilised intelligent but bored young ladies into action. They had grown up in a frenetic city that was expanding exponentially and attracted a wide variety of people. Glittering emblems of vast wealth like the majestic hotels and shiny stores of Fifth Avenue sat precariously close to the grinding poverty of the tenement slums. In New York, a step in the wrong direction could transport a visitor to another world, for the haves and have-nots lived as disaffected neighbours thrown together in a melting-pot.

For the moment, the ideas of 'The Downtrodden' and other social forces challenging the establishment would remain just that. Consuelo may have seen the parallels between America's upper class with its relationship to the servants and workers it depended on for its fortune, and the English aristocracy with its feudal undertones. Her decision to voice her opinions may have been driven by a desire to create conflict and illuminate her unsuitability as a potential bride or by a genuine desire to highlight the need for social change. However, if she had hoped that her challenge to the great Marlborough traditions and values that Sunny held dear would provoke an impassioned response, she was wrong. He simply appeared amused by the young American. Consuelo wrote, '… whether he considered them [her remarks] witty or naive I never knew.'[3]

The previous evening she had sat in the Long Library at Blenheim listening to the Duke's organist, Charles William Perkins, play the great organ that Duchess Lily's American money had paid for. Consuelo wondered what plans Sunny had for the large dowry he was sure to receive if a marriage between the two of them went ahead. Lily's fortune had gone a long way to modernising Blenheim and saving it from financial ruin, but the remarkable decline of the rural economy in England in the late nineteenth century had left an unprepared aristocracy floundering.

'In 1873 four hundred peers and peeresses owned 5,729,000 acres of England and Wales, over 15 per cent of the total area,'[4] explains John Bateman in his book *The Great Landowners of Great Britain*. This highlights how susceptible the nobility were to rural price fluctuations. The great landowners, of which Sunny was now one, had suffered large-scale loss of capital income due to the increase in production of grain by the United States. Great Britain relied on its wheat crops and other grains, leaving it vulnerable to price decreases inflicted by cheaper imports. With the industrial surge forwards of the railways and steamships that provided good refrigeration, meat sales were also hit, as cheaper imports from North and South America poured into England in ever-greater numbers. Tenants could no longer afford their rents, leaving landlords desperate to uncover other sources of income.

'In 1855–9 agriculture in the form of wages and profits had provided 20% of net national income, in 1895–9 it was 6%.'[5] The shift from England's rural economy to the frenzied and profitable activity of the burgeoning cities, driven by the industrial revolution, was clear. Their political power base had dominated until now, but the aristocracy was also experiencing a transformation with the extension of the franchise in the Third Reform Act in 1884 which increased the electorate from around three million men to six million. Peerages were accorded to men who weren't of the traditional landed elite and political movements allied to the middle and working classes were agitating for change. The pendulum of power was swinging away from the aristocracy and rural power, and the great landowners were in trouble.

Throughout the evening, while she had been engaging in conversation with Sunny's sisters Lady Lillian and Lady Norah Spencer-Churchill, Consuelo had noticed her mother and Minnie locked in their own conversation, peppered with frequent glances in her direction. The Duke had invited other young men to make up the party, including Lord Landsdowne's heir, Kerry, but nonetheless she couldn't help feeling the vastness of the Palace. Its large state rooms seemed immense to house such a small party, and the 320 rooms that Blenheim boasted was a scale still incomprehensible to Consuelo, who was no stranger to enormous mansions. Even filled with the thunderous sound of the organ and the lively chatter of guests, it retained its cold and lonely air.

At dinner, she noted that Minnie Paget had been very keen to inform Sunny and the Vanderbilts of the marriage at the end of April of Josephine Chamberlain to Thomas Talbot Scarisbrick, the only son and heir of Charles Scarisbrick, Justice of the Peace for Lancashire. Minnie seemed to take some credit for the match, comparing it to her endeavours on behalf of the Chamberlains' other daughter Jennie, some years before. Although she had been somewhat inconveniently detained in America when the wedding took place, she delighted in informing the assembled party of all the details. The wedding had taken place at St John the Baptist church in Hillingdon, before the couple and their guests had retired to Hillingdon Court in West Drayton, the country residence of Captain and Mrs Naylor-Leyland, who had now both recovered from their terrible bout of typhoid fever. The Naylor-Leylands had presented Josephine with a dazzling diamond collar as a wedding gift, which had hung dramatically around her neck, offset by a turned-back deep collar of old point lace. The dress,

Minnie went on, was made of very heavy white satin and had a long train. It was beautifully embroidered with a design of silver lilies that was replicated around the entire skirt and bodice. The bride had held a bouquet of rare orchids and a wreath of orange blossoms, and a diamond tiara sat atop a delicate tulle veil. Consuelo had watched her mother masterfully absorbing every detail that dripped from Minnie's mouth, her eyes lighting up when Minnie mentioned that the Scarisbricks were enormously rich. A passport to the aristocracy and a fortune waiting for her, little Josephine Chamberlain had done well for herself, Minnie declared. Consuelo stole a look at Sunny, who was paying particular attention to his place setting, seemingly oblivious and wholly bored with the conversation.

The emotional strain of maintaining a social position seemed to be a favourite topic of Minnie and Alva, who had discussed the subject on the trip from London to Blenheim. Once in a while they would remind Consuelo that the obstacles they faced now would be hers very soon. She should listen, learn and garner as much as knowledge as she could, to be sure she would succeed. Consuelo felt confident that a lifetime of witnessing such masters of manipulation in full swing would be enough to arm her with a host of behaviours she did not care to duplicate. Her mother declared, 'I know of no profession, art or trade that women are working at today, as taxing on mental resources as being a leader of society.'[6] Minnie agreed: she knew that hostesses had to be fully functioning and at the top of their game to negotiate the complex web of etiquette and connections that lay at the heart of society. Her own venture was increasingly coming under threat from forces beyond her control, such as the media and meddlesome English dowagers, keen to protect their daughters' rights to the prime of the Season's unmarried gentlemen. 'There are social guerrillas in London just as there are martial guerrillas in the Philippines, who still keep up a fragmentary fight against the stars and stripes,' *Harper's Magazine* observed. 'You will hear from time to time a resentful wailing over some fresh American victory, another ancestral domain seized and occupied, another prize snapped up.'[7]

The last few years had seen a steady stream of American faces become stalwarts of the London society scene. The financial strain the aristocracy had been under for decades had tipped the scales of power in favour of wealth over lineage. The musical *The Dollar Princess*, which opened in London in 1909, satirised the trend:

> For gold is the now the God of the Earth,
> It's the dollar, dollar, dollar!
> There's no more use for rank or for birth,
> It's the dollar, dollar, dollar!
> Though your pedigree may be old,
> What is that unless you have gold?
> For the noble, the artist, the scholar,
> Have to bow down to the dollar!
> You kow-tow to the King of the dollar,
> And no less
> To the dollar princess![8]

Throughout the late nineteenth century, London society was preoccupied with speculation over which dollar princess would be joining their ranks next and the presence of the Vanderbilt girl over the past couple of Seasons had not gone unnoticed. The Vanderbilt fortune was legendary and it was only a matter of time before she was offered a title in exchange for her money. But what kind of title could she purchase with her millions? *The Baltimore American* assured its readers in March 1895, 'It is somewhat gratifying that American heiresses are demanding a rather better article of foreign title than was accepted a few years ago.'[9] Heiresses had become much more savvy than the first buccaneers. The young ladies and their ambitious mothers knew what they were worth, and for Consuelo Vanderbilt that meant Alva would accept nothing less than a duke. She had communicated this to Minnie in no uncertain terms and Minnie had responded by reminding Alva how crucial it was that Consuelo toed the line this weekend. Sunny must be able to imagine Consuelo as duchess of this ancient and majestic family seat.

As they turned to head back to the palace, Consuelo no doubt felt a pang of guilt for the comments she had made. If Sunny happened to repeat them to her mother or Minnie, they would both be furious at her foolishness. The Oxfordshire countryside rolled past them, providing a seemingly eternal backdrop which overwhelmed Consuelo with its beauty. This was a piece of England she could learn to love, she thought, but the man beside her would always fall short of her affections. There was a man waiting for her in America and, despite the pretence of the last few days, she would never become a duchess, of that she was certain.

The Promise of Romance

July 1895, Newport, Rhode Island

*'I have never even dreamt of such luxury as I have seen
in Newport. It is like walking on gold. An enchanted
island.'* – GRAND DUKE BORIS OF RUSSIA

The Newport Casino was already in full swing. In every corner of the
club on Bellevue Avenue, the elite lingered at leisure. They clustered in
corners with pitchers of iced tea or lounged in chairs concentrating on
the morning newspaper; they prepared for a quiet game of billiards or
indulged in a hand of cards. Whatever their chosen pursuit, they had
one thing in common. All kept a constant watch on those who came
and went, for any visitor to the Casino was there for one purpose only:
to observe their friends and be noticed by those they had yet to win
over. A mental note would be made of the movements of each member
of society that graced the Casino's Japanese-ivy-clad walls, with a
particular murmur of excitement reverberating around the club if one
of Mrs Astor's inner sanctum chose to appear. It was all conducted

in a deeply civilised manner, Newport society operating with a practised restraint gained from years of suppressing natural impulses. A surreptitious glance, a stealthy further check for confirmation, then a combined look of recognition with their companion was all it took to commit to memory the day's attendees, then with a nod of approval the morning's activities were resumed. That was the way life was conducted in Newport, and Pauline Whitney, who sat on the Casino's grandstand in a delicate Worth gown, surveying the efforts of the lawn-tennis players below, was no different.

As the daughter of William C Whitney, a wealthy and influential lawyer and politician, Pauline's place was assured at the club. The Whitneys were an integral part of the Newport set and Pauline had an expectant poise radiating from her this year in particular, knowing that she was in possession of a secret. One that would silence her doubters and enable her to claim her place as one of the most eligible young heiresses The Four Hundred had to offer. Her friend Consuelo Vanderbilt was talked about incessantly everywhere that Pauline went. Of course she had her ambitious mother, Alva, to propel her forward, an advantage that Pauline, after the death of her mother Flora three years previously, was lacking. Now more than ever she longed for that steadying maternal hand to guide her through the next few months. She almost envied Consuelo, even though she knew Alva ruled her daughter's life not so much with a gentle hand as with an iron fist, resulting in few choices for the young Vanderbilt. Rumours had begun to circulate that Consuelo was set to marry a duke. If only the ladies who quietly repeated the gossip in that very grandstand, as they looked out over the immaculately groomed courts, knew that Pauline, poor, delicate Pauline, had already captured the heart of an English aristocrat and was sure to set a date before the Vanderbilt lawyers had even decided on terms with the Marlboroughs.

Almeric Hugh Paget was the younger brother of Arthur Paget, Minnie Paget's husband. At thirty-three years old, he was thirteen years older than Pauline, but the age difference seemed to matter little. The two were in love and planned to announce their engagement at the end of the month. Although Almeric hailed from one of England's most distinguished families, he had no title to speak of and had actually been living in Minnesota for many years, where he had prospered in the town of St Paul through real estate and insurance interests. As Arthur's brother, he had become a favourite with Marietta Stevens, who was delighted by his affable charm and cordial manner. Everyone who met Almeric immediately warmed to him and Pauline had quickly been won over by the attentive English gentlemen who suddenly appeared in her circle. Almost from the moment they had been introduced, she had known that Almeric was the man she wanted to marry, and fervently prayed that circumstances would make it so.

'It seems likely that they had met in England through Minnie Stevens [Paget],'[1] Pauline Whitney's biographer, W A Swanberg, determined in his book *Whitney Father, Whitney Heiress*. Indeed, the connections between the Whitney, Stevens and Paget families were long and had endured the many twists and turns that New York society had presented. Pauline's parents, Flora and William, had met at Paran Stevens's Fifth Avenue Hotel in 1868 and Flora immediately struck up a friendship with the lively and vivacious wife of the proprietor, Marietta, who so resolutely fought to become accepted into Mrs Astor's closed society. When Flora died, Marietta, with her customary loyalty, made it her business to keep a watchful eye over the young and impressionable Pauline.

Pauline made her debut on 10 December 1892 at a lavish reception at the Whitneys' mansion on Fifth Avenue and 57th Street. Although Pauline was still considered very young by society's standards to be presented as a debutante, her mother's health had been increasingly deteriorating, necessitating William to bring forward the occasion. He knew that Flora's greatest wish was to witness Pauline moving effortlessly through the grand white and gold Whitney ballroom and so, with the knowledge of the severity of his wife's illness, he defied convention and set a date. The finest artisans had been drafted in to transform the tired-looking residence, which the Whitneys had recently invested in, into an opulent private house, with stained-glass windows imported from European cathedrals, priceless Flemish tapestries that hung over the balustrades and a banquet-hall floor that originally occupied an Italian palace in Genoa. These all provided a dramatic backdrop to the festivities, with the obligatory floral decorations adorning almost every inch of the mansion. Tall palms strained to reach the ceiling while undulating garlands of orchids and American Beauty roses intertwined around the room. Pauline suffering from a last-minute spell of nerves, belatedly discovered her poise and performed her duties with consummate ease in a stylish white silk gown. Four weeks later, Flora Whitney was dead.

William C Whitney had once written to Flora, 'Pauline, withal so affectionate and sweet, is headstrong and decided and I always fear for her.'[2] Those stubborn tendencies may have stood her in good stead now, as she assumed the role of responsible adult. Despite her tender years, she immersed herself in trying to take her mother's place. She was a judicious companion to her father, mother to her little sister Dorothy (who was only five years old when Flora died), older sister to her brothers Harry and Payne and affectionate niece to her wealthy uncle Oliver Payne, whose promises of a handsome inheritance were strategically dangled before the Whitneys whenever their father's speculations on the stock market incurred heavy losses. In 1894, Pauline and her father sailed for Europe where, upon arriving in England, they visited both Consuelo Manchester and Minnie Paget. In addition to undertaking excursions to Windsor, Oxford and Stratford, the Whitneys also visited Scotland, where William owned a country shooting bolthole masquerading as an extravagant country estate. At some point in June, the press reported that Pauline was 'painfully and dangerously ill with rheumatism… the result of a coaching trip and the neglect of being properly protected against the chilly English air'[3]. William immediately retained the services of two nurses to attend to Pauline day and night. She eventually recovered enough to return to America in time for the social Season to begin in earnest, attending a dinner given in her honour in Newport later in the summer, at which Alva, Consuelo and Marietta were also present, and the popular horse show at Madison Square Garden in November, where they all watched the annual parade from their family boxes.

By 5 December 1894, Pauline was on board the *Majestic*, setting sail again for Europe. This time her companions included her father, her brother Harry, family friends Alexander Gunn and Miss Davidge and one Almeric Paget. The exchanges that William and Pauline had engaged in with Minnie and Consuelo during their visit to England, whose sentiments had been echoed by Marietta in New York on their return, had had the desired effect. Pauline and Almeric had been strategically placed together, and now it was a waiting game to see if affection could blossom.

The crossing over the Atlantic was stormy and the assembled party found themselves playing endless rounds of cards to stifle boredom and distract themselves from their inevitable nausea. William kept a careful eye on Almeric and Pauline, wondering if this young man could perhaps win his daughter's heart. One reporter described Almeric as a 'straightforward, hardworking, manly fellow, whose self-reliance is due wholly to achievement'[4], all qualities that William, who had fought hard to accomplish his position, admired. There would be no raffish noble with an aversion to hard work for his daughter. When the ship docked in England William had already decided that he was ready to allow the marriage of Almeric to his beloved daughter, Pauline. The Whitneys continued to the Mediterranean before moving on to Cairo.

During the next month, Pauline and Almeric spent idyllic languid days together sailing down the Nile on the charming *dahabeah* boat Pauline's father had hired for the trip. Extended canoeing trips provided a precious chance for them to engineer stolen moments alone and before long Pauline had fallen in love. 'The attachment intensifies,'[5] wrote their companion Alexander Gunn about the young couple. By the time they had left Egypt and travelled to Greece, he was reporting that Pauline and Almeric were '… earnestly engaged… there could never be a more political place for troth plighting… her face is filled with rosy light. I am sure the engagement is settled.'[6]

As she sat on the Newport grandstand, Pauline smiled at the memory of those heady days spent with her fiancé appreciating this occasion too. It wouldn't be long until they had to leave for Bailey's Beach. There was always a strict timetable to a Newport day. It began with a visit from the maid with a breakfast tray and a chance to catch up on any correspondence, followed by the obligatory morning call to the Casino, where the fashionable set would enjoy tennis, bowling or promenading with friends accompanied by the sound of one of the Casino's many orchestras. Henry Conrad's Society Orchestra was just one of the outfits that kept patrons entertained from morning until night, when weary ladies and gentlemen finally called for their carriages to transport them home. An excursion to Bailey's Beach would occupy the hours between eleven and one o'clock. The private club was frequented by the Vanderbilts, Goelets and Astors, who had all purchased a bathhouse to enable a swift change into cumbersome bathing suits in absolute privacy. Before any of its members appeared, the beach manager, Old Sam, would instruct his workers, bedecked in crisp white uniforms, to groom the sand, lest it should be precariously uneven for its patrons. After any planned luncheons, often scheduled on one of the throngs of majestic yachts that filled the Newport harbour, the elite would ready themselves for the formal afternoon carriage parade. The great spectacle limited itself to Bellevue Avenue, the beating thoroughfare of Newport, where occupants flanked by liveried servants could inspect the newest addition to the Avenue's real estate. And they had much to scrutinise. Increasingly opulent mansions sprang up every year in a never-ending competitive rush to ensure each of Newport's superior families built a residence befitting their status.

During the course of the afternoon, it was the custom to drop in calling cards on friends and acquaintances and fulfil any visits that had been arranged, then ladies would retire to their palatial houses – referred to in Newport, somewhat disingenuously, as 'cottages' – while their errant husbands could excuse themselves to the Newport Country Club for a few precious hours of peace from the perpetual social frenzy. There they could practise the latest leisure pursuit of golf or while away the humid afternoon smoking cigars at the Reading Room. Without fail, every evening there would be a dinner party or ball to attend. Each event required formal attire, leaving many society ladies requiring up to six outfit changes a day, depending on their activities. Some ladies found the constant flurry of engagements overwhelming, as Eleanor Belmont recalled in her memoirs: 'I found such an endless round of strangers and entertainment was frequently more exhausting than previous hard work had been.'[7]

Newport's rise as the pre-eminent leisure resort of the American aristocracy had been swift and decisive. In 1881, Ward McAllister had persuaded Mrs Astor to purchase 'Beechwood', a charming and not inconsequential 'cottage' situated on Bellevue Avenue. She commissioned the architect Richard Morris Hunt, beloved by Gilded Age matrons, to extend the house to accommodate a ballroom, and so rendered it appropriate for society functions. McAllister presented Newport as the answer to the problem of society during the summer months, when it was too stifling to remain in New York. The upper classes looked to Mrs Astor and McAllister to provide guidance as to the destination of choice when society's inevitable exodus from the city came. They needed somewhere that could manage an influx of the upper classes in a dignified and befitting manner, somewhere so exclusive that any social upstarts tempted to make the journey would be unable to force their way in. The Rhode Island town was small enough to curtail any visitors to a select group. It would be easy, McAllister reasoned, to keep any undesirables out. Any Swells that were on the verge of being accepted into society could expect to spend three Seasons trying to break in to Newport, said McAllister, and then they would only do so if they were very lucky or had an impeccable social sponsor. 'You can launch them into the social sea, but can they float?'[8] he asked. Newport was the ultimate test of a newcomer's mettle. In many ways it was more difficult than New York to gain a social foothold, as its size rendered it much more exclusive. Socialite Elizabeth Drexel Lehr wrote, 'Newport was the very holy of holies, the playground of the great ones of the Earth from which all intruders were ruthlessly excluded by a set of cast-iron rules.'[9]

Once accepted into Newport society, the smart set were plunged into a cluster of entertainments, whose sole purpose was to entertain and impress. Ostentatious displays of wealth were an everyday occurrence, as hostesses rivalled each other to conjure up the most lavish occasion. It wasn't just the nightly round of balls that laid bare the great fortunes of America's wealthiest families for all to see. From yachts to mansions, gowns to private clubs, everything about Newport emanated excessive wealth.

'I have never even dreamt of such luxury as I have seen in Newport. It is like walking on gold. An enchanted island,'[10] commented the Grand Duke Boris of Russia when he visited the resort. The French writer Paul Bourget was slightly less enamoured with the earnest devotion of the fabulously rich to an extravagant lifestyle when he visited Newport, writing, 'It revolts you or it ravishes you accordingly, as you are nearer to socialism or snobbery.'[11]

Town Topics delighted in appraising its readers of the details of the summer entertainments, writing in 1895, 'The sumptuous banquets, to which I have alluded several times as having been the feature of July at Newport, continue and grow if possible more magnificent than ever. By a sort of common consent certain evenings have been allotted to certain houses for these banquets and with them no one else interferes.'[12]

Of course, the sheer number of servants it required to guide such occasions and ensure the wealthy were well attended to every summer crept ever higher. In 1895, around 2,200 servants worked for the summer visitors from New York, making up ten per cent of the total population of Newport. The Four Hundred employed only the most experienced and qualified staff to do their bidding. Alva Vanderbilt drafted in a renowned French chef, Rammeau, to ensure her banquets were the most sumptuous and talked-about in Newport, happily paying him the exorbitant ten thousand dollars a year he demanded for his services.

As Pauline Whitney rose gracefully from her seat and descended from the grandstand, heading towards the Worth boutique housed in the Casino's main building, she considered the evening ahead. The smart set had been assigned to Mrs Stuyvesant Fish's house for dinner this evening. Mamie, as she was fondly known, favoured fun and frivolity over the tiresome entertainments preferred by other society matrons. There was sure to be a quirky flavour or unique diversion to lift the evening. Pauline would smile, she would regale acquaintances with exotic tales from her travels, yet she would keep her most interesting story from her companions and close to her heart. Her engagement would be announced soon enough. Some in society would wonder why William Whitney hadn't insisted on a titled aristocrat for his daughter; after all, they were one of America's most influential families. Pauline, however, remained unconcerned. She knew from Minnie's experience that the Pagets were perfectly placed in English society to offer her a seamless transition into the upper echelons of the nobility. Besides, she had managed to find an aristocrat and love, a rare combination and one she was unlikely to discard for the prospect of an unhappy union with a viscount or marquess. She knew that soon all of society would be analysing the union, but for the moment she would take a delightful pleasure in keeping the information to herself. It was a secret that would remain hers for just a little longer, until she was ready to share it with the world.

Britannia Versus *Meteor*

August 1895, Cowes, Isle of Wight

> '*The explanation of the mystery of her resources
> which is offered in court circles is that she represents
> a secret syndicate of millionaires... these gentlemen
> jointly foot the bills, it is asserted, each contributing
> an agreed-upon sum.*' – NEW YORK WORLD

Consuelo Manchester read the note that had arrived from her sister Natica once more. She was asking for advice on the guest list for that evening's dinner party and there was no better person to ask for guidance than Consuelo. From her wicker chair on the lawn of the Royal Yacht Squadron, she glanced at the names Natica had proposed, which read like a roll-call of the most prestigious aristocracy. Preparations would have to be made for the Prince of Wales, of course, although it was unclear whether Bertie would make an appearance. At Cowes, his schedule was always so brimming with invitations that his closest friends knew that engagements might not be confirmed until the last minute. Their role was simply to be on call for whenever Bertie might need diverting, whenever he became tired of the formality required at Queen Victoria's Osborne House and retreated to the rented house of one of his favourite hostesses, where he would expect the lavish welcome that was customary to assure his presence. An opulent entertainment in the manner that befitted a future King was demanded by Bertie and he could count on his entourage of aristocratic friends to provide it.

Although it had only been a matter of months since Consuelo had buried her beloved daughter Mary, she had decided to separate herself from her remaining children and take a house in Cowes for the annual regatta, as had been her habit for many years. For society it was a principal feature of the summer calendar, and it had grown from a modest social occasion cherished by the royal family for its intimate and informal nature to an event so large that the bustling, sporting coastal town groaned under the weight of its annual visitors. It had become so popular that its duration had been increased from a week to a fortnight, yet still events, dinners and garden parties competed with each other for space in the diaries of prestigious guests. Cowes during the regatta was frenetic, and attracted the highest calibre of European royalty, the nobility and increasingly wealthy pretenders who bankrolled the yachts that provided the sport for all of society to witness. This year, Crown Princess Stephanie of Austria and the Crown Princess of Romania were in attendance to watch the Royal Yacht *Osborne* with its jet-black hull and two canary-yellow funnels glide into the harbour, closely followed by Bertie's beloved racing yacht, *Britannia*, adorned with a garland of twenty-one winner's flags, advertising its intention to compete in the scheduled daily races. The royal yachts were the prize attractions among the flotilla that descended on Cowes in preparation for the races. 'The yachts lay slooping quietly on the bosom of the estuary,'[1] a reporter from the *Daily Telegraph*, who had been dispatched to cover the entire fortnight's festivities, told its readers on 5 August 1895. The English weather, true to form, alternated between glorious sunshine and thundery downpours, as more yachts arrived every hour to take up their positions.

From her vantage point, Consuelo Manchester could surreptitiously evaluate the masses who had turned out in force for an afternoon at the club. She was pleased that her sister Natica, now Lady Lister-Kaye, was in residence at Cowes to support her through the myriad of functions she would be expected to attend. Of course, that role extended to ensuring that the sisters' position was maintained in society, as well as in Bertie's affections, as relations between Consuelo and Bertie remained strained after the Daisy Warwick affair. It was imperative, now more than ever, that Natica play her part as the final link in the chain that brought favour to Consuelo's protégés. Besides, Natica was better equipped to present the warm and lively front that had served the sisters so well in British society. Consuelo, who for so long provided Natica with an accomplished example to follow, was well aware that the charm and sparkle that had once radiated out of her like a warm Southern afternoon had abandoned her and, while she remained pleasant and dignified, she knew she seemed adrift, somehow lessened. Yet she was here, as she had always been, inspecting society, accepting invitations, quietly making connections, all with the most pleasing of landscapes as her view.

In the intervening months since her last foray into society, Minnie had taken great pleasure in appraising Consuelo Manchester of the details of her visit to Blenheim with Alva and Consuelo Manchester's god-daughter, the younger Consuelo. Consuelo Manchester had felt a curious mix of interest and alarm for her namesake on the news that an engagement to Sunny, Duke of Marlborough was imminent. She knew just how difficult it was to be an English duchess. There was nothing, of course, that could be done to prevent it now, especially if Alva was resolved to engineer the match. Consuelo Manchester knew Alva well enough to know that her ambition would rationalise every misgiving the young Vanderbilt girl had about Sunny. For when it came to securing her position in New York society, Alva was determined and unyielding, something she had witnessed first-hand when she had aided her plans to blindside Mrs Astor at Alva's costume ball a decade earlier. Society, back then, had all seemed a game. As an American heiress with an English title, Consuelo Manchester had felt that there was nothing she couldn't accomplish. If only she'd known the sheer hard work it would take to forge a position without the support of her husband and then generate a fortune to maintain it.

The timetable of events at Cowes took their usual course. The Sunday before the races had begun, society descended on the fashionable Trinity Church and with the church's bells ringing in the distance, all made their way to Cowes Castle, where the club of the Royal Yacht Squadron was located, to parade on its sloping lawns in the very latest fashions from Paris.

As one reporter commented, '… the yachting gowns, they are neater, prettier and more becoming than ever.'[2] The 'Britannia costume' was, not surprisingly, the most popular choice for ladies in 1895, featuring a sailor collar, full sleeves and long cuffs, and made from white linen. The attention that society paid to its yachting attire created a spectacular procession of nautical splendour and, once Queen Victoria had raised the royal standard over Osborne House, Cowes was quickly festooned in rivers of white and blue. The guns sounded the salute to signify the official start of the first race and then, if they had not been fortunate enough to receive an invitation to race on board *Britannia*, the Marlborough House Set would dutifully position themselves so that they could avidly follow her progress. By day the aristocracy could be seen obsessively monitoring *Britannia*'s duels with rival racer *Ailsa*, or cruising on one of the luxurious yachts that were at their disposal. By night, the anchorage was luminous with twinkling lights to guide them to parties on shore, culminating in glittering firework displays that were a customary feature of Cowes.

The regatta had been given added significance in recent years by the competitive rivalry between Bertie and his nephew, Kaiser Wilhelm II, who in 1895 arrived at Cowes through dense mist and rain aboard the imperial German yacht, the *Hohenzollern*, flanked by his racing yacht, *Meteor*, which he intended to pit against the *Britannia* in the Queen's Cup. Wilhelm used his exploits at Cowes as a means of encouraging public interest in his plans to bolster Germany's navy and to heighten the mutual antipathy that existed between himself and Bertie. On his arrival, Wilhelm immediately irritated Bertie by giving a speech commemorating the German victory at Worth during the Franco-Prussian war, in which he 'pointed out that in this battle, at the very outset of the campaign, the union of the German races had already commenced'[3].

Bertie was duty-bound to entertain the Kaiser, who was Queen Victoria's grandson, at Cowes so, as commodore of the Royal Yacht Squadron, he arranged for a banquet to be given in his honour. 'The dinner was laid in the glass-house on the balcony, and the tables were adorned with statuettes emblematic of English naval and military victories,' a reporter from *The Times* described to its readers. 'In a temporary enclosure adjoining the dining-room the band of the *Hohenzollern* performed at intervals.'[4]

Despite such occasions, Bertie bemoaned the way that the arrogant and ambitious Wilhelm had seized his beloved regatta as a nationalistic platform. Bertie also greatly resented his unflattering comments when he heard that Wilhelm referred to him as an 'old peacock'[5]. Wilhelm's entourage went even further, with a diplomat calling Bertie 'Fat Wales'[6] and 'inconceivably rude'[7], while a despairing Bertie, irritated that his nephew had drained the pleasure out of his favourite hobby, called Wilhelm the 'boss of Cowes'[8]. In 1895, Bertie was to be the victor, winning the Queen's Cup, but the following year Wilhelm was back with a new yacht, the *Meteor II*, which was modelled on *Britannia* but ultimately eclipsed her. Wounded by the defeat, in 1897 Bertie decided to withdraw *Britannia* from racing at Cowes.

The obvious animosity between the two simmered and spread into wider society and presented some of its members with a dilemma as to how to entertain Wilhelm in the proper manner without offending Bertie. Daisy, Princess of Pless, an Englishwoman who had made a fortuitous match when she had married Hans Heinrich XV, Prince of Pless, son to one of the wealthiest and most prominent families in Germany in 1891, was forced to tread a perilous tightrope between her long-standing friendship with Bertie and her husband's loyalty to the insufferable Wilhelm in the years preceding the First World War. When she found herself in possession of conflicting invitations to entertainments hosted by both royal camps at Cowes in the summer of 1894, she wrote in her diary, 'I wonder how this Emperor business will end & what I shall write in my diary in years to come… The Emperor seems to think he is a God wherever he goes to be worshipped by all the world.'[9]

Despite the presence of the Kaiser, Cowes still provided society with a glorious extension to the London Season, Consuelo Manchester thought. While London's endless round of parties simply relocated to the Isle of Wight, it did so in a leisurely fashion. Like the Saratoga Springs of her girlhood, Consuelo knew that resorts such as Cowes, where society was clustered together, likely to encounter acquaintances and friends at every turn, provided a unique opportunity for an intermediary to engineer matches. Those young ladies who had been unsuccessful in London, where occasions were so plentiful that it might be impossible to ascertain the movements of an intended target, looked to Cowes. It was conveniently compact and the event's short duration gave a heightened sense of urgency that galvanised love-struck beaus into rash declarations of affection. It was at Cowes in the summer of 1873 that Jennie Jerome had first met and fallen in love with Randolph Churchill, becoming engaged after a swift three-day courtship. Consuelo had found that here it was infinitely easier to introduce new faces to the aristocratic scene. Some of those faces were young ladies searching for a titled husband, while others were important men in their own right, wealthy American plutocrats, anxious for the opportunity to be introduced to royalty and gain access to the British upper classes. At Cowes, Consuelo Manchester was confident that the opportunities to accomplish her objectives were plentiful indeed.

Of course, the question of the nationality of her charges remained a significant hurdle. Even after so many years of welcoming American brides and American dollars to England, there were still those among the nobility who resented their presence in society. Unlike Minnie, who had assimilated herself seamlessly into the aristocracy, Consuelo had never lost her sense of otherness, preferring to accentuate her heritage rather than paint over it with a refined accent and English manners. Her presence and position within the aristocracy was now so entrenched and valued that she was considered one of them but, on occasion, she still had the discomfort of being privy to European prejudice towards her compatriots. An incident involving an Italian baron at the British Embassy in Rome only served to confirm her suspicions. Despite their superior education, extensive travel and lavish lifestyle, American heiresses would never be completely accepted among the upper classes on the other side of the Atlantic. The Baron, who had assumed by her title that she was English, said: 'Ah! How glad I am to get away from those Americans there! We come across them everywhere don't we Duchess? You can't imagine how happy I am to converse with you – there is such a contrast between the manners of English and American women!' Consuelo had taken great pleasure in retorting, 'Perhaps you are right Baron; but being myself an American I am no doubt incapable of judging.'

The exchange reminded her of her former self, the vivacious, witty, enchanting girl from the South who had dazzled a British aristocrat and taken London society by storm. Consuelo was well aware that to survive, she needed to recapture the Yznaga family spirit of her youth, something she had lost over the past few months. Her plan was to spend the autumn in Scotland with the Earl and Countess of Dudley at Invermark Lodge in Forfarshire. By the time September came, the British aristocracy would retreat to the countryside, where weekend shooting parties would replace fashionable dinners in town. Some might follow Bertie to the Continent and to the spa town of Marienbad to recuperate from the vigours of the Season, but others would content themselves with fishing trips, horse riding and a seeming obsession with surpassing the previous year's shooting haul. Inded, at Sandringham during the shooting season, it was not unusual for Bertie's party to shoot over 2,000 pheasants in one day. In Scotland, Consuelo would regain her strength, catch up on her correspondence and check in with contacts both old and new before alighting in London just in time to take advantage of the fresh waves of Swells that would be sure to wash up on English shores.

In later years, the *New York World* would wonder how Consuelo Manchester managed to run houses in Grosvenor Square, Richmond, Ascot and Biarritz and, after having regained his favour, put them at the disposal of Bertie, now King Edward VII. The reporter estimated that she spent around twenty-five thousand dollars a week to maintain a property for the duration of Ascot or Cowes, where she favoured renting the impressive Egypt House, and speculated that the King would often dine with her up to three times a week while in London. 'The explanation of the mystery of her resources which is offered in court circles is that she represents a secret syndicate of millionaires... these gentlemen jointly foot the bills, it is asserted, each contributing an agreed-upon sum.'[10]

It was an interesting theory and one firmly rooted in the truth, but in 1895 Consuelo's introductions venture was being refined. It was still susceptible to the human frailties and shadow of loss that had plagued Consuelo and her friends, the rest of the original buccaneers, that year. Minnie had lost Marietta, Jennie Churchill had buried her husband Randolph and her mother Clara, and Consuelo Manchester had experienced the death of her beloved daughter Mary. All had lost their nearest and dearest, yet all rose up again, renewed their commitment to the social game and blazed a trail for others to follow. The year had delivered searing grief and unimaginable sorrow, yet it had somehow produced limitless possibilities for these American women. There, at Cowes, Consuelo Manchester pledged to start anew.

20

Confrontation

September 1895, Newport, Rhode Island

*'A marble palace is the right place for a woman
with a marble heart.'* – ANONYMOUS
RESIDENT OF NEWPORT

The gardens of Marble House looked resplendent in their summer
bloom and from the shade of a copper-beech tree, Consuelo Vanderbilt
would have appraised the newly constructed mansion that was her
mother's masterpiece. Its imposing façade, entirely of marble, stood
defiantly on Bellevue Avenue, its Corinthian pillars rising endlessly
to meet the sky. Alva's statement to all of Newport was clear: exclude
me at your peril. Consuelo had heard the rather uncomplimentary
views of Marble House. An anonymous resident of Newport had been
reported to say, 'A marble palace is the right place for a woman with
a marble heart.'[1] Now, she sadly contemplated whether this statement
possessed more than a grain of truth.

Alva had collaborated with Richard Morris Hunt on the project, their third mansion together, after Willie K had presented her with a blank cheque for the project on her thirty-fifth birthday some years before. The project was so ambitious that it had outlived their ill-fated marriage. By its completion, Alva had spent almost eleven million dollars[2] on a neoclassical-inspired palace that proudly claimed its place among Newport's other summer houses, all competing for the accolade of most spectacular. French author Paul Bourget wrote, 'The same outbreak of individuality which reared the palaces of Fifth Avenue in New York, almost as by Aladdin's lamp, created in a flash of miracle this town of cottages.'[3]

Italian and French artisans had been drafted in to ensure the five hundred thousand cubic feet of fine marble was shaped into a remarkable and accomplished palatial residence that eclipsed the dramatic turrets of Ochre Court, the Goelets' Hunt-designed French chateau. It had taken numerous workers years to realise Alva's dream, but almost as soon as the last piece of furniture had been placed in the perfect position, life had changed immeasurably. The Vanderbilts' divorce had been controversial and public. Alva seemed oblivious to the gossip and hurt that the constant presence of Oliver Belmont at her side created for her daughter. Consuelo Vanderbilt would have considered how her own life was on the cusp of change; she was almost certainly bound for England. It must have seemed to Consuelo as though, while her mother busily gave instructions to construct the most impressive and enduring statement of the Vanderbilts' wealth and position, she had been just as diligently dismantling the foundations on which their lives were built. The Vanderbilts had risen and prospered together, now they were at war.

In the messy aftermath of Alva and Willie K's divorce, there had been many casualties. The Vanderbilts were no stranger to being the subject of spurious reports in the popular press, in fact they had courted journalists and furnished them with titbits about their lives, but until now they hadn't been exposed to a sustained period of scandal. While Alva and Willie K had separately left for long sojourns to Europe, it was Willie K's brother Cornelius and his wife Alice who had endured the daily gossip propagated about the family and then been forced to face the rest of New York society at numerous social functions. It was safe to say that Alice Vanderbilt and Alva had never been close, but now the tension was palpable as they both converged on Newport for the summer Season. At a dance at the Newport Casino on 8 August 1895, *Town Topics* had commented on Alva, who 'looked remarkably well in green', and Alice, who was 'becomingly gowned in black'[4]. Keen to capitalise on the Vanderbilts' evident rift, the report went on to tell its readers, 'They both held courts of their own in their respective corners of the room where they sat.'[5]

It wasn't long before the two camps could no longer avoid each other and *Town Topics* again delighted in informing its readers when Cornelius Vanderbilt came face to face with his former sister-in-law Alva and her rumoured lover, Oliver Belmont, on the steps of the Casino. Cornelius was on his way back to his mansion, The Breakers, which had recently been designed and reconstructed by Richard Morris Hunt. Its very existence typified the feud between Alva and Alice. The Breakers and Marble House were prodigious, both in size and cost, and vied with each other for the distinction of most lavish addition to Newport's real estate, as their mistresses competed to be crowned queen of society. Meanwhile, Alva drove up to the Casino with Oliver, who some said had been audacious and most ungentlemanly in his attentions towards Mrs Vanderbilt. On noticing Cornelius, she was said to react 'calmly'[6]; he, however, could barely contain his emotions, eventually furnishing Alva with a 'sarcastic smile'[7].

The subject of Alva and Oliver's abiding companionship had been a source of endless speculation in the gossip columns of New York's newspapers for many months. Consuelo Vanderbilt had witnessed their affection for each other grow when Oliver, as one of Willie K's friends and confidants, had accompanied the family on a long voyage aboard the *Valiant* to India in 1893. Consuelo remembered the trip well. It was the trip that signalled the awakening of her own passionate feelings for Winthrop, who had also been on board the yacht. When, disorientated and beguiled by the beauty and the bedlam of the East, she had fallen in love. Seen through the prism of her own undeniable affections for Winthrop, while duty pushed her towards Sunny, she finally understood her mother's refusal to cast Oliver to one side. No matter what it cost her. If only Consuelo had the luxury of choice.

It wasn't just the Vanderbilts who avidly followed the whereabouts of Alva and Oliver during the summer of 1895. The press, now wise to the increasing popularity of society gossip amongst its readers, pursued The Four Hundred relentlessly, wherever they went. Alva was used to utilising the media to her advantage, feeding them stories to increase her social standing, but she bitterly resented their pursuit of her when she lost control of the story. Newspapers were rumoured to install spies in the households of the wealthy, pay waiters and receptionists at hotels for information and put telegraph operators on the payroll. All in the pursuit of a good story.

'The dogging of the footsteps of Mr and Mrs Vanderbilt and Mr Belmont... that has already begun at Newport would hardly be possible in any other civilised country on the face of the globe,' wrote one reporter rather sympathetically. 'The wonder to my mind is that more of our very wealthy and prominent American men and women do not resent or combat this detective business... by exiling themselves to Europe.'[8]

Alva, Willie K and Oliver had all exiled themselves in Europe for long enough. Now they were back to reclaim their places in society, showing faith that the scandal and speculation over their respective affairs would disappear and the order they were all accustomed to would be restored. Willie K resided on his yacht and entertained widely, surrounded by his friends and family, seemingly untainted by the stories of his affairs with Parisian courtesans. Oliver ensconced himself at Belcourt, his unconventional sixty-room mansion that gave his beloved horses pride of place in stables on the ground floor, with the mansion's only bedroom reserved for their master, who was situated directly above them. Alva retreated to Marble House, where she approached the Season with the fortitude and chutzpah that she had employed in every moment of crisis throughout her life. She made a conscious effort to be seen at all of Newport's social occasions and made a note of those who welcomed her and those who didn't. She adhered to the plan she had so carefully constructed with Minnie in England and began to make the necessary arrangements for the finest ball Newport had ever seen. Just as she had in 1883, when her costume ball had compelled Mrs Astor to extend the hand of friendship, Alva was determined her 'Bal Blanc' would restore her to greatness among the American aristocracy and capture the heart of the British aristocracy too. If Sunny was in any doubt about Consuelo, Alva would demonstrate just what the Vanderbilt millions could buy, with the most luxurious manifestation she could fashion.

Consuelo was fully aware of her mother's scheme. She had endured the humiliation that accompanied scandal in society and seemed to follow them wherever they went, with whispers at the Casino or silent stares from matrons and their charges burning through her from the comfort of their carriages. She had done as she was instructed, attending picnic parties at Lawton's Valley, cycling with her mother in the countryside and pretending to enjoy an excursion to Narragansett Pier, but it was Winthrop who occupied her thoughts. It had been months since she had seen or heard from him and, since leaving England, Alva had determined that Consuelo should not be granted permission to see any friends or attend events alone, thwarting all her attempts to engineer a meeting. 'On reaching Newport my life became that of a prisoner, with my mother and my governess as wardens,' she wrote. 'I was never out of their sight. Friends called but were told I was not at home.'[9]

Then suddenly he was there, standing in front of her. Consuelo had dressed for yet another ball, inattentive to the nightly instructions from her mother that had become a feature of the early evening. She began the evening with the sense of impending monotony that had begun to consume her thoughts in Newport as she spent more and more hours alone and isolated, and dutifully followed Alva into the ballroom, back straight, eyes ahead, always a few steps behind. She sensed Winthrop rather than saw him as she moved deeper into the throngs of people, and then he was before her, asking her if he could claim this dance. For several minutes they glided around the room, undisturbed while Alva was temporarily distracted, engaging in social niceties with Newport's smart set. Winthrop assured her that his feelings had not altered and Consuelo gave a gentle nod of agreement and then abruptly the dance was over. The strains of the violins fell silent and immediately Consuelo felt Alva at her side. Firmly gripping Consuelo's elbow, Alva rushed her away from Winthrop without saying a word. Anxious not to make a scene, the whole manoeuvre was executed swiftly, masterfully, before Consuelo could protest. The carriage was readied and Alva and Consuelo quickly returned to Marble House.

The ceiling of Alva's boudoir at Marble House had been painted to her exacting instructions with an elaborate and intricate painting of Athene, the Greek goddess of wisdom and power. Consuelo looked up at the image and wondered whether any of the fabled power would help her summon the courage to face her mother. Amongst the heavy damask that covered the walls and windows, in a voice rendered faint with emotion, Consuelo carefully and calmly explained her intention to marry Winthrop. 'These words the bravest I had ever uttered, brought down a frightful storm of protest,'[10] Consuelo revealed in her memoirs. Unused to anything but compliance from her passive daughter, Alva quickly lost her temper. She railed against Winthrop, accusing him of being a flirt, engaging in adulterous affairs and liaisons with different ladies. She warned Consuelo that he was only after a fortune, a charge she didn't seem to think applied to the impoverished aristocrat Sunny. She told her daughter that there was madness in the Rutherfurd family and that Winthrop couldn't have children. And when her catalogue of insults seemed to have no effect, she finally told Consuelo that she would rather shoot Winthrop than see him married to her daughter. Alva's desperate measures, as she contemplated the disappearance of her carefully laid plans, continued throughout the night. 'We reached a stage where arguments were futile, and I left her then in the cold dawn of morning feeling as if all my youth had been drained away,'[11] Consuelo recalled.

Despite her mother's pleas, when Consuelo finally retired to her austere, oak-panelled bedroom at the rear of Marble House, she had been resolute. She must marry Winthrop. However, Alva had one last card to play and sent her old friend Mrs William Jay to deliver the final blow. 'Mrs Jay… came to talk to me… she informed me that my mother had had a heart attack brought about by my callous indifference to her feelings.… In utter misery I asked Mrs Jay to let X know that I could not marry him. How sad those summer days of disgrace and unhappiness…'[12]

In the weeks that followed, Consuelo had not seen or heard from Winthrop and became resigned to a life without him. The gatekeeper at Marble House had been instructed that she should not be permitted to leave the grounds. Her mother's 'heart attack' passed without any further comment and soon Alva was consumed with planning the details of her 'Bal Blanc' once more. Consuelo watched as the liveried servants moved quickly back and forth, diligently taking delivery of decorations, favours and flowers. All the ingredients for a spectacular occasion. Consuelo remained seated, wondering whether anyone would be sent to search for her. All those around her were preparing for a momentous event, the night when a duke would be guest of honour at a ball to be hosted at Alva Vanderbilt's Marble House. Consuelo thought of Sunny, small and disagreeable, and hoped that all of society would not be as bitterly disappointed with him as she was.

A Second-Class Duke

October 1895, New York

*'She has placed no seal upon the lips of the lucky
tradesmen and tradeswomen who have furnished forth
the marriage feast, and consequently a wealth of
information has been poured out.'* – TOWN TOPICS

The newspapers had been crammed with speculation about the Vanderbilt wedding for weeks and today was no different. Alva Vanderbilt had organised the press campaign with the precision and skill of a military commander, with the desired result playing itself out on the newsstands, a daily piece of gossip for all of New York to read. From the poorest workers to The Four Hundred, the clamour for information about Consuelo's fairytale wedding to Sunny, the Duke of Marlborough, continued unabated.

'She has placed no seal upon the lips of the lucky tradesmen and tradeswomen who have furnished forth the marriage feast, and consequently a wealth of information has been poured out,'[1] remarked

Town Topics, in one of its numerous reports on the wedding preparations. It was exactly how Alva had planned it. Consuelo would get the wedding that Alva didn't have to Willie K, when the Vanderbilts were still considered social upstarts and largely irrelevant. She would get the wedding she would never have with Oliver, for as a divorcee, it would be considered unseemly to make a fuss. Consuelo, however, would get it all and it would be thanks to Alva's efforts. She would understand that some day, Alva thought confidently. When her daughter was installed at Blenheim, as the great Duchess of Marlborough, with a son and heir produced to continue the family line, Alva felt sure she would think of this moment and radiate the gratitude that was so unforthcoming now.

After the engagement was announced, Sunny had remained in America to travel, feeling sure he would never deign to grace its shores again. Like his father Blandford, he failed to ingratiate himself with the press, which, despite being enthralled by the romanticism of its American princess marrying into the British aristocracy, had begun to show signs of dissent when it came to millions of American money disappearing over the Atlantic. In 1893, a financial panic had hit America, causing around three million Americans to become unemployed. While colossal fortunes like the Vanderbilts' remained intact, others in society suffered and ordinary workers began to struggle to scratch out an existence on their meagre wages. Social unrest swept the country in the form of strikes, which affected a range of industries, and tensions between ethnic groups, such as the Italians and Irish, combusted amidst the strain. As the economy began to recover, feelings still ran high, with the prospect of American dollars being used to prop up the British aristocracy increasingly unappealing. Powerful voices began to denounce the trend, with J Potter writing to his friend and fellow founder of the National Association of Manufacturers in September 1895, '[The British] come over here every day and trade us a second-class Duke or a third-class Earl for a first-class American girl and get several million dollars to boot. And the very next day the entire outfit goes back to Liverpool on a British vessel.'[2]

Americans were becoming wise to the fact that huge sums of money were being drained from their economy by transatlantic marriages. Some estimates put the figure lost through dowries to England and other European countries at around 220 million dollars[3] by the time the phenomenon was coming to its natural conclusion. By 1908, Representative Sabath of Chicago introduced a bill to Congress which sought to put an end to the practice, in the form of a tax placed on the dowries that were accompanying American heiresses across the pond. After witnessing several transatlantic marriages flounder, the *Washington Post* wrote, 'there is no gain, either for the country or the girl. The former [United States] loses money and the latter happiness, with an empty title as her only compensation.'[4]

Although Alva was pragmatic about the personal happiness her daughter could expect from this arranged marriage, she remained hopeful that, given time, the couple would find a level of contentment in each other that had been lacking in her union with Willie K. First, she had to secure the union, which meant entering into lengthy negotiations with Sunny's lawyer, George Lewis, who had made the pilgrimage over from England to ensure that the Marlboroughs were handsomely compensated for the title they offered. Willie K was drafted in to enter a suitably generous opening offer to Lewis, who then countered for the Marlboroughs. By the time the negotiations had been concluded, Sunny had been promised two and a half million dollars in Beech Creek railway stocks, with a guaranteed yield of four per cent annually. The Vanderbilts had also agreed to provide one hundred thousand dollars a year for the couple and to purchase a town house for them in London. In total, the value of Consuelo's dowry was estimated to total fifteen million dollars[5]. Amid the negotiations and talk of business, Alva concentrated on the performance. Where she could detract from the financial aspect of the deal by focusing attention on the bride's toilette or the expected guest list, she would. Nothing must spoil the day.

In the end, Sunny had proposed to Consuelo amid the cold stone and carved wood of the Gothic Room at Marble House after a summer of keeping everyone guessing. Large stained-glass windows and a statue of St George slaying the dragon provided the backdrop for the moment when both parties sacrificed their future happiness for the sake of the prestige and honour of their families. Afterwards, a reporter wrote, 'Miss Vanderbilt had all the servants in the Marble House summoned to the servants' hall, and then, in a few words, she told them the heart-hustling news. "And now," she added, "I want you each, and all to take a holiday. Go out and tell everyone you know and every one you meet.'[6] This account seems unlikely given Consuelo's evident reluctance to marry Sunny, unless she was acting on Alva's instructions, who was no doubt desperate to spread the news as quickly and widely as possible.

Many in society had expected that Alva's 'Bal Blanc' would be the setting for the engagement announcement. Five hundred invitations had been sent out for the event that would form the centrepiece of the 1895 Newport Season. It was the first time that many of the upper class would be granted a glimpse inside the lavish Marble Palace and, just as it had proved when Alva had invited society into her Fifth Avenue mansion, the chance to step inside this new imposing mansion was irresistible. Alva knew the ball provided a crucial opportunity to prove to society that she was back on top and that no amount of scandal or public cold-shoulder by the Vanderbilts would wrest the mantle of society leader from her immovable grip. The attendance of Sunny just intensified her belief in the importance of the occasion. She would leave nothing to chance and money would be no object.

'All the world knows that Mrs Vanderbilt lavished an extraordinary amount of expense and attention upon this ball to make it if possible the event of the Newport Season and to complete the coup, the visit of the Duke of Marlborough was so timed that he naturally became the guest of honor at the ball,'[7] observed *Town Topics*.

Long before the night of the ball, Alva had imagined Sunny's face when he witnessed the magnificent scale of the festivities for the first time. He wasn't a man to show much expression, she knew that by now, but even he, the great Duke of Marlborough, couldn't fail to be impressed and no doubt his aristocratic head would be quietly calculating what the Vanderbilt money could achieve back in England to save Blenheim Palace. The night was still and warm, a perfect evening for Alva, who had concentrated the festivities around the mansion's marble terrace, overlooking immaculately tended lawns that stretched out far beyond towards the ocean. Hundreds of white silk Chinese lanterns lit up the terrace, swaying gently in the summer breeze. The similarities between Marble House and Versailles weren't subtle and they weren't intended to be. There was a marble sculpture of Louis XIV situated at the top of the mansion's imposing staircase, flanked by an oil painting of Louis XV no doubt to remind guests of the hostess's limitless aspirations. Alva ensured her footmen were dressed in Louis XIV costumes and powdered wigs to lead guests into the great hall, where one of three orchestras Alva had engaged for the party played. Nine French chefs had been drafted in to prepare a first dinner at midnight, with a larger sumptuous supper served at three o'clock in the morning. Vast swathes of Marble House had been transformed with a profusion of decorations, creating a visually stunning backdrop that positively encouraged comparisons between Alva's achievement and the vision of the Sun King. A large bronze fountain filled with floating lotus of the Nile, lilac water hyacinths and pale-pink hollyhocks danced with groups of artificial hummingbirds, bees and butterflies. Afterwards, there were rumours that some of the ladies in attendance had pocketed favours, which were laid out on great shields in the ballroom. Alva had spent five thousand dollars and imported the favours from Paris and they included fans, mirrors, watch cases and sashes of ribbons, all stamped with a medallion of Marble House and the date. They were lavish and covetable and few guests could resist the enticement to abandon their principles and acquire an extra souvenir.

In the midst of it all, Alva stood serenely in a striking gown of jade-green satin trimmed with white satin and intricate Spanish lace. As she directed proceedings and watched over Sunny, she wore over her shoulder her three-foot pearl necklace, which once belonged to

Catherine the Great. Her point had been made. Alva's Marble House, her clothes, her jewellery and her 'Bal Blanc' all exuded a renewed confidence in her own social position that came from knowing her daughter would soon be a duchess. It rankled that another gentleman had led Consuelo in the first cotillion after Sunny had declined, but it was a minor detail that she could put aside on such a night. When the last guest had left in the early hours of the morning, it was clear that no announcement would be forthcoming. Sunny had taken longer than expected to make a decision about his future bride, something that Alva had not anticipated, after all her efforts to welcome him as her honoured guest. She had tortured herself with thoughts that his hesitance to entangle his future with that of the Vanderbilts had been caused by her divorce from Willie K. Perhaps Sunny thought the English aristocracy would be reluctant to accept the daughter of divorced social upstarts as their new Duchess of Marlborough. Alva knew that there was nothing she could do to change the circumstances, so she pressed on with her plans, in the manner she always had. Determined and resolute, she continued to present Sunny with a feast of entertainments, the finest that Newport had to offer. She demonstrated that she was equal to any challenge or obstacle. When Sunny requested Consuelo's presence in the Gothic Room, she knew she had triumphed. The 'Bal Blanc' that summer in Newport had proved to be Alva's crowning glory, welcoming her back to the pinnacle of society, but the wedding would be the final step in her pursuit of distinction.

In the weeks that followed the proposal, various dates for the wedding were discussed and finally agreed upon: 6 November, at the beginning of the busy winter Season, would play host to the most lavish and prestigious wedding New York had ever seen. Alva consumed herself with wedding preparations, managing the press and entertaining Sunny, organising a coaching trip to West Point in New York state with Oliver, Colonel and Mrs Jay, and Consuelo and Sunny, where Sunny watched his first game of American football. When the party returned to New York in mid-October, Sunny ensconced himself at the Plaza Hotel and set about discovering the city. The newspapers gleefully described his brush with the authorities when he was pursued and detained by Central Park's policemen who did not approve of his coasting downhill on his bicycle. He was eventually released with a warning, but the humiliating episode was widely reported and only sought to highlight how little Sunny was acquainted with his future wife's homeland.

Alva shook her head in disbelief at Sunny's treatment. It had become difficult to predict what these indecent reporters would write next, which made her increasingly anxious as the wedding day approached. The New York press, in its irrational way, lurched from glowing articles that detailed every aspect of the approaching nuptials to subtle condemnations of a feeble aristocracy that was intent on stealing away a jewel in the democracy's crown. Alva's task would be to maintain the delicate balance between the two, removing the threat that spiteful criticism posed to Sunny's resolve, and to ensure her reluctant daughter did her duty. It was a difficult task, but not insurmountable. If anyone could pull it off, Alva could.

Pomp and Ceremony

November 1895, New York

*'It was estimated that the chrysanthemum blossoms, if
piled up, would equal in bulk an ordinary haystack,
and the roses, if placed from end to end, would extend
over a distance of eight miles.'* – THE TIMES

The bride was described as 'one of America's fairest young women'[1] in
The New York Times's report of the Vanderbilt-Marlborough wedding.
The newspaper devoted four pages to the nuptials of one of its city's
most distinguished families to an English aristocrat, a duke, no less.
One of theirs would be mistress of Blenheim Palace.

For those that paid particular attention to these things, and there
were many of them, the New York newspapers had duly covered every
little detail of the wedding preparations. Speculation gave way to
fabrication until the press had worked itself into a frenzy over what
was billed as the most lavish nuptials the city had ever seen. One
report went so far as to allege that the bride's garters had gold clasps

studded with diamonds, at which Consuelo Vanderbilt began to wonder how she 'should live down such vulgarities'[1]. However, the spurious rumours were the least of Consuelo's worries. She was about to enter into a marriage contract that would bind her to a man she did not love and a country she did not know. The finer details of her lingerie were of little concern.

'I spent the morning of my wedding day in tears and alone; no one came near me,'[2] admitted Consuelo in her memoirs, *The Glitter and the Gold*. The soon-to-be Duchess had risen early, to prepare for the day ahead. With a footman posted at the door, she slowly began to assemble and don the bridal wear that was estimated to have cost her mother eighty thousand dollars. The lace lingerie was first, followed by white silk stockings and shoes. The Worth wedding dress, which had been ordered by a supremely confident Alva in Paris the spring before Consuelo and the Duke had even met, came next. Consuelo watched impassively as her maid helped her into the exquisite white satin bodice and skirt with its several tiers of cascading Brussels lace. Perhaps fittingly for this wedding, the collar was high, the sleeves were tight. There was also a five-foot train intricately embroidered with seed pearls and silver that hung in double box pleats from her shoulders. The delicate tulle veil was secured with a wreath of orange blossoms to symbolise fertility, serving as a reminder to Consuelo of the duties she would be required to fulfil. The long, gauzy material fell over her face and down to her knees. Concealed beneath the elegant layer Consuelo's eyes grew puffy and swollen as the tears continued to flow.

Consuelo's father, Willie K, had been banished from the house leading up to the wedding and was under strict instructions from Alva that his duties extended only to escorting Consuelo to the church, formally giving her away and signing the register. Then he was required to disappear out of sight, his role completed. The tension between the recently divorced couple had been heightened by the summer's sojourn to Newport, causing relations to further sour between Willie K and his former wife. In light of such hostilities, it was considered prudent for Willie K to time his arrival to escort Consuelo to the church only after Alva had left. The mother of the bride had entered St Thomas's dressed spectacularly in a pale-blue satin flared skirt edged with Russian sable, complemented by a sable collar and a lace and silver hat finished with a pale blue aigrette. It was noted by onlookers that 'she wore a decided expression of satisfaction, as she entered the church.'[3]

In stark contrast, at Alva's recently acquired town house on 72nd Street and Madison Avenue, her daughter was still struggling to contain her emotions as the noon deadline fast approached. Having been informed that her father was downstairs, Consuelo composed herself and made her way to greet him. She felt 'cold and numb'[4] as she left her room, but her self-control failed her as soon as she laid eyes on Willie K. Once more, tears pricked her eyes and once more her face had to be sponged and calmed before the wedding party could leave for the church. When they finally emerged, now almost twenty minutes late, several reporters noted the downcast appearance of both father and daughter. 'She looked sad and appeared to have been crying,' commented *The Herald*, before quickly adding, 'a natural proceeding with brides'[5]. According to *The New York Times*, 'There was a grave look upon his face as if his short talk with the future Duchess had been of a serious nature.'[6] Despite Consuelo's obvious distress, Willie K, always reluctant to challenge Alva's authority when it came to their children, reasoned with himself that there was too much at stake to offer his daughter a way out now. The show would go on.

'I suppose that no American or Anglo-American wedding ever excited so much interest among people of all sorts and conditions, nor was any such ceremony in this city ever so splendid and elaborate. If there be any prejudices in this country against rank and wealth, or against the union of the two, they have on this occasion been suppressed. The marriage is extremely popular,'[7] wrote *The Times*.

If the press had exaggerated the contents of the bride's trousseau in the weeks leading up to the wedding, it for once couldn't be accused of inflating the enthusiasm for the nuptials among the general public. The crowds had begun to arrive at nine o'clock and by half past ten there were around two thousand people lining the route. From every window, women jostled for position, opera glasses in hand, desperate for a view of the American version of royalty, the irrepressible Vanderbilts.

In an attempt to stop huge swells of onlookers congregating outside the church to watch proceedings, the streets between Alva's residence on 72nd Street and St Thomas Church on Fifth Avenue were lined with policemen, who had been given orders to hold the crowds back. In the preceding years, one society bride had become trapped inside the fashionable church by the curious masses outside and the authorities didn't want a repeat performance. An awning had been erected directly outside the church so that the bride was all but concealed from prying eyes, but the sheer numbers of fervent spectators still threatened to overwhelm officers during the day. The *World* reported that when 'the women heard the rumble of heavy wheels,' they 'seemed to become possessed of demons. They struggled like so many drowning persons and there being such a tremendous pressure behind them they pushed the police line further and further towards the church.'[8]

Its reporter described an officer, Acting Inspector Courtright, who tried to take control of the deteriorating situation, shouting, 'Here, that won't do. Push those women back, every one of them – back they go. Quick, now.'[9] Enthralled by the inspector's heroic efforts, the reporter recounted how the policeman laid his hands on the shoulders of a woman who was trying to push her way between two officers and shoved her back into the crowd 'until her ribs ached'[10].

The bridesmaids had proceeded to the church before the carriage carrying Consuelo and Willie K. There were eight in total, selected by Alva from among her friends. Edith Morton, Evelyn Burden, Marie Winthrop, Katherine Duer, Elsa Bronson, May Goelet, Julia Jay (daughter of Mrs Jay, who had finally persuaded Consuelo to give up Winthrop) and Daisy Post all wore long dresses of white satin with blue sashes and all waited patiently for the bride to arrive.

St Thomas on Fifth Avenue wasn't the Vanderbilts' usual church, but it was *de rigueur*, definitely *the* place for society weddings. Alva had decreed that it was the only church big enough to seat the fifteen hundred people who had been invited to the service, the sixty members of the choir and the celebrated conductor Walter Damrosch and his fifty-piece orchestra.

Scores of florists had worked for days beforehand to ensure that when the church doors were flung open at ten o'clock that morning, a breath-taking sight greeted each and every guest. Flowers or foliage adorned almost every inch of woodwork and stone column, every pew and arch, creating a spectacular effect, which was highly unlikely to be replicated. Every fifth pew had a huge floral torch of pink and white roses surmounted by a four-foot palm gathered with a huge pink and white satin bow with ends that lightly touched the floor. The aisle from the vestibule to the chancel was an avenue of pink and white blooms and the *pièce de résistance* was a floral dome that hung over the marrying couple.

'From the great dome gracefully hung six massive strands of foliage and flowers, lilies, roses, and chrysanthemums being used. The ends of these garlands reached to the north and south galleries, to the right and left transepts, and to the organ alcoves. It took thousands of yards of smilax and holly and hundreds of posies to weave these garlands,'[11] said *The New York Times* in admiration.

Afterwards, people would comment that the wedding was 'without exception the most magnificent ever celebrated in this country'[12] and that was exactly what Alva had set out to achieve. Of course the rest of the Vanderbilt family wouldn't see such splendour and neither would the Marlboroughs, as both families were not attending the nuptials. The Vanderbilts, including Willie K's brother Cornelius and his wife Alice, had been unceremoniously banned from the proceedings by Alva, and the Marlboroughs had simply had not been inclined to make the journey across the Atlantic for such a match. They would wait and see how the American girl and her money fared at Blenheim.

For those arriving early, Walter Damrosch, his orchestra and the choir mounted an ambitious musical programme to entertain the crowds. Many guests were determined to secure their place so they could be sure to see the most distinguished guests, who duly took their seats just in time before the mother of the bride made her appearance. Indeed, many female guests were so keen for a better view of the fashionable gowns on parade that they clambered onto their seats, standing on tiptoe, craning their necks in anticipation, whenever a member of the Four Hundred made their way down the aisle.

Alva checked her watch one more time: twenty minutes late. What on earth could have happened to Consuelo? And then she heard it, the roar of the crowd outside, signalling her daughter's arrival. The bells were pealing when Willie K stepped out of the carriage, blinking into the daylight, astounded by the spectacle he was witnessing. Scores of people, cheering, waving, smiling and waiting for his daughter. When Consuelo appeared, an even louder cheer greeted her. She wrestled her enormous train out of the carriage, leaned on her father and finally gave the crowd what they wanted, a weak and lacklustre smile. It was all she could manage.

With her bridesmaids leading the way, Consuelo slowly walked into the church. Throngs of expectant faces turned around and fixed their eyes on the bride. Now she was thankful for the long veil that covered her small, swollen face. Consuelo and her bridesmaids all carried bouquets of roses and orchids that had arrived from Blenheim Palace a few days before, according to Marlborough family tradition. Consuelo's bouquet was overwhelming at nearly three feet wide and was made wholly of orchids. Years later, in her autobiography, Consuelo would say that the orchids had never arrived from Blenheim, that even on her wedding day there had been signs to indicate the marriage would not be a happy one. However, contemporary press reports are full of descriptions of the flowers, saying they were 'one of the most talked about features of the wedding breakfast'[13].

Inch by inch, Consuelo and Willie K made their way down the aisle, Consuelo slowly pressing her father's arm, signalling him to slow down. When she reached Sunny, standing with his best man and cousin Ivor Guest, she noted that his 'eyes were fixed in space'[14]. For Sunny's part, he later described his bride as looking 'much troubled'[15].

After so much pomp and ceremony, the formalities of the wedding service were quickly over and the bridal party retired to the vestry to sign the register. As soon as his part was done, Willie K took his leave, slipping out of a side door and taking a carriage back to his club. He had parted with millions of Vanderbilt money and his only daughter, with no fuss and seemingly no documented objections. Once more he had avoided confrontation and given his daughter to a man who he must have seriously doubted could ever bring her happiness. The bride and groom soon returned from the vestry and walked back down the aisle to the march from Wagner's *Tannhäuser*. The deed was done.

'As we came out of the church the crowd surged towards us and women tried to snatch flowers from my bouquet,'[16] Consuelo remembered. She was quickly bundled into the carriage and flanked by police officers who tussled with the crowds. The liveried coachmen forged their way through the melee and sped back to 72nd Street. Back at St Thomas, some onlookers attempted to force their way into the church and take flowers as souvenirs, but the police held them back, before eventually the excitement died down and everyone packed up and went home, 'worn out in mind and body'[17].

Readers of *The Times* in London were treated to a detailed description of the decorations that had been so painstakingly prepared at Alva's house for the wedding breakfast. 'It was estimated that the chrysanthemum blossoms, if piled up, would equal in bulk an ordinary haystack, and the roses, if placed from end to end, would extend over a distance of eight miles. Twenty thousand sprays of lilies of the valley were used,'[18] reported their correspondent eagerly.

For Alva the wedding wasn't just about the marriage of her daughter to a man of distinction. This day was the culmination of years of planning. Years spent on the fringes of New York society clamouring to get in. Years spent carefully maintaining her position before scandal threatened to take it all away. This was the day she would solidify her standing and command the respect that, even as the all-conquering wife of Willie K Vanderbilt, certain elements of old New York had continued to deny her. Alva's journey from social outcast to one of them was complete and every inch of her newly bought town house would show that she was the mother of a Duchess. And if swarms of pushy newspaper men were there to report it to the world, then so much the better.

'The predominating tint was pink, the dining room being decorated solely with pink and white blossoms,' went on *The Times* in breathless excitement. 'In the decoration of the hall palms were disposed among banks of chrysanthemums. The marble trellis of the staircase was draped with ferns, banked with pink and yellow chrysanthemums, and edged with pink roses of a deeper colour. In the reception room South American tree ferns were disposed in front of all the windows.'[19]

The tree ferns were in fact around ten feet high, immersing the guests in luscious foliage that transformed the dining room from a rather impersonal marble expanse into a glorious garden. Five ferns were made into a canopy, from which a bell of lilies of the valley, with an eight-foot circumference, was suspended. Beneath this opulent centrepiece stood the diminutive Sunny and an ashen-faced Consuelo, primed to receive their guests.

Alva had ensured that only the very best of New York society gained an invite to the wedding breakfast. While 1,500 invitations had gone out for the church service at St Thomas Church, there were only 115 golden tickets to the reception. Of course Mrs Astor was present and was duly seated at Alva's table next to the first British Ambassador to the United States, Sir Julian Pauncefote, who read out congratulatory notices from both Queen Victoria and Bertie during the festivities. The Governor of New York, Governor Morton, Bishop Littlejohn of New Jersey and a certain politician, William Whitney, his daughter Pauline and her fiancé Almeric Paget, were also notable attendees guaranteed to bring credibility to the occasion, since none of the Vanderbilts were invited and Willie K was banished to his club.

Willie K did manage to leave his daughter a diamond tiara with large pear-shaped stones, one of a swathe of opulent gifts the couple received. Alva presented Consuelo with her string of magnificent pearls, whose owner had once been Catherine the Great of Russia, perhaps a nod to the woman she hoped her daughter would become. It must have pained Consuelo greatly to open a present from Winthrop, the man she could have been sharing her wedding day with, if Alva had given her the choice. He gave the couple a pair of antique silver candlesticks, which were a family heirloom that had been carefully passed down the generations. An enduring symbol perhaps of family, duty and tradition, with a meaning observers could only speculate on.

While the guests dined, outside there were skirmishes between police and scores of women who were impatiently awaiting another chance to see the bride and groom. When the time finally came, there were chaotic scenes, as Consuelo and Sunny attempted to avoid the traditional shower of rice from the ushers. Sunny, who bore the brunt of the celebrations with the barrage hitting him in the back of the neck, was described as following his wife into the carriage 'with more speed than grace'[20]. Another over-enthusiastic guest threw a pale-blue satin shoe, nearly knocking off the coachman's hat.

Eventually the couple made it into their carriage, accompanied by loud cheers from the gathered crowds. Sunny had chosen to remain in the frock coat he had worn for the wedding, while Consuelo had changed into an elegant navy and crimson velvet travelling dress. She took a long look at Sunny, her Duke, wondering what life now had in store for her. For so long she had had her movements planned out for her with military precision by her mother and she longed to break free from the constraints that governed every aspect of her life. Despite the circumstances that had so cruelly robbed her of happiness with Winthrop, she had been given the chance to begin her life again in earnest with some degree of autonomy. So, why, at this moment, did she yearn to be back inside the New York townhouse with its occupant who loomed so large?

'Driving away from home I looked back,' Consuelo recalled. 'My mother was at the window. She was hiding behind the curtain, but I saw that she was in tears. "And yet," I thought, "she has attained the goal she set herself, she has experienced the satisfactions wealth can confer, she has ensconced me in the niche she so early assigned me, and she is now free to let ambition give way to a gentler passion."'[21]

Perhaps Alva knew the arduous road that lay ahead of her eighteen-year-old daughter, or perhaps she was simply overtaken by the emotion of the day. Maybe her years of scheming, planning and controlling had caught up with her and she was mourning the new Duchess's departure to a land far away. Either way it didn't matter, Consuelo was gone.

The Marriage Business

November 1895, London

'*Society means the same thing all over the world – the same ambitions, the same small jealousies, the same ceaseless struggle to get ahead of someone else, the same climbing, climbing! That is human nature and that is society in every land.*' – MINNIE PAGET

Number 35 Belgrave Square had been buzzing with activity all day in preparation for the evening ahead. Now, as the remains of the bright autumn day gave way to the encroaching gloom of the cold, dark night, Minnie Paget would have taken advantage of the pause in duties. She glanced down at her notebook, checked the menu once more and began to stalk slowly around the table that was already set for dinner. She checked that the place cards she had handwritten herself corresponded with the guest list and adjusted the seating arrangements more than once. She had spent a great deal of time calculating the most beneficial layout. *Town Topics* had remarked in 1894 that Minnie's 'cheeky little card parties' had 'helped to pass the winter'[1] and she intended to channel her efforts into the same intimate occasions this year. She would be ready to entertain aristocrats and royalty, politicians and plutocrats, all weary of the dreary London weather, all temporarily stranded in town on their way to more enticing destinations – the Continent perhaps or a lively county house party. Irrespective of their destination, Minnie knew her role and, although London had a sort of eerie quietness about it as it embedded itself in the swirling winter fog, the game of society never stopped. While those around her might retreat for the winter, Minnie would forge ahead, laying the foundations for the Season to come.

When Minnie reflected on 1895, she would have been gratified to note that it had been a most successful year. She had engineered and arranged, cajoled and manipulated, and had been rewarded with several marriages that she had played a part in and had seen her financial position drastically improved into the bargain. With the increasing interest of the world's press in American heiresses who had captured the hearts of dashing English aristocrats, more and more daughters of Swells were making the journey on the steamship to England, bound for a life of love, acceptance and a social superiority that they believed they could never achieve at home. Minnie knew the image peddled by newspapers that had culminated in the feverish coverage of the Vanderbilt-Marlborough wedding was little more than a fairytale, conjured up by those who wished to disguise the realities of the phenomenon. The uncomfortable truth was that such marriages were simple transactions that required months and sometime years of complicated machinations by those surrounding the couple. Those who had their very best interests at heart. Those who knew that love was more often than not wholly unobtainable in the ruthless world they all inhabited. Whether they lived in New York, Paris or London, the upper classes bore intolerable scrutiny from their peers and the wider world that dictated their every move. Anyone who wished to truly succeed in society needed to master the rules quickly and display the same ruthless streak as all those who had come before them and now occupied the upper echelons of society.

'Society means the same thing all over the world,' Minnie told a reporter when asked to reveal her thoughts on the subject. 'The same ambitions, the same small jealousies, the same ceaseless struggle to get ahead of someone else, the same climbing, climbing! That is human nature and that is society in every land.'[2] She had always known how to read those around her, how to study and prosper in a society that valued huge fortunes and impeccable lineage, when she could lay claim to neither. Her mother's fortitude and example had served her well, all the way to the pinnacle of the most fashionable set in London. Her achievements had even extended to engineering the match of the decade. The spectacle of Consuelo's wedding to Sunny had been handled masterfully by Alva, Minnie had to admit, and as she read the acres of newspaper coverage given to all the details, she luxuriated in the moment, her greatest triumph. When Pauline Whitney's wedding took place just a week later in the same church, St Thomas in New York, with almost as much pomp and ceremony, Minnie's feat was complete.

The similarities between the two weddings would not have been lost on the crowds of onlookers that again turned out to witness another member of the American aristocracy marry into the British one. While William Whitney was not so adept at briefing the press on arrangements as Alva Vanderbilt was, Pauline's wedding nonetheless generated enormous publicity from an insatiable press and public who hadn't lost their appetite for the intricate details of such occasions. Unlike the Vanderbilts, who were still occupying themselves with infighting between Alva and Willie K, the Whitneys were popular in society and two pre-wedding dinners were organised in advance of the day. Perhaps to highlight her glaring absence from Consuelo's wedding, Mrs Cornelius Vanderbilt hosted a dinner for Pauline, and William arranged for a celebration to be given at the Metropolitan Club in Almeric's honour, to which Winthrop Rutherfurd was invited as a guest. The financial considerations had been agreed between

William and the Paget family, with Pauline's dowry estimated at two million dollars.

It was a cool, bright day when Almeric arrived at noon to the sight of a large crowd at the now infamous Fifth Avenue church. Onlookers would note that the crowds were not as large as Consuelo had attracted the week before, but more guests were in attendance to appreciate the great arches of white roses and chrysanthemums that hung over the central aisle. Comparisons between the two friends' weddings were numerous, reports on both occasions noting the presence of Mrs Astor and Bishop Potter's careful handling of the service; it was also remarked that Pauline's wedding boasted a superior calibre of guest, with President Cleveland and Lady Colebrooke, Almeric's sister, among those who heard Edouard de Reszke sing *Ave Maria* accompanied by the renowned Nathan Franko's orchestra before the bride arrived.

Pauline was beautiful in a white satin dress with a high neck and long, dramatic train trimmed with point lace. Her fine veil was held in place by a small diamond pin, a gift from Almeric, and she carried a bouquet of white orchids and roses. Six bridesmaids, including Gertrude Vanderbilt and Miss Emily Sloane, wore identical poplin dresses trimmed with sable in varying pastel shades of pink, blue, green, yellow, lilac and, white with dainty velvet hats, and carried pretty muffs decorated with lace frills. Afterwards, guests retired to the Whitneys' residence on West 57th Street, where the bridal party observed their several hundred guests from a crescent-shaped table situated in the window at the west end of the palatial ballroom. The wedding breakfast, which was catered by the fashionable Sherry's restaurant, indulged guests with a menu encompassing *oeufs brouillés aux truffes* [scrambled eggs with truffles] and *carré d'agneau à la bourgeoise* [rack of lamb].

Minnie had ensured that her gift of a silver breakfast service had arrived at the Whitney mansion on the appointed day, an essential token of her appreciation for their lucrative friendship. It joined an antique silver urn from President Cleveland, a white feather fan with a mother-of-pearl handle from Willie K and a silver vase from Lady

Colebrooke. William Whitney gave Pauline part of his wife's extensive jewellery collection, including a collar of sapphires and diamonds, a corsage of diamonds that draped for four inches and a brand-new diamond and pearl necklace.

Despite the profusion of wealth on display, and against the general grain of such matches, the young couple radiated happiness. They had been calculatingly laid in each other's path, but against the odds, Minnie thought, real affection had blossomed. She had to acknowledge that Almeric and Pauline, while not representing the highest position among the aristocracy, made a promising match. Almeric was not yet titled, but Minnie suspected it would not be long before he would be, particularly now that he had Pauline's fortune to utilise and fund his ambitions. Minnie believed with every fibre of her being that marriage, when applied to the upper classes, was all about finances. Money was the heart that beat at the centre of every match, driving young people, some unsuspecting and some with their eyes wide open, down the aisle. Yet Pauline and Almeric disproved her theory. Yes, money and station had certainly been a consideration but there was romance there too. Frederick Martin agreed in his memoir, arguing, '… marriage with American women infuses vitality, personality, beauty and money into the peerage, although money is not always the factor in the case.'[3] Indeed, Minnie's own marriage with Arthur, despite Marietta's longing for something better, had been built on affection, prompting Minnie's friend Lady Decies to declare in her autobiography, *Turn of the World*, that 'when she married Arthur Paget, [she] had married for love'.[4]

Not all of the American heiresses who married that year did so publicly and in the glare of the world's press. While Consuelo and Pauline were planning their nuptials, Minnie noted that a certain Colonel Howland Roberts and Elizabeth La Roche had got married in Kensington on 21 October 1895. The La Roches were not conspicuous in society but there had been some effort to bolster their status in recent years, with *The New York Times* reporting on the first of a series of dinners hosted by Dr and Mrs La Roche at their home on Madison Avenue in November 1894. 'The dinner will be in yellow and blue, the floral decorations consisting of violets and yellow chrysanthemums,'[5] readers were informed. Minnie sensed that this was an effort to raise their profile among New York's elite, after all a series of dinners reported on in the society pages was a statement of intent, a sign that the family wished to partake in the round of occasions that characterised the winter Season. Perhaps it was an attempt to attract a husband for their daughter Elizabeth, who, at thirty years old, was in serious danger of being classed a spinster. It was clear the tactics had worked: Elizabeth was now married and living in England. Colonel Roberts was connected to the London Irish Rifles and was twenty years older than his bride. Maybe Arthur could use his military connections to discover more about the pair and whether they needed guidance to be embraced by London society?

Minnie understood that at least two more marriages between English gentlemen and American heiresses were scheduled to take place by year's end. Keen evangelist Leonora Van Marter was due to marry the eccentric Lord Bennet, the future Earl of Tankerville, while Cara Rogers, whose father had made his fortune in oil, had accepted the wealthy English civil engineer Urban Hanlon Broughton. Even by Minnie's standards, the year had been an extraordinary one. With more American women marrying into the British aristocracy than ever before, the clamour for respectability garnered from acceptance by the nobility was worth its weight in gold. Minnie had long ago foreseen the potential for profit from such alliances and realised that, with a little guts and guile, she could assist naive and objectionable upstarts blinded by ambition and mystified by the ordered world that she ruled. She had been the first to understand that dukes with high overheads and hard hearts would enthusiastically respond to the prospect of a renewed fortune and a cast-iron guarantee of their favourable place in family folklore. Later, a reporter would comment on Minnie's calculated move into society.

'While her husband was attending to his military duties abroad, this calm, observing, far-sighted woman was arranging her own outposts and defenses at home, and before long London became aware that a very strong and attractive personality had been established in its midst.'[6]

As she turned her attentions to that evening's objectives, she must have smiled at the thought of the crop of heiresses who had joined her in England that year. All so different, all searching for something – acceptance, love, respectability, influence – in this land that was in some ways so familiar, yet demanded things from them they couldn't begin to fathom. They had money and now had a title, but they would need resilience more than anything else to survive the transition. Minnie wondered whether they would be happy, as she had been with Arthur, and immediately berated herself for being so indulgent. The rules of high society were simple and clear. Marriage was a business, and for Minnie Paget that business had been, and would continue to be, a lucrative one.

Epilogue

On 1 August 1904 Minnie Paget returned home to Belgrave Square from a dinner party, impeccably and elegantly dressed as usual. She opened the door to the house lift, anxious to retire to bed, and – in a move uncharacteristic of the perceptive woman who fills the pages of this book – she failed to notice that the lift was actually at the top of the house and, stepping out into the darkness, fell twenty feet to the bottom of the elevator shaft. When her servants found her, she was a huddled and broken figure. She had fractured her thigh and kneecap and was in tremendous pain. Although she received the best medical attention England had to offer, Minnie's bones failed to heal and it would take two years, fifteen operations, a trip to Berlin to see the renowned bone specialist Professor Hoffa and a course of excruciating treatment before her condition improved. Letters poured in from all over the world, wishing Minnie a speedy recovery. Bertie would take a personal interest in her health, asking for updates from her doctors on her progress. Friends would comment that she showed 'superhuman fortitude'[1] during her period of self-exile from society and remembered that, despite the notes she received from the royal family, it was a 'dirty little note'[2] from her washerwoman that she most cherished. 'I don't think anything has delighted me more than that she should have thought of me,'[3] she was reported to have said.

With the tenacity that was so characteristic of her personality, Minnie recovered, and continued to dominate British society, pressing on with the unique service she covertly offered to the American parvenus. Consuelo Vanderbilt's first summer as Duchess of Marlborough was punctuated by a visit from Minnie and afterwards the master and her reluctant protégé would often work together with other American notables in London, organising charity bazaars for good causes. In January 1896, Minnie was spotted with the newly married Pauline Whitney in Nice on the French Riviera. 'Mrs Arthur Paget… is one of the most distinguished Americans here, and with her are Mr and Mrs Almeric Paget… Both women are handsome and carry themselves most beautifully.'[4]

What her role was at this point – whether she was giving Pauline advice on the steps she should now take to conquer British society or basking in the light of her obvious success the previous year – isn't clear, but in any case the names of many of the heiresses who had made matches that year were intrinsically linked with Minnie's for many years to come. Perhaps that isn't surprising, given the intimate nature of the British aristocracy and the American colony within it, yet Minnie's position as social godmother and confidante to many of the women was an enduring relationship, and in some cases friendship, which transcended the financial transactions that had dominated their earlier dealings.

She was also credited for other high-profile marriages, like that of Anna Gould, daughter of the notorious speculator Jay Gould, to the French Count Boni de Castallane in 1895 and railroad heiress Alice Thaw to the Earl of Yarmouth in 1903. Both marriages ended unhappily, the former leading to divorce after the adulterous count spent one million dollars[5] of the Gould fortune in a single year and the latter granted an annulment for non-consummation. However, Minnie's social reach extended further than just arranging marriages. She continued to be a cherished friend and confidante of the royal family. Queen Alexandra wrote to her in 1915, commenting, 'You have never changed since the time I first knew you at court in our happy youth.'[6] The Paget papers at the British Library are a testament to the numerous friendships she enjoyed with high-profile public figures, including letters from President Roosevelt, Woodrow Wilson, Herbert Asquith and Queen Mary, as well as numerous society figures and members of the aristocracy. Her opinion and insight was often respected and sought out. Edith Wharton, who had clearly maintained a friendship with Minnie despite her failed engagement to Minnie's brother, asked for her advice on the accuracy of the descriptions of racing at the popular resort of Saratoga Springs in her novel *The Buccaneers*. 'Please pick up as many points for me as you can on this subject,'[7] she implored. There were rumblings in the press that Minnie's influence wasn't what it used to be when Bertie died and his son ascended the throne as King George V. Some reports suggested she was going 'out of vogue'[8] and that she had 'overdone the running of American nobodies'[9]. Yet she persisted in acting as a social sponsor right up until the end of her life.

On 17 April 1919, Minnie left London for Paris with the American social climber Nancy Leeds, whom she had been chaperoning around society. The pair had arranged an opulent dinner at the Ritz for Prince Christopher of Greece when Minnie suddenly succumbed to the flu pandemic that had been sweeping the continent. She died of pneumonia on 21 May 1919 at the age of sixty-six. In an echo of the aftermath of her mother's death in New York some twenty-five years earlier, Nancy Leeds, after some debate ('It seems so dreadful to give the party with her lying dead here'[10]), decided to continue with her long-planned dinner on the advice of Ward McAllister's successor, social arbiter Harry Lehr, who told her to keep Minnie's death a secret until the occasion was over. 'No whisper of the tragedy was allowed to cloud the atmosphere of the dinner,'[11] remembered Elizabeth Drexel Lehr.

The funeral took place in Paris a few days later, with a memorial service planned at St Peter's Church, Eaton Square, in London afterwards. A few months later Minnie's treasured wardrobe, which included numerous Worth gowns and priceless costumes exquisitely made by artisans for famous costume balls, was auctioned off. 'Many articles fetched low prices,' the newspapers reported. A celebrated Cleopatra costume that had been the talk of London when Minnie had worn it for the Duchess of Devonshire's ball in 1897 made just nine pounds.

Minnie had outlived her old friend Consuelo Manchester, who died of heart failure after neuritis on 22 November 1909 at her home in Grosvenor Square in London. She was fifty-six years old. The once lively and unconventional beauty had suffered further tragedy when in 1900 her surviving daughter, Lady Alice, died of tuberculosis, aged only twenty. While Consuelo again returned to the life of a society hostess, the loss of her twin daughters profoundly changed her. It was said that, 'as she lost or suffered, so she braced herself to the day, even where it involved an effort of giving pleasure to others…'[12]

Later that year, on 14 November 1900, Consuelo's son, Little Kim, who had inherited his father's love of extravagance, again followed in his footsteps when he married Helen Zimmerman, daughter of a Cincinnati railroad magnate, Eugene Zimmerman, without informing his mother – who completed the circle by making her disapproval of Miss Zimmerman's unrefined background well known. The unhappy marriage ended in divorce in 1931. Four years later, in debt again, Little Kim would serve time at Wormwood Scrubs for attempting to pawn some jewellery that belonged to the trustees of the Manchester estate.

In 1901, Consuelo Manchester was finally relieved of the constant money worries that had plagued her life in England. Her brother Fernando died, and in his will he named her as the sole benefactor of his considerable fortune, eliminating the need for her to profit from society. With her innate sense of fairness, she shared the inheritance with her sisters Emily and Natica, but the money meant that she would never again be forced to rely on the kindness of friends to bring dishes for dinner. She continued to entertain and even in 1907 it was noted that, 'Other favourites might come and go but she was always as she is to-day *persona gratissima* to Albert Edward [Bertie].'[13]

Consuelo and Minnie had been in the game for so long, they didn't know how to do anything else. The fact that they were so different yet perfectly complemented each other did not go unnoticed. *The New York Times* described Consuelo Manchester as 'all sunshine and glitter', Minnie as 'more cool and calm in her methods. It was the difference between a summer morning and a moonlit night, each charming in its way and full of great possibilities.'[14] They had been at the forefront of Anglo-American relations for over thirty years, each in their unique way, each wielding extraordinary power through their ambition, need for survival and fantastic ingenuity. 'They were the pioneers of the American woman's influence in England, an influence which in these two distinct influences has gone far beyond mere ballroom popularity or royal favor, and has come as close as woman may to affairs of State and Cabinet councils.'[15]

Together they had pioneered a new way in for Americans seeking acceptance within the British aristocracy. In their varying ways, either exploiting or concealing their differences to the typical English lady, they had won the affections of a prince and the whole of the royal family, while outfoxing the unsuspecting and rather staid competition. They used their friendship to gossip, hone their skills and share contacts and connections, cementing a partnership that had begun in a schoolroom in Paris and had endured isolation, tragedy, illness and the ruthlessness of the fashionable set. The handwritten card that Minnie sent with her flowers to Consuelo Manchester's funeral read: 'In sorrowing, and most loving memory of our lifelong friendship. – Minnie'[16]

The heiresses that married into the British aristocracy in 1895 met markedly varied fortunes. As was largely expected by those around them at the time, many of their marriages ended in divorce after long years of unhappiness. In relationships devoid of love and romance, they would look elsewhere for affection and many shed their puritanical American morality to embark on affairs in the accepted way of the upper classes of their adopted country. As married women, once their duty to provide an 'heir and a spare', as Consuelo Vanderbilt would later put it, was fulfilled, they were largely free to discreetly take a lover and pursue pet projects that would extend their influence in society. Some chose politics, charity or the arts, and found that in England they were not banished to the drawing room and encouraged to remain solely in the realms of society. Instead they could exert real power, using the long-nurtured education of their youth for individual and collective gain.

As Consuelo Vanderbilt, now Duchess of Marlborough, arrived at the station at Woodstock, the small town nearest to Blenheim Palace, in early 1896, she was greeted with a glorious reception, including crowds of ordinary people eager to lay eyes on the beautiful Duchess they had read so much about. The Lord Mayor greeted them, schoolchildren presented Consuelo with bouquets of flowers and the Duke's carriage was dragged through the streets to the Town Hall by Woodstock's finest and most robust men in tribute to the newlyweds. The celebrations continued with a reception and a procession to the palace, escorted by the Oxfordshire Hussars yeomanry and a local band. The welcome they received was undoubtedly warm; it was just a pity an icy chill had already begun to permeate the Marlboroughs' marriage.

When not entertaining at Blenheim – in November 1896 the Marlboroughs hosted Bertie and a large shooting party of over one hundred guests including Mary and George Curzon, requiring months of preparation and refurbishment of Blenheim – they would endure long dinners together when Sunny would push his laden plate away, causing the food to go cold, and endlessly twirl the ring on his little finger, deep in thought. Consuelo took to knitting at the table to relieve the boredom, while the butler read detective stories outside in the hall. Consuelo produced two sons in quick succession to secure the Marlborough dynasty: John Albert Edward William, known as the Marquess of Blandford, in November 1897, followed by Ivor in October 1898. Once she had performed that duty, the chasm that existed between the pair became ever more apparent. Consuelo wrote that they were 'people of different temperament condemned to live together'[17] and consoled herself with brief respites from the misery with a series of affairs. She was rumoured to have had a liaison with French portrait painter Paul Helleu and a more serious affair with Sunny's cousin Lord Castlereagh.

After spending large swathes of time avoiding each other, both contenting themselves with long periods away from Blenheim, it was clear that the Marlboroughs could no longer endure their marriage. They separated in October 1906, with Winston Churchill, who held Consuelo in high esteem, helping to broker a separation agreement. Despite the agreement, the separation became very public and friends found it increasingly difficult not to take sides. Jennie Churchill's second husband, George Cornwallis-West (whom she married in 1900), wrote to Winston, saying: 'I heard every little detail, unsavoury and otherwise, from a man today who was told by Minnie Paget who got it all from Sarah [Lady Sarah Wilson]... Surely the obvious line for all your family to take is to decline all discussion on the matter, let alone volunteering disgusting gossip with the most renowned of gossip mongers.'[18]

This time Minnie, for reasons known only to her, was disinclined to help Consuelo and Sunny manage their separation discreetly. Instead, Cornwallis-West suggests she was peddling the salacious gossip that made the period intolerable for them both. Consuelo used the time as a single woman to focus on philanthropy, which opened her eyes to the social problems caused by industrialisation. She supported Winston's Liberal government and its programme of social reforms, and used her influential position on charitable boards and the financial support afforded by her father Willie K to venture into public life, calling for better working conditions for women and extolling the merits of female suffrage. In 1917, she met French aviator Jacques Balsan, who had been at the Duc de Gramont's ball in 1894 where Consuelo had made her French debut. Since Consuelo now wanted to remarry and Sunny had long been in a relationship with the American Gladys

Deacon, the Marlboroughs finally divorced on 13 May 1921. Sunny married Gladys on 25 June 1921, and Consuelo and Jacques followed just over a week later on 4 July. Consuelo then left behind England, the country that had provided her with so much purpose and heartache, where she had arrived a young woman of eighteen charged with the responsibilities of a duchess, and departed for France and a new life.

However, before long it became clear that Jacques's family, who were staunch Catholics, would not recognise his marriage to a divorcee. Sunny, too, had developed an interest in converting to Catholicism and so, five years after their divorce, they applied to the Pope to annul their marriage on the grounds of coercion. The Rota, comprising members of the Church who would decide on whether the annulment application would be successful, heard testimony from several people, but the star witness was Alva. Knowing that the whole episode would be widely and unflatteringly reported in the press, she finally atoned for her scheming thirty years earlier and stated for the Rota: 'I forced my daughter to marry the Duke... I have always had absolute power over my daughter... I, therefore, did not beg, but ordered her to marry the Duke... She was very much upset... I considered myself justified in overriding her opposition.'[19] After such a dramatic testimony, which would forever vilify Alva, the annulment was duly granted.

Consuelo moved back to America in 1940 and divided her time between Florida and Long Island. She died on 6 December 1964 at the age of eighty-seven and asked to be buried at Bladon in Oxfordshire, close to Blenheim Palace, a little corner of England that, for better or worse, had defined the course of her life.

Alva Vanderbilt married Oliver Belmont in January 1896, almost as soon as Consuelo was installed at Blenheim Palace. She found a kind of contentment with Oliver that had been lacking with Willie K and, although their relationship could often be tempestuous, they were well matched and genuinely happy. Her social rivalries continued but during the years of her second marriage, with a duchess for a daughter, she was firmly established as one of the most prominent leaders of society and seems to have concentrated her efforts on giving ever more lavish entertainments, as the Gilded Age hostesses continually strove to eclipse one another. Oliver's death on 10 June 1908 led Alva to re-evaluate her chosen course and, with her characteristic verve, she put all her energies and financial support into the fight for women's suffrage. Motivated as always by the challenge, she was a leading member of the National Woman's Party and worked tirelessly on the Nineteenth Amendment that granted women the vote in the United States in 1919.

When Alva died on 26 January 1933 of a stroke, with Consuelo by her side, the only possible place for her funeral to take place was St Thomas Church, where so many of the defining moments of her life had unfolded. Female pallbearers carried her coffin draped with an old suffrage banner that read 'Failure is impossible'. For the girl from Alabama who had taken on the establishment and risen to the very top of the American aristocracy, it was a fitting tribute.

Maud Cunard (née Burke) arrived at Cunard's country estate only for her husband to be told by an elderly family friend to 'take her away!'. The bleak grey stone of Nevill Holt through the autumn and winter months that Cunard adored for the hunting and racing opportunities was not what Maud had envisaged when she had imagined her life as a lady of the aristocracy. Cunard's eccentricities and attempts at romance went unappreciated by his perky young wife. He adored tinkering around with metalwork in a tower above the gateway, which housed a workroom, and worked studiously on an ornamental gate with the words 'Come into the garden, Maud' (taken from the Tennyson poem and popular song) carefully crafted out of small horseshoes. Unsurprisingly, his plea went unheeded by Maud, who immersed herself in European literature and playing the piano. From March 1896, after producing a daughter, Nancy, who would grow up to become a notorious bohemian and have a fractious relationship with her mother, Maud took a number of lovers and then eventually fled Leicestershire and Cunard altogether in 1911 for the alluring and fashionable society of London, a place where she felt certain she could climb the social ladder.

There she embarked upon establishing a salon where she supported the arts and favoured intellectuals. Her love affair with Thomas Beecham and her consequent championing of the opera earned her the nickname the 'Duchess of Covent Garden' from Evelyn Waugh. She was loved or loathed in equal measure and divided society, with Diana Cooper referring to her as 'a jewelled bird uncaged' whereas Virginia Woolf labelled her a 'ridiculous little parakeet-faced woman'. Deciding one day that Maud was not a suitable name for a woman of her calibre, she changed it to Emerald, her favourite jewel, and was never again referred to as plain old Maud. Emerald was to become an influential society hostess and was popular with Edward VIII and his paramour Wallis Simpson. When the then Prince of Wales ascended the throne, she was confident that her friendship with the couple would ensure her place at court, possibly in the influential position of Mistress of the Robes. It was a shame for Emerald that she backed the wrong horse. When she heard of the abdication, she cried, 'How could he do this to me?'[20]. Afterwards, she was ostracised by the more conservative George VI, who cared little for Americans. Emerald died of pleurisy at the Dorchester Hotel on 10 July 1948.

Mary Curzon (née Leiter) found herself quickly pregnant after her wedding to George Curzon, welcoming a daughter, Mary Irene, on 20 January 1896. She was followed by Cynthia Blanche in August 1898 and Alexandra Naldera in March 1904. Mary turned out to be everything George had hoped for. Consuelo Vanderbilt would comment that she 'had subordinated her personality to his to a degree I would have considered beyond an American woman's power of self-abnegation'[21]. George did prove to be every bit as controlling and domineering as his behaviour during their long courtship had suggested, but there is no evidence that Mary wasn't a willing participant in the mechanics of their marriage. When George was named as Lord Elgin's replacement as Viceroy of India in 1898, he was overjoyed, feeling that all his hard work and extensive travel in the East had finally paid off. Mary made the perfect Vicereine, the highest position other than the Queen in the British Empire. She performed her duties with aplomb and with the appropriate regal air, particularly during the prodigious Delhi Durbar to celebrate the accession of Edward VII that lasted two weeks, involved 150,000 people and a great deal of imperial pomp and ceremony. Her obvious popularity with the aristocracy and Indians alike was something that her pompous husband witnessed with increasing awe. He wrote, 'You are everything and the sole thing in the world and I go on existing in order to come back and try to make you happy.'[22] She had become his confidante, greatest friend and fiercest champion. However, her time in India and her third pregnancy left her health increasingly fragile. After suffering an illness in 1904 from which she would never really recover, she died prematurely of heart failure on 18 July 1906. George was devastated, writing to Jennie Churchill of his 'utter desolation'[23]. He would marry another American in 1917, Grace Duggan, but would never get over losing Mary and was buried next to her in the family vault at their Derbyshire seat, Kedleston.

The twice-widowed Lily, Duchess of Marlborough, finally found the happiness she craved third time around, with William Beresford. Many had speculated that Lily had married once for money, twice for a title and the third time for love, and, given the path that her marriages navigated, it seems likely that this was the case. At their country estate, Deepdene in Surrey, the Beresfords enjoyed a life together untroubled by financial problems or concerns about their place in society. They were popular and content and eventually, after years of trying without success with her previous husbands, Lily found herself pregnant at the age of forty-two and gave birth to a son, William Warren de la Poer Beresford, in February 1897. Their happiness was to be short-lived. William senior had a history of health problems after contracting dysentery during his years in India, which now recurred, causing him increasingly to take to his bed at Deepdene. On 28 December 1900, he contracted peritonitis and promptly died. In a horrible coincidence, Lily had lost her final husband after only five years, the same amount of time she was married to Louis Hamersley and to the 8th Duke of

Marlborough. She spent her final years at Deepdene, seldom seen in London, devoted to her son and with regular visits from friends like Consuelo Manchester and Winston Churchill, who never forgot the kindness Lily had shown him when his father, Randolph, died. On 11 January 1909, she died of heart failure. She was fifty-five years old.

After Pauline Whitney and Almeric Paget were married in November 1895 they travelled to the Continent, where they spent January on the French Riviera with Minnie. They lived in America until 1901, when they decided to make a permanent move to England, dividing their time between Suffolk and Berkeley Square in London. By this time the couple had one daughter, Olive Cecilia, born in 1899, and there was another daughter to follow in 1905, Dorothy Wyndham, named after Pauline's younger sister. Although the marriage had begun so promisingly, it soon became apparent that Pauline and Almeric weren't entirely suited. Pauline's continued ill health plagued the marriage and she spent long periods at health spas in an attempt to restore herself. Almeric leased Deepdene in 1911 after Lily Beresford's death, perhaps in the hope that the country air and spectacular display of rhododendrons and glasshouses of exotic flowers that Lily had favoured would lift Pauline's spirits. She eventually died on 22 November 1916. Almeric got his title when he was elevated to the peerage as Baron Queenborough. He embarked on another unhappy marriage to an American, Edith Starr Miller, in 1921, which ended in separation in 1932.

Another of the 1895 heiresses, Leonora Van Marter, gained the title of Countess of Tankerville in 1899 when her husband, George, succeeded to the earldom. Throughout their lives they were devoted to evangelicalism, the cause that had initially brought them together and which dominated their courtship. They held meetings in Northumberland, near the family seat of Chillingham Castle. Leonora had four children and generally shunned society for a simpler life in the country. George died in 1931, while Leonora lived until 15 February 1949.

Josephine Chamberlain's marriage to Thomas Talbot Scarisbrick was to produce two sons, Everard in 1896 and Ronald in 1899. Although tragedy would strike when Ronald died in 1900, the Scarisbrick's appear to have had a happy marriage. Thomas Talbot was made Baron Scarisbrick in 1909.

American Cara Rogers, who had also married towards the end of 1895, continued to live in America with her husband, Urban, until 1912, when they took their two sons to live in England. Like her father, she retained a keen interest in philanthropy and donated land to the town of Fairhaven, Massachusetts for the purpose of creating a park. Her marriage to Urban was a genuinely happy one and when he died in 1929 and was posthumously created Baron Fairhaven, the new Lady Fairhaven donated Runnymede, the site of the signing of the Magna Carta, to the National Trust in his memory. Cara died in March 1939.

Elizabeth La Roche appears to have led a long and quiet life in England with Sir Howland Roberts. Very little is known about the two and Elizabeth seems to have made no impression on the English aristocracy, although they did travel regularly between England and America, and had two sons. She died on 11 April 1949.

The great Mrs Astor died in 1908 at the age of seventy-eight, after years of decline and failing memory following a fall down her famous marble staircase. The once all-powerful queen of New York society took to planning menus and discussing guest lists with her loyal and devoted servants for imaginary balls and dinners. After a lifetime of hosting New York's elite in her vast mansion, she wandered its opulent rooms, carefully organising the most prestigious occasions of a faraway New York Season right until the very end. A ten-thousand-strong crowd of New Yorkers gathered in the cold outside her iconic residence on Fifth Avenue on the day of her funeral to pay their respects to a legend.

The impression that American heiresses left on the aristocracy was long and enduring. Today, their influence and their dollars can still be felt in many stately homes around Great Britain, although others, such as Deepdene in Surrey, no longer exist, having made way for urban expansion after the Second World War. It is certainly true that great palaces such as Blenheim would not have survived in the regal splendour that greets visitors now if it hadn't been for the timely injection of American cash that Lily and Consuelo brought with them. Sites like Runnymede, donated by Cara Rogers, were also safeguarded for future generations by American money. Indeed, the dowries that accompanied many of the heiresses across the Atlantic saved several aristocratic families from bankruptcy in a time when the accepted order of patrician influence was being challenged by the advent of the industrial age. The 1895 heiresses were a product of industrialisation, their new money generally derived from the spoils that rapid expansion after the American Civil War provided, yet in England they sought to provide an answer to the problems that industrialisation caused for the aristocracy. For a price, of course.

That price was a title, which equalled social acceptance, something that in their own country had evaded them. The parvenus who had enormous financial resources at their fingertips discovered that their wealth wasn't quite enough when it came to the close scrutiny of their heritage to which they were subjected by Mrs Astor, Ward McAllister and the rest of The Four Hundred. In England they found a floundering aristocracy and a bored heir to the throne more welcoming and willing to overlook their questionable background. That's not to say that the heiresses found their path to a title or the marriage thereafter easy. In some cases the journey was fraught with complications and one social mis-step could see promising debutantes banished to the sidelines. That was why many turned to women experienced in the art of society to help them forge a way forward. Ladies, like Minnie Paget, who had a wealth of resources, the intelligence and the guile, and crucially were American, so understood the complexities of both societies, were primed and ready to assist and benefit from the heiresses' predicament.

The introduction of these women changed the appearance of the British aristocracy and its behaviour immeasurably. The fun and frivolity that characterised the American upper classes throughout the

Gilded Age now extended over the pond to Great Britain, and those stalwarts of the nobility who had entertained their guests conservatively and prudently before soon found that their efforts were no longer good enough to attract the most desirable guests. Not everyone agreed that the vitality, extravagance and direct challenge to the conservative status that the heiresses introduced was for the better. 'Take away their millions from Americans and how much would one hear of them in the great world? They might have made London society brighter, but they have also made it shallower, more extravagant and more vulgar than it was before,'[24] wrote 'Colonial' in the *Contemporary Review*. However, there is no doubt that these American invaders made English society more open, cosmopolitan and interesting than it had been.

It was the end of the Victorian period and the Edwardian era that saw the social phenomenon of transatlantic marriages. In total over one hundred heiresses married into the aristocracy, with 1895 the year that the trend reached its peak. There are several explanations for this, stemming from the time that had elapsed between the making of vast fortunes by the original Swells, like the ambitious workaholic Commodore Vanderbilt, to the leisure generation of their grandchildren and great-grandchildren, who were by now accustomed to their wealth and demanded a position in society commensurate with their money. It was also more than twenty years since the original buccaneers, Consuelo Manchester, Jennie Churchill and Minnie Paget, had made their journey to England and taken society by storm. They had made their mistakes, yet risen through the ranks to become influential society leaders and now extended an experienced hand to the daughters of friends and contacts who wished to replicate their success. These buccaneers were also now in a position to earn their own income, so had a financial motivation for encouraging the practice. Furthermore, the role of the Prince of Wales in the admittance of Americans into British society cannot be overstated. His penchant for American ladies and his obvious predilection for their company was noted and copied by wider society. And finally, while much of the aristocracy had been suffering from reduced incomes for some years, by the 1890s the financial pressures that had thus far been absorbed finally began to catch up on those with large estates and extended families to support. Faced with the unrelenting pace of social change bearing down upon them, there was little choice but to evolve or perish. One of the options available to unmarried male heirs was to eschew an English bride for an American one, who could provide the estate with a much-needed financial boost.

Whether it was the heiresses themselves or, in Consuelo Vanderbilt's case, her mother who had desired a title, the life that they had imagined for themselves as part of the aristocracy did not always live up to the ideal. Many were trapped in loveless marriages, in cold and ancient houses that bore no resemblance to the palatial mansions they had left at home. They found the complicated social etiquette difficult to master and made countless mistakes as mistresses of their estates, where an experienced butler who had served the family for years could with a single remark make them feel out of place and irrelevant, and delighted in doing so. However, England did offer them the opportunity to play a more active role in social and political affairs, whether that was through politics, philanthropy or discreet commercial enterprises, and the easy morality applied to married aristocratic women afforded them the chance to experience genuine love and affection. Whether the sacrifices were worth it is difficult to ascertain.

Many of the heiresses' personal recollections of the period do not survive, so biographers are forced to piece together the fragments of their lives like a hazy jigsaw puzzle. Even personal accounts such as Consuelo Vanderbilt's are undoubtedly coloured by her own point of view and feelings towards persons involved and, when written so many years after events, can prove unreliable as source material. As was so typical of Minnie Paget, she left very little evidence of her activities arranging Anglo-American marriages, knowing the sensitivity of such information. Resolutely careful and discreet to the very end, these women largely left it to others, through memoirs and contemporary press reports, to provide the evidence of this lucrative sideline.

Indeed, it was a feature of the period for instructions to be left for any potentially scandalous personal papers to be destroyed after death, and in many instances theses wishes were meticulously carried out.

The question remains as to why Anglo-American marriages began to decline in popularity. Even in 1895 there were dissenting voices which called into question the merits of such matches. The press variously alternated between extolling their romance and highlighting the blatant transaction of cash for titles that lay at the heart of many of them. Marriages like Consuelo Manchester's had already proved to be disastrous and the image of a sacrificial American debutante rendered desperately unhappy by a rakish and bankrupt English aristocrat added to their unpopularity. There was also the matter of vast amounts of American dollars leaving the country to prop up the English economy. The United States began to find its feet on the world stage and was no longer a country unsure of its national identity in the wake of the Civil War. It was a burgeoning superpower whose plutocrats no longer needed the respectability and stature that an English title brought. The decline of the British Empire was beginning, while America's star was on the rise. As was probably to be expected, ambitious mothers looked increasingly at the opportunities for their daughters available on their own shores.

For Minnie Paget and the crop of heiresses that made England their home at the end of the nineteenth century, life securing a transatlantic marriage and its consequences were complex and not always happy. However, very few of the heiresses returned to the land of their birth and, despite the challenges, they seemed to relish the life they built for themselves in their new country. Minnie understood more than most that the future she was offering the heiresses who walked through her door at Belgrave Square was rarely straightforward and would present many twists and turns, which only the most industrious and tenacious would navigate successfully. Judging by the legacy they left behind, it seems the pleasure and the pain of life as a buccaneer was worth it.

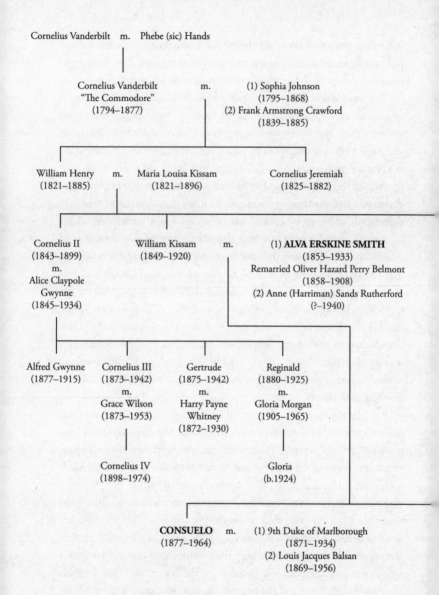

Cornelius Vanderbilt   m.   Phebe (sic) Hands

Cornelius Vanderbilt
"The Commodore"
(1794–1877)
m.
(1) Sophia Johnson
(1795–1868)
(2) Frank Armstrong Crawford
(1839–1885)

William Henry   m.   Maria Louisa Kissam
(1821–1885)   (1821–1896)

Cornelius Jeremiah
(1825–1882)

Cornelius II
(1843–1899)
m.
Alice Claypole
Gwynne
(1845–1934)

William Kissam   m.
(1849–1920)

(1) **ALVA ERSKINE SMITH**
(1853–1933)
Remarried Oliver Hazard Perry Belmont
(1858–1908)
(2) Anne (Harriman) Sands Rutherford
(?–1940)

Alfred Gwynne
(1877–1915)

Cornelius III
(1873–1942)
m.
Grace Wilson
(1873–1953)

Gertrude
(1875–1942)
m.
Harry Payne
Whitney
(1872–1930)

Reginald
(1880–1925)
m.
Gloria Morgan
(1905–1965)

Cornelius IV
(1898–1974)

Gloria
(b.1924)

CONSUELO   m.   (1) 9th Duke of Marlborough
(1877–1964)   (1871–1934)
(2) Louis Jacques Balsan
(1869–1956)

Select Vanderbilt Family Tree

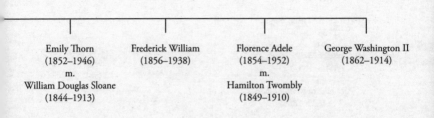

Emily Thorn
(1852–1946)
m.
William Douglas Sloane
(1844–1913)

Frederick William
(1856–1938)

Florence Adele
(1854–1952)
m.
Hamilton Twombly
(1849–1910)

George Washington II
(1862–1914)

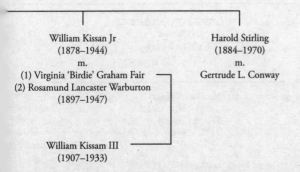

William Kissan Jr
(1878–1944)
m.
(1) Virginia 'Birdie' Graham Fair
(2) Rosamund Lancaster Warburton
(1897–1947)

Harold Stirling
(1884–1970)
m.
Gertrude L. Conway

William Kissam III
(1907–1933)

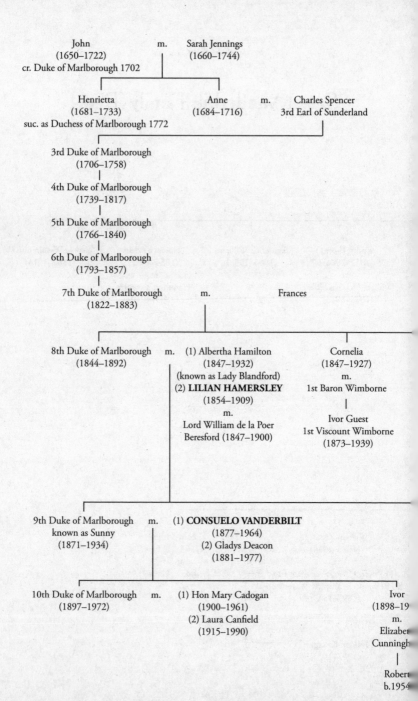

John
(1650–1722)
cr. Duke of Marlborough 1702

m.

Sarah Jennings
(1660–1744)

Henrietta
(1681–1733)
suc. as Duchess of Marlborough 1772

Anne
(1684–1716)

m.

Charles Spencer
3rd Earl of Sunderland

3rd Duke of Marlborough
(1706–1758)

4th Duke of Marlborough
(1739–1817)

5th Duke of Marlborough
(1766–1840)

6th Duke of Marlborough
(1793–1857)

7th Duke of Marlborough
(1822–1883)

m.

Frances

8th Duke of Marlborough
(1844–1892)

m.

(1) Albertha Hamilton
(1847–1932)
(known as Lady Blandford)
(2) **LILIAN HAMERSLEY**
(1854–1909)
m.
Lord William de la Poer
Beresford (1847–1900)

Cornelia
(1847–1927)
m.
1st Baron Wimborne

Ivor Guest
1st Viscount Wimborne
(1873–1939)

9th Duke of Marlborough
known as Sunny
(1871–1934)

m.

(1) **CONSUELO VANDERBILT**
(1877–1964)
(2) Gladys Deacon
(1881–1977)

10th Duke of Marlborough
(1897–1972)

m.

(1) Hon Mary Cadogan
(1900–1961)
(2) Laura Canfield
(1915–1990)

Ivor
(1898–19
m.
Elizabet
Cunningh

Robert
b.1954

APPENDIX 2

Select Marlborough Family Tree

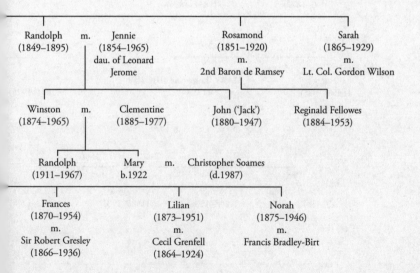

Randolph (1849–1895) m. Jennie (1854–1965) dau. of Leonard Jerome

Rosamond (1851–1920) m. 2nd Baron de Ramsey

Sarah (1865–1929) m. Lt. Col. Gordon Wilson

Winston (1874–1965) m. Clementine (1885–1977)

John ('Jack') (1880–1947)

Reginald Fellowes (1884–1953)

Randolph (1911–1967)

Mary b.1922 m. Christopher Soames (d.1987)

Frances (1870–1954) m. Sir Robert Gresley (1866–1936)

Lilian (1873–1951) m. Cecil Grenfell (1864–1924)

Norah (1875–1946) m. Francis Bradley-Birt

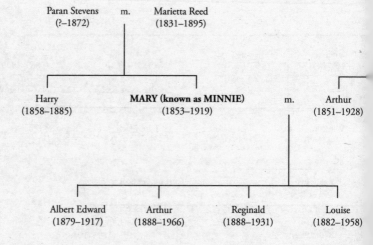

Paran Stevens   m.   Marietta Reed
(?–1872)   (1831–1895)

Harry   **MARY (known as MINNIE)**   m.   Arthur
(1858–1885)   (1853–1919)   (1851–1928)

Albert Edward   Arthur   Reginald   Louise
(1879–1917)   (1888–1966)   (1888–1931)   (1882–1958)

Select Paget Family Tree

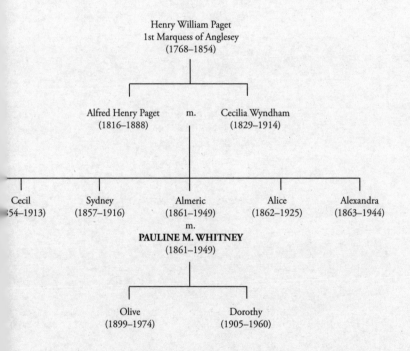

Henry William Paget
1st Marquess of Anglesey
(1768–1854)

Alfred Henry Paget   m.   Cecilia Wyndham
(1816–1888)   (1829–1914)

Cecil	Sydney	Almeric	Alice	Alexandra
(1854–1913)	(1857–1916)	(1861–1949)	(1862–1925)	(1863–1944)

m.
PAULINE M. WHITNEY
(1861–1949)

Olive   Dorothy
(1899–1974)   (1905–1960)

Notes

1   *Personal Letters of Edward VII*, Sewell, p.64

PROLOGUE
1   *Alva Vanderbilt Belmont*, Hoffert, p.45
2   Cited in *Gilded Prostitution*, Montgomery, p.144
3   Cited in *Gilded Prostitution*, Montgomery, p.137
4   *Titled Americans*, p.253
5   *Harper's Bazaar*, July 1905
6   *Harper's Bazaar*, July 1905
7   *The Buccaneers*, Wharton, p.83
8   *The Glitter and the Gold*, Balsan, p.32
9   *Harper's Magazine*, November 1908
10   *Harper's Magazine*, November 1908
11   *The Buccaneers*, Wharton, p.82
12   *The Buccaneers*, Wharton, p.82
13   *The New York Times*, 7 November 1895
14   *The Glitter and the Gold*, Balsan, p.32
15   *Chicago Tribune*, 21 July 1891

CHAPTER 1: SOCIETY GATHERS
1   *New York Tribune* cited in *They All Married Well*, Elizabeth Eliot, p.85
2   *Things I Remember*, Martin, p.63
3   *Things I Remember*, Martin, p.63
4   *Incredible New York*, Morris, p.142
5   *Incredible New York*, Morris, p.142
6   *Things I Remember*, Martin, p.65
7   *Things I Remember*, Martin, p.63
8   *Diary of a Union Lady*, Daly, p.320
9   Charles P. Daly Papers, Maria Lydig Daly journal entry, 15 February 1866
10   *The Best Circles*, Davidoff, p.63
11   *Society As I Have Found It*, McAllister, p.245
12   *The New York Times*, 16 December 1894

CHAPTER 2: THE ART OF DISCRETION
1   *Society As I Have Found It*, McAllister, p.214
2   *Society As I Have Found It*, McAllister, p.215.
3   *King Lehr*, Drexel Lehr, p.11–12
4   Ward McAllister cited in *Season of Splendor*, King, p.116
5   *Society As I Have Found It*, Ward McAllister, p.223
6   *King Lehr and the Gilded Age*, Drexel Lehr, p.84
7   *Society as I Have Found It*, McAllister, p.127

8   *King Lehr and the Gilded Age,* Drexel Lehr, p.87

9   *King Lehr and the Gilded Age,* Drexel Lehr, p.87

10   *New York Tribune,* 24 March 1888

11   *The New York Times,* 14 January 1894

12   *The New York Times,* 14 January 1894

13   *The New York Times,* 1 February 1895

14   *Fabric of Memory,* Belmont, p.85

15   *The New York Times,* 4 November 1894

16   *The New York Times,* 2 December 1894

17   *The New York Times,* 2 December 1894

CHAPTER 3: FORTUNE
FAVOURS THE BRAVE

1   *New York World,* 16 January 1895

2   Cited in *Alva Vanderbilt Belmont,* Hoffert, p.5

3   Cited in *Consuelo and Alva,* MacKenzie Stuart, p.40

4   *Fortune's Children,* Arthur T Vanderbilt, p.87

5   Cited in *Consuelo and Alva,* MacKenzie Stuart, p.19

6   *Fortune's Children,* Arthur T Vanderbilt, p.87

7   *Gilded,* Davis, p.80

CHAPTER 4: THE
YOUNG PRETENDER

1   Cited in *Consuelo and Alva,* MacKenzie Stuart, p.105

2   *Consuelo and Alva,* MacKenzie Stuart, p.57

3   *Consuelo and Alva,* MacKenzie Stuart, p.57

4   Cited in *A Season of Splendor,* King, p.153

5   Cited in *A Season of Splendor,* King, p.130

6   Three million dollars was around seventy five million dollars in 2015

7   *The Vanderbilts and the Story of their Fortune,* Croffut, p.194

8   *The New York Times,* 27 March 1883

9   Cited in *Consuelo and Alva,* MacKenzie Stuart, p.62

10   *The New York Times,* 27 March 1883

11   *The New York Times,* 27 March 1883

12   *The New York Times,* 27 March 1883

13   *King Lehr and the Gilded Age,* Drexel Lehr, p.69

14   Cited in *Incredible New York,* Morris, p.253

CHAPTER 5: BERTIE'S WHIMS

1   *Harper's Magazine,* November 1908

2   *Town Topics,* 25 July 1895

3   *Vanity Fair,* 6 July 1905

4   *Harper's Magazine,* November 1908

5   *Society in London* cited in *Gilded Prostitution,* Montgomery, p.22

6   Cited in *The Rise of the Plutocrats,* Caplin, p.180

7   Cited in *A Season of Splendor,* King, p.378

8   *Personal Letters of Edward VII,* Sewell, p.63

9   *The Washington Times,* 6 March 1904

10   *The House of Mirth,* Wharton, p.39

11   *The Decline and Fall of the British Aristocracy,* Cannadine, p.347

12   *Free Opinions, Freely Expressed,* Corelli, p.100

13   *Morning Post,* 2 February 1895

14   *Town Topics,* 31 May 1894

CHAPTER 6: PROTÉGÉS AND PLANS

1   Cited in *They All Married Well,* Eliot, p.207

2   Cited in *They All Married Well,* Eliot, p.207

3   *Cosmopolitan,* 1904,

4   *Things I Remember,* Martin, p.179

5   *Harper's Magazine,* November 1908

6   *The Evening Telegram,* 19 March 1895

7   Cited in *They all Married Well,* Eliot, p.206

CHAPTER 7: AN
IMPASSIONED PROPOSAL

1   Cited in *Consuelo and Alva,* MacKenzie Stuart, p.43

2   *The Age of Innocence,* Wharton, p.34

3   *The Glitter and the Gold,* Balsan, p. 34

4   *My Candid Recollections,* Manchester, p.87

5   *The Vanderbilt Women,* Stasz, p.166

6   *The New York Times,* 23 July 1920

7   Cited in *Consuelo,* Brough, p. 58

8   *The Glitter and the Gold,* Balsan, p.35
9   Cited in *Consuelo and Alva,*
     MacKenzie Stuart, p.152
10   *The Glitter and the Gold,* Balsan, p.35
11   *The Glitter and the Gold,* Balsan, p.35

CHAPTER 8: A MOST
SUPERIOR PERSON

1   *The Realm,* 8 March 1895
2   *Town Topics,* March 1895
3   Cited in *Mary Curzon,* Nicholson, p.62
4   Cited in *Informal Ambassadors,*
     Cooper, p.94
5   *Famous American Belles of the
     19th Century,* Peacock, p.270
6   *Mary Curzon,* Nicolson, p.28
7   *Romantic Adventure,* Elinor Glyn, p.51
8   *Mary Curzon,* Nicolson, p.37
9   *Mary Curzon,* Nicolson, p.37
10   *Sheffield Daily Telegraph,* 11 July 1890
11   *Mary Curzon,* Nicolson, p.38
12   *Curzon,* Gilmour, p.100
13   Cited in *Curzon,* Gilmour, p.109
14   *Mary Curzon,* Nicolson, p.40
15   Cited in *Curzon,* Gilmour, p.107
16   *Chicago Daily Tribune,* 26 May 1891
17   *To Marry an English Lord,*
     MacColl/Wallace, p.115
18   Cited in *To Marry an English
     Lord,* MacColl/Wallace, p.114
19   Cited in *Curzon,* Gilmour, p. 113
20   *American Belles of the 19th
     Century,* Peacock, p.266
21   *Titled Americans,* p.254

CHAPTER 9: FAITH,
FIGURES AND FRANCS

1   *The Times,* 12 March 1895
2   *Town Topics,* 14 March 1895
3   Cited in *Age of Worth,* Saunders, p.182
4   *Age of Worth,* Saunders, p.194
5   *Harper's Magazine* cited in *Gilded
     Prostitution,* Montgomery, p.142
6    $20,000 is around $500,000
     in today's money
7   *The Glitter and the Gold,*
     Balsan, p.31–32
8   *The Glitter and the Gold,* Balsan, p.32
9   *The Glitter and the Gold,* Balsan, p.32
10   *Romantic Adventure,* Glyn, p.208

11   Cited in *Consuelo,* Brough, p.65
12   *The Glitter and the Gold,* Balsan, p.33
13   Cited in *Lily, Duchess of
     Marlborough,* Svenson, p.229
14   *The Glitter and the Gold,* Balsan, p.35
15   *The Glitter and the Gold,* Balsan, p.35
16   *The Glitter and the Gold,* Balsan, p.35

CHAPTER 10: ROGUEY
POGUEY STORIES

1   *Things I Remember,* Martin, p.181
2   Letter from Jennie Jerome to
     Lord Randolph Churchill,
     March 1874, Churchill Archives,
     CHAR 28/94/106-108
3   *The New York Times,* 7 August 1907
4   *Strange to Say,* Mrs Carter H
     Harrison cited in *Plantation Life on
     the Mississippi,* Clement, p.132
5   Duke of Manchester diary entries cited
     in *In a Gilded Cage,* Fowler, p.16
6   *The New York Times,* 23 May 1876
7   *Free Opinions Freely Expressed,*
     Corelli, p.119
8   Cited in *In a Gilded Cage,* Fowler, p.27
9   Cited in *In a Gilded Cage,* Fowler, p.25
10   *Affair of State,* Vane, p.101
11   *The Days I Knew,* Langtry, p.50
12   *Dundee Evening Telegraph,* 8 July 1878
13   *Queen Victoria's Journal,* Vol
     75, 7 October 1881, p.77
14   Cited in *In a Gilded Cage,* Fowler, p.32
15   Cited in *They All Married
     Well,* Eliot, p.90
16   *Things I Remember,* Martin, p.181
17   Letter from Consuelo Manchester
     to Kim, undated, Manchester
     Collection, M2/114/14
18   Letter from Consuelo Manchester to
     Kim, 25 December 1886,
     Manchester Collection, MII/114
19   *Cincinnati Enquirer,* 23 March 1890
20   Cited in *Affair of State,* Vane, p.186
21   *My Candid Recollections,*
     Manchester, p.26
22   *Town Topics,* 21 March 1895
23   *Town Topics,* 21 March 1895
24   *Town Topics,* 11 April 1895
25   *Town Topics,* 12 July 1894
26   Cited in *Consuelo and Alva,*
     MacKenzie Stuart, p.109

27   Cited in *Consuelo and Alva*,
     MacKenzie Stuart, p.109

CHAPTER 11: THE
CHANGING GUARD
1   Around two million dollars
     in today's money
2   *The New York Times*, 2 April 1895
3   *The New York Times*, 28 March 1895
4   *The New York Times*, 22
     November 1891
5   *The New York Times*, 22
     November 1891
6   *Town Topics*, 1 February 1894
7   *Sunday Herald*, 27 July 1890
8   *The Age of Innocence*, Wharton, p.60
9   *The New York Times*, 21 June 1885
10   Cited in *Edith Wharton*,
     Auchincloss, p.44
11   Cited in *No Gifts from
     Chance*, Benstock, p.46
12   *Romantic Adventure*, Hardwick, p.56
13   *Romantic Adventure*, Hardwick, p.56
14   *Things I Remember*, Martin, p.228

CHAPTER 12: LOVE IS BOURGEOIS
1   Cited in *Great Hostesses*, Masters, p.109
2   *New York Herald*, 18 April 1895
3   *Town Topics*, April 1895
4   *The Title-Mart*, Churchill, Act Three
5   Cited in *Emerald and
     Nancy*, Fielding, p.6
6   Cited in *Emerald and
     Nancy*, Fielding, p.2
7   *Emerald and Nancy*, Fielding, p.2
8   *Great Hostesses*, Masters, p.112
9   Two million dollars is around fifty
     eight million dollars in today's money
10   *Emerald and Nancy*, Fielding, p.1
11   *Great Hostesses*, Masters, p.113
12   *Letters*, Moore, p.13
13   *Town Topics*, 28 June 1894
14   *Letters*, Moore, p.34
15   *Things I Remember*, Martin, p.175

CHAPTER 13: A RARE
MISCALCULATION
1   *Personal Letters of Edward
     VII*, Sewell, p.31

2   *Personal Letters of Edward
     VII*, Sewell, p.57
3   *Things I Remember*, Martin, p.175
4   *Things I Remember*, Martin, p.175
5   *Free Opinions Freely Expressed*,
     Corelli, p.122
6   *They all Married Well*, Eliot, p.88
7   *They all Married Well*, Eliot, p.88
8   Paget Papers, Letter from
     Prince Leopold to Minnie,
     dated early Spring 1878
9   Paget papers, Letter from Prince
     Leopold to Minnie, 9 June 1878
10   *The House of Mirth*, Wharton, p.87
11   Cited in *Warren House
     Tales*, Good, p.103
12   Cited in *Things I Remember*,
     Martin, p.176
13   Paget Papers, Letter from Prince
     Leopold to Minnie, 7 June 1878
14   Cited in *Personal Letters of
     Edward VII*, Sewell, p.61
15   Paget Papers, Letter from Prince
     Leopold to Minnie, 21 June 1878
16   Paget papers, Letter from Prince
     Leopold to Minnie, Undated but
     written between 1878-1882
17   *The New York Times*, 30 July 1878
18   *The New York Times*, 30 July 1878
19   *Harper's Magazine*, November 1908
20   *Them and Us*, Jennings, p.44

CHAPTER 14: LILY OF TROY
1   Letter from Winston Churchill
     to Lady Randolph Churchill, 2
     May 1895, Churchill Archives,
     CHAR 28/21/31-33
2   *Lord William Beresford*, Menzies,
     p.vi of Introduction
3   *Lord William Beresford*, Menzies,
     p.vii of Introduction
4   Cited in *In a Gilded Cage*, Fowler, p.77
5   *The Brooklyn Eagle*, 6 May 1888
6   *The Title Mart*, Act 1
7   Cited in *The Churchills: In Love
     and War*, Lovell, p.103
8   Cited in *Lily, Duchess of
     Marlborough*, Svenson, p.99
9   *Cosmopolitan*, September 1890
10   Cited in *To Marry an English
     Lord*, MacColl/Wallace, p.130

11   Cited in *Them and Us*, Jennings, p.52
12   Cited in *Them and Us*, Jennings, p.90

CHAPTER 15: TO CONQUER
THE SEASON
1   *My Candid Recollections*,
    Manchester, p.75
2   *Queen Alexandra*, Trowbridge, p.199
3   *The Buccaneers*, Wharton, p.256
4   Cited in *The Best Circles*, Davidoff, p.54
5   Cited in *They All Married
    Well*, Eliot, p.94
6   Cited in *The Best Circles*, Davidoff, p.63
7   *The Best Circles*, Davidoff, p.50
8   *Harper's Magazine*, November 1908

CHAPTER 16: THE
INTRODUCTIONS MARKET
1   £95,000 in 1895 is around ten
    million pounds in today's money
2   Two thousand pounds in 1895 is
    around £200,000 in today's money
3   *St Louis Post*, 6 May 1888
4   *San Francisco Chronicle*, 15 March 1890
5   *New York World*, 16 March 1890
6   *In a Gilded Cage*, Fowler, p.40-41
7   *Bertie*, Ridley, p.268
8   *Affair of State*, Vane, p.188
9   Cited in *In a Gilded Cage*, Fowler, p.65
10 Cited in *In a Gilded Cage*, Fowler, p.47
11 *The Buccaneers*, Wharton, p.251

CHAPTER 17: MASTERS
OF MANIPULATION
1   *The Glitter and the Gold*, Balsan, p. 38
2   *The Glitter and the Gold*, Balsan, p.38
3   *The Glitter and the Gold*, Balsan, p.39
4   Cited in *Old World, New
    World*, Burk, p.746
5   *The Rise of the Plutocrats*, Caplin, p.30
6   *The Vanderbilt Legend*, Andrews, p.286
7   *Harper's magazine*, November 1908
8   *The Dollar Princess*, Act 2,
9   *The Baltimore American*,
    11 March 1895

CHAPTER 18: THE PROMISE
OF ROMANCE
1   *Whitney Father, Whitney
    Heiress*, Swanberg, p.121
2   *Whitney Father, Whitney
    Heiress*, Swanberg, p.80
3   *Kansas City Star*, 9 August 1894
4   *Boston Herald*, 25 July 1895
5   Cited in *Whitney Father, Whitney
    Heiress*, Swanberg, p.123
6   Cited in *Whitney Father, Whitney
    Heiress*, Swanberg, p.124
7   *The Fabric of Memory*, Belmont, p.82
8   Cited in *Gilded City*, Davis, p.38
9   *King Lehr and the Gilded
    Age*, Drexel Lehr, p.113
10 Cited in *Great Hostesses*, Masters, p.63
11 Cited in *Gilded City*, Davis, p.51
12 *Town Topics*, 15 August 1895

CHAPTER 19: *BRITANNIA*
VERSUS *METEOR*
1   *Daily Telegraph*, 5 August 1895
2   *Daily Telegraph*, 5 August 1895
3   *The Times*, 7 August 1895
4   *The Times*, 7 August 1895
5   Cited in *Royalty and Diplomacy
    in Europe*, McLean, p.86
6   Cited in *Royalty and Diplomacy
    in Europe*, McLean, p.86
7   Cited in *Bertie*, Ridley, p.317
8   Cited in *Royalty and Diplomacy
    in Europe*, McLean, p.86
9   Cited in *Daisy, Princess
    of Pless*, Koch, p.49
10 Cited in *Gilded Prostitution*,
    Montgomery, p.77

CHAPTER 20: CONFRONTATION
1   Cited in *Great Hostesses*, Masters, p.62
2   Approximately $280 million
    in today's money
3   *Outres mer*, Bourget, p.45
4   *Town Topics*, 8 August 1895
5   *Town Topics*, 8 August 1895
6   *Town Topics*, 29 August 1895
7   *Town Topics*, 29 August 1895
8   *Town Topics*, 11 July 1895
9   *The Glitter and the Gold*, Balsan, p.39
10 *The Glitter and the Gold*, Balsan, p.39

11 *The Glitter and the Gold*, Balsan, p.40

12 *The Glitter and the Gold,* Balsan, p.40

CHAPTER 21: A
SECOND-CLASS DUKE

1   *Town Topics*, 7 November 1895

2   Cited in *Old World, New World*, Burk, p.529

3   220 million dollars in 1895 is around six billion dollars in today's money

4   *Washington Post*, 26 January 1908

5   Fifteen million dollars in 1895 is around 400 millions dollars in today's money

6   *Town Topics*, 7 November 1895

7   *Town Topics*, 5 September 1895

CHAPTER 22: POMP AND CEREMONY

1   *The Glitter and the Gold*, Balsan, p.45

2   *The Glitter and the Gold*, Balsan, p.45

3   *The New York Times*, 7 November, 1895

4   *The Glitter and the Gold*, Balsan, p.45

5   Cited in *Consuelo and Alva*, MacKenzie Stuart, p. 145

6   *The New York Times*, 7 November 1895

7   *The Times*, 7 November 1895

8   *World*, 7 November 1895

9   *World*, 7 November 1895

10 *World*, 7 November 1895

11 *The New York Times*, 7 November 1895

12 *The New York Times*, 7 November 1895

13 *The New York Times*, 7 November 1895

14 *The Glitter and the Gold*, Balsan, p.46

15 *The New York Times*, 25 November 1926

16 *The Glitter and the Gold*, Balsan, p.46

17 *World*, 7 November 1895

18 *The Times*, 7 November 1895

19 *The Times*, 7 November 1895

20 *The New York Times*, 7 November 1895

21 *The Glitter and the Gold*, Balsan, p.46

CHAPTER 23: THE
MARRIAGE BUSINESS

1   *Town Topics*, 10 May 1894

2   *New York World*, January 1904

3   *Things I Remember,* Martin, p.181

4   *Turn of the World*, Decies, p.252

5   *The New York Times,* 11 November 1894

6   *The New York Times*, 7 April 1907

EPILOGUE

1   *Things I Remember*, Martin, p.176

2   *Things I Remember,* Martin, p.176

3   *Things I Remember,* Martin, p.176

4   *The Sunday Herald*, 9 February 1896

5   One million dollars would be around 29 million dollars in today's money

6   Paget papers, Letter from Queen Alexandra to Minnie

7   Cited in *Edith Wharton*, Lee, p.724

8   *Indianapolis Star*, 24 August 1903

9   *Indianapolis Star*, 24 August 1903

10 *King Lehr and the Gilded Age*, Drexel Lehr, p.285

11 *King Lehr and the Gilded Age*, Drexel Lehr, p.286

12 Cited in *In a Gilded Cage*, Fowler, p.69

13 *The New York Times*, 7 August 1907

14 *The New York Times*, 7 August 1907

15 *The New York Times*, 7 August 1907

16 Montagu Family papers, Huntingdon Archives

17 *The Glitter and the Gold*, Balsan, p.158

18 Cited in *Consuelo and Alva*, MacKenzie Stuart, p.271

19 Cited in *Consuelo and Alva*, MacKenzie Stuart, p.420

20 Cited in *Emerald and Nancy*, Fielding, p.120

21 *The Glitter and the Gold*, Balsan, p.147

22 Cited in *The Marrying Americans*, Pearson, p.112

23 Letter from George Curzon to Lady Randolph Churchill, 21 July 1906, Churchill Archive, CHAR 28/78/46

24 Cited in *Harper's Magazine*, November 1908

Picture Credits

Index

Bibliography

PRINTED SOURCES

Books – Non-fiction

Amory, Cleveland. *Who Killed Society?* Harper and Brothers; New York, 1960

Anand, Sushila. *Daisy – The Life and Loves of the Countess of Warwick.* Piatkus; London, 2008

Andrews, Wayne. *The Vanderbilt Legend.* Harcourt, Brace and Company; New York, 1941

Auchincloss, Louis. *Edith Wharton – A Woman in her Time.* Michael Joseph; London, 1971

Auchincloss, Louis. *The Vanderbilt Era.* Charles Scribner's Sons; New York, 1989

Balsan, Consuelo Vanderbilt. *The Glitter and the Gold.* George Mann; London, 1973

Belmont, Eleanor Robson. *The Fabric of Memory.* Farrer, Straus and Cudahy; New York, 1957

Benstock, Shari. *No Gifts from Chance.* University of Texas Press; Austin, 2004

Biddle, Flora Miller. *The Whitney Women and the Museum They Made.* Arcade; New York, 1999

Bourget, Paul. *Outer-Mer – Impressions of America.* T Fisher Unwin; London, 1895

Brandon, Ruth. *The Dollar Princesses.* Alfred A Knopf Inc; New York, 1980

Brough, James. *Consuelo – Portrait of an American Heiress.* Coward, McCann and Geoghegan Inc; New York, 1979

Brough, James. *The Prince and the Lily.* Hodder and Stoughton; London, 1975

Burk, Kathleen. *Old World, New World – The Story of Britain and America.* Abacus; London, 2007

Cannadine, David. *The Decline and Fall of the British Aristocracy.* Yale University Press; New Haven, 1990

Caplin, Jamie. *The Rise of the Plutocrats.* Constable and Company; London, 1978

Chisholm, Anne. *Nancy Cunard.* Sidgwick and Jackson; London, 1979

Clement, William E. *Plantation Life on the Mississippi.* Pelican; New Orleans, 1952

Cooper, Dana. *Informal Ambassadors.* The Kent State University Press; Kent, Ohio,1977

Cornwallis-West, George. *Edwardian Hey-Days.* Putnam; London, 1930

Corelli, Marie. *Free Opinions, Freely Expressed on Certain Phases of Modern Social Life and Conduct.* Archibald, Constable and Co Ltd; London, 1905

Courcy, Anne de. *Society's Queen – The Life of Edith, Marchioness of Londonderry.* Phoenix; London, 1992

Courcy, Anne de. *The Viceroy's Daughters.* Orion Books; London, 2000

Cowles, Virginia. *Edward VII and his Circle.* Hamish Hamilton; London, 1956

Croffut, W A. *The Vanderbilts and the Story of their Fortune.* Belford, Clarke and Company; Chicago, 1886

Daly, Maria Lydig. *Diary of a Union Lady 1861–1865.* University of Nebraska Press; Lincoln, 2000

Davis, Deborah. *Gilded – How Newport Became America's Richest Resort.* John Wiley and Sons; Hoboken, 2009

Davidoff, Leonore. *The Best Circles – Society Etiquette and the Season.* Croom Helm; London, 1973

Decies, Elizabeth, Lady. *Turn of the World.* J B Lippincott; Philadelphia, 1937

Drexel Lehr, Elizabeth. *King Lehr and the Gilded Age.* Applewood Books; Bedford, 1935

Dunlop, M H. *Gilded City.* William Morrow; New York, 2000

Eliot, Elizabeth. *They All Married Well.* Cassell and Company; London. 1960

Escott, T H S. *Society in the Country House.* T Fisher Unwin; London, 1906

Fielding, Daphne. *The Duchess of Jermyn Street.* Eyre and Spottiswode; London, 1964

Fielding, Daphne. *Emerald and Nancy.* Eyre and Spottiswode; London, 1968

Fiske, Stephen. *Off-hand Portraits of Prominent New Yorkers.* Geo R Lockwood and Son; New York, 1884

Forster, Margaret Elizabeth. *Churchill's Grandmama.* The History Press; Stroud, 2010

Fowler, Marian. *In a Gilded Cage,*Vintage Books; Toronto, 1994

Gilmour, David. *Curzon.* John Murray; London, 1994

Gittelman, Steven H. *Willie K Vanderbilt II.* McFarland and Company; Jefferson, North Carolina, 2010

Glyn, Elinor. *Romantic Adventure.* Ivor Nicholson and Watson; London, 1934

Good, V K L. *The Warren House Tales.* Third Millennium Publishing; London, 2014

Hamilton, Elizabeth. *The Warwickshire Scandal.* Michael Russell; London, 1999

Hardwick, Joan. *Addicted to Romance, The Life and Adventures of Elinor Glyn.* Andre Deutsch; London, 1994

Hoffert, Sylvia D. *Alva Vanderbilt Belmont.* Indiana University Press; Bloomington, 2012

Homberger, Eric. *Mrs Astor's New York.* Yale University Press; New Haven, 2002

Homberger, Eric. *New York City.* Signal Books; Oxford, 2002

Homberger, Eric (introduction by). *Titled Americans – The Real Heiresses' Guide to Marrying an Aristocrat*. Old House; Oxford. 2013

Howarth, Patrick. *When the Riviera Was Ours*. Routledge and Kegan Paul; London, 1977

Hubert, Christopher. *Edward VII*. Allen Lane; London, 1976

Jennings, Charles. *Them and Us, The American Invasion of British High Society*. Sutton Publishing; Stroud, 2007

Kehoe, Elisabeth. *Fortune's Daughters*. Atlantic; London, 2005

Kennedy, A L (ed). *My Dear Duchess – Social and Political Letters to the Duchess of Manchester 1858–1869*. John Murray; London, 1956

King, Greg. *A Season of Splendor*. John Wiley and Sons; Hoboken, 2009

Langtry, Lillie. *The Days I Knew*. Redberry Press; St John, 1989

Lee, Hermione. *Edith Wharton*. Chatto and Windus; London, 2007

Leslie, Anita. *Edwardians in Love*. Hutchinson; London, 1972

Lewis, Alfred Allan. *Ladies and Not-So-Gentle Women*. Penguin; New York, 2000

Lovell, Mary S. *The Churchills – In Love and War*. W W Norton and Company; New York, 2011

MacColl, Gail and Wallace, Carol McD. *To Marry an English Lord*. Workman Publishing; New York, 2012

MacKenzie Stuart, Amanda. *Consuelo and Alva*. Harper Perennial; London, 2006

Magnus, Philip. *King Edward the Seventh*. John Murray; London, 1964

Manchester, Duke of. *My Candid Recollections*. Grayson and Grayson; London, 1932

Manchester, William. *The Last Lion – Winston Spencer Churchill, Visions of Glory, 1874–1932*. Little Brown and Company; New York, 1983

Martin, Frederick Townsend. *Things I Remember*. Eveleigh Nash; London, 1913

Martin, Ralph G. *Lady Randolph Churchill*. Cassell and Company; London, 1969

Masters, Brian. *Great Hostesses*. Constable and Company; London, 1982

Matthews, Joseph J. *George W. Smalley – Forty Years a Foreign Correspondent*. The University of North Carolina Press; Chapel Hill, 1973

McAllister, Ward. *Society as I Have Found It*. Cassell Publishing; New York, 1890

McAuliffe, Mary. *Dawn of the Belle Epoque*. Rowman and Littlefield; Lanham, 2014

McLean, Roderick R. *Royalty and Diplomacy in Europe*. Cambridge University Press; New York, 2007

Menzies, Mrs Stuart. *Lord William Beresford V C*. Herbert Jenkins Ltd; London, 1917

Milne-Smith, A. *London Clubland – A Cultural History of Gender and Class in late-Victorian Britain*. Palgrave Macmillan; New York, 2011

Montgomery, Maureen. *Gilded Prostitution*. Routledge; London, 1989

Moore, George. *Letters to Lady Cunard*. Rupert Hart-Davis; London, 1957

Morris, Lloyd. *Incredible New York*. Syracuse University Press; New York, 1996

Mowat, R W. *Americans in England*. George G Harrap and Co Ltd; London, 1935

Murphy, Sophia. *The Duchess of Devonshire's Ball*. Sidgwick and Jackson Ltd; London, 1984

Nevill, Ralph. *London Clubs*. Chatto & Windus; London, 1911

Nevill, Ralph (ed). *The Reminiscences of Lady Dorothy Nevill*. Edward Arnold; London, 1906

Neville, Amelia Ransome. *The Fantastic City*. Houghton Mifflin Company; Boston, 1932

Nicolson, Nigel. *Mary Curzon*. Phoenix; London, 1977

Peacock, Virginia. *Famous American Belles of the Nineteenth Century*. Books for Libraries Press; New York, 1900

Pearson, Hesketh. *The Marrying Americans*. Coward McCann Inc; New York, 1961

Pullar, Philippa. *Gilded Butterflies – The Rise and Fall of the London Season*. Hamish Hamilton; London, 1978

Reid, Wemyss. *Memoirs and Correspondence of Lyon Playfair*. Harper and Brothers; New York, 1899

Ridley, Jane. *Bertie – A Life of Edward VII*. Vintage Books; London, 2013

Robinson, John Martin. *Felling the Ancient Oaks*. Aurum Press; London, 2011

Rosslyn, Earl of. *My Gamble with Life*. Cassell and Company; London, 1928

Rudorff, Raymond. *Belle Epoque – Paris in the Nineties*. Hamilton; London, 1972

Saunders, Edith. *The Age of Worth*. Longmans, Green and Co Ltd; London, 1954

Sebba, Anne. *Jennie Churchill – Winston's American Mother*. John Murray; London, 2007

Sewell, J P C. *Personal Letters of King Edward VII*. Hutchinson and Co; London, 1931

Stasz, Clarice. *The Vanderbilt Women*. St Martin's Press; New York, 1991

Stuart, Denis. *Dear Duchess – Millicent Duchess of Sutherland 1867–1955*. Victor Gollancz Ltd; London, 1982

Swanberg, W A. *Whitney Father, Whitney Heiress*. Charles Scribner's Sons; New York, 1980

Svenson, Sally. *Lily, Duchess of Marlborough*. Dog Ear Publishing; Indianapolis, 2012

Trowbridge, W R H. *Queen Alexandra*, T Fisher Unwin; London, 1921

Twain, Mark and Dudley Warner, Charles. *The Gilded Age*. Chatto and Windus; London, 1885

Vanderbilt, Arthur T. *Fortune's Children – The Fall of the House of Vanderbilt*. William Morrow and Co; New York, 1989

Vanderbilt Jr, Cornelius. *Farewell to Fifth Avenue*. Simon and Schuster; New York, 1935

Vanderbilt Jr, Cornelius. *Queen of the Golden Age*. George Mann; Maidstone, 1999

Vane, Henry. *Affair of State*. Peter Owen; London, 2004

Wharton, Edith. *A Backward Glance*. Constable; London, 1972

Zacks, Richard. *Chasing the Last Laugh*. Doubleday; New York, 2016

Zeepvat, Charlotte. *Queen Victoria's Youngest Son*. Sutton Publishing; Stroud, 1998

Fiction

Atherton, Gertrude. *American Wives and English Husbands*. Service and Paton; London, 1898

Harrison, Constance Cary. *The Anglomaniacs*. Cassel Publishing Co; New York, 1890

James, Henry. *Daisy Miller and the Turn of the Screw*. Penguin English Library; London, 2012

Wharton, Edith. *The Age of Innocence*. Canterbury Classics; San Diego, 2014

Wharton Edith. *The Buccaneers*. Penguin Books; London, 1995

Wharton, Edith. *The House of Mirth*. Penguin English Library; London, 2012

Plays and musicals

Churchill, Winston. *The Title Mart*. Macmillan; London, 1905

Grunbaum F and Willner, A M. *The Dollar Princess*. Ascherberg, Hogwood and Crew Ltd; London, 1909

Manuscript sources consulted

Bennet Family Papers, Northumberland Archives Service

Blenheim Palace Visitor Book

Costume Ball archive, New York Historical Society

Churchill papers, Churchill Archives, Churchill College, University of Cambridge

Dorking Museum and Heritage Centre

Manchester Collection, Huntingdonshire Archives, Huntingdon Library

The Millicent Library, Fairhaven, USA

Nancy Cunard Collection, Harry Ransom Center, The University of Texas at Austin, Austin USA

New York Public Library Collections, Maria Lydig Daly Journal, Charles P Daly Papers, Maunscripts and Archives. The New York Public Library. Astor, Lenox, and Tilden Foundations

Paget Family Papers, British Library

Queen Victoria's Journal, Royal Archives

Dissertations

Bibby, Emily Katherine. *Making the American Aristocracy: Women, Cultural Capital and High Society in New York City, 1870–1900*. Virginia Polytechnic Institute and State University, 2009

Periodicals

The Baltimore American

Boston Herald

The Brooklyn Eagle

Chicago Tribune

Chicago Daily Tribune

The Cincinnati Enquirer

Cosmopolitan

The Daily Telegraph

Dundee Evening Telegraph

The Evening Telegram

Harper's Magazine

Kansas City Star

The Morning Post

New York Evening Post

The New York Herald
The New York Times
New York Tribune
New York World
San Francisco Chronicle
Sheffield Daily Telegraph
St Louis Post
Sunday Herald

The Realm
The Throne
The Times
Town Topics
Truth
Vanity Fair
World

Acknowledgements

When I first came across Minnie Paget, I wasn't thinking about transatlantic marriages or American heiresses. I was researching a different project and had immersed myself in reading around the subject. However, almost as soon as I came across Minnie and her title as unofficial marriage broker for the wealthy but socially excluded Swells of America, I was intrigued to know more and began a research tangent that would ultimately lead me to write my first book. Minnie, her mother Marietta, then the two Consuelos and Alva Vanderbilt began to open up a world that excited and enchanted me – I feel very privileged to have spent so much time in their company. Nevertheless, these accomplished society hostesses and their protégés have challenged me as a researcher and writer, the covert nature of their business and constant preoccupation with keeping up appearances, led to sometimes frustrating gaps in source material. Equally, the large number of women who inhabited this world in 1895 and the different names at various points of their lives, provided numerous obstacles when trying to decide on a coherent structure for the book, while also illuminating their diverse stories. While I have only been able to provide a glimpse of each heiress and the original buccaneers who helped them to assimilate into the British upper classes, my hope is that collectively they provide a window into the intrinsic relationship between England and America in the Gilded Age and the burgeoning roles aristocratic women were carving out for themselves as the nineteenth century drew to a close.

The Transatlantic Marriage Bureau would not have been possible without the keen assistance of many people. First, I would like to thank Aurum Press for providing me with such a welcoming home for my first book. The team have been unfailingly supportive and my warm thanks go particularly to my incisive copyeditor, Catherine Rubinstein, my meticulous proofreader, Philip Parker, and of course, my brilliant editor Jennifer Barr, who has done a sterling job of holding my hand throughout the whole process. Any errors that remain are mine alone.

I owe a great debt to my agent, Carrie Kania, who immediately fell in love with the women in this book, as much as I did. She helped me to develop the idea, wholly committed herself to the book and has taught me an enormous amount along the way.

I have used many different libraries and archives during the course of my research and have without exception found them to be informative, engaging and utterly professional. Special thanks go to Jason Baumann at the New York Public Library who made my visit there infinitely easier than it likely would have been without his help. I would also like to thank the librarians and archivists at the British Library, Huntingdonshire Archives, Northumberland Archive Service, Blenheim Palace, Newport Historical Society, Newport Tree Society, New York Historical Society, Museum of the City of New York, Millicent Library and my local library in Henleaze, Bristol who were always willing to track down forgotten books from other libraries for me. Its bustling walls are a constant hub of activity and a reminder of just how vital libraries are to a community.

I would like to acknowledge the kind permission of Her Majesty The Queen Elizabeth to quote from the journal of Queen Victoria and the Estate of Consuelo Vanderbilt Balsan © 2011 reproduced by Hodder and Stoughton Limited for extracts from *The Glitter and the Gold*, HarperCollins Publishers for extracts from *Consuelo and Alva Vanderbilt* by Amanda MacKenzie Stuart © 2006; John Murray Press, an imprint of Hodder and Stoughton for extracts from *Curzon* by David Gilmour © 1994, Curtis Brown Group Ltd, London on behalf of the beneficiaries of the Estate of Nigel Nicholson Copyright © Nigel Nicholson, 1977, for extracts from *Mary Curzon* by Nigel Nicholson and Workman Publishing Co., Inc., New York for excerpts from *To Marry an English Lord* ©1989, 2012 by Gail MacColl and Carol McD Wallace, all rights reserved. I have endeavoured to contact all copyright holders for the relevant permissions, however if there are any omissions, please contact myself or the publishers.

I would like to thank Sir Humphry Wakefield for his interest in the project and Peter Czernin, whose early enthusiasm for the characters, continually spurred me on. I would like to pay tribute to my parents – my Dad, Bob, for a childhood spent discussing royalty and society, war and politics, engendering me with an enquiring mind and a love of history that has helped me in the preparation of this book. To my Mum, Elaine, for showing me that you can achieve anything with hard work and dedication. Thanks also go to Carol and Alastair MacDonald who were always willing to make themselves available for babysitting duties, which was very much appreciated. To my wonderful friends and family, including my sister, Donna, for their advice and encouragement throughout and to my children, Evie and Arlo, who, when I was in danger of becoming too immersed in 1895, happily pulled me back into the present, with their unique blend of fun and vitality.

Finally, the biggest thank you must go to my husband, James. In many ways this book has been a joint effort and achievement. It would have been impossible to research and write with two young children without his enduring love, support and reassurance. I feel enormously lucky to have someone who believes in me so emphatically by my side.

JULIE FERRY is a freelance journalist and has
written for a wide range of national newspapers
and magazines. She lives with her husband and two
children in Bristol. This is her first book.